KRISTEN KISH COOKING

RECIPES AND TECHNIQUES

KRISTEN KISH WITH MEREDITH ERICKSON

CLARKSON POTTER/PUBLISHERS
NEW YORK

Photograph on page 15 by Gillian Laub
Photographs on pages 16 and 19 by Bravo/
David Moir/©2012/NBC Universal/Getty Images

Names: Kish, Kristen, 1983- author. | Erickson,
Meredith, 1980- author.
Title: Kristen Kish cooking : recipes and techniques /
Kristen Kish with Meredith Erickson ; photographs by
Kristin Teig. Description: New York : Clarkson Potter/
Publishers, [2017] | Includes index.
Identifiers: LCCN 2016055343 (print) | LCCN
2017006417 (ebook) | ISBN
  9780553459760 (hard cover) | ISBN 9780553459777
(Ebook)
Subjects: LCSH: Cooking—Technique. | Creative ability
in cooking. | LCGFT:
  Cookbooks.
Classification: LCC TX714 .K56665 2017 (print) | LCC
TX714 (ebook) | DDC
  641.5--dc23
LC record available at https://lccn.loc
.gov/2016055343

ISBN 978-0-553-45976-0
Ebook ISBN 978-0-553-45977-7

Printed in China

Book design by Marysarah Quinn
Cover photography by Kristin Teig

10 9 8 7 6 5 4 3 2 1

First Edition

FOR MOM, DAD, AND Jon

CONTENTS

I was born in a small town just outside of Seoul. My birth mother delivered me in Room 2 of a busy, tiny clinic, and then she promptly left. What I know about her is only what I have seen in the police record:

> Height: 5'4"
> Oval face
> Black hair set in a permanent
> Arrived wearing navy jogging suit

No other details are available. The police department and clinic waited four days for her to come back. "Some people change their mind," they said. But she didn't. On day five I was officially handed over to the state and was named—it was the first name I was given— Kwon Yung Ran. From there I passed through a few different orphanages around Seoul.

On April 22, 1984, at four months old, I flew with an older Korean woman, a chaperone, to Detroit, Michigan, where my new family was eagerly waiting for me. They had already seen pictures of me and had been preparing for my arrival, and so they say I felt like theirs long before they got to take me home. They jumped through hoops to get me, went through the process of interviews and home visits, and then waited for me for months. They truly wanted me to join their family. As I grew up, I realized just how incredible it was to go from unwanted and abandoned by my birth mother to being part of a new, welcoming family, who felt only joy at my arrival. This is a bond we adoptees share.

April 25, 1985, is my adoption day, when everything became official. On September 18, 1987, I was granted US citizenship. All kids have a birthday, but adopted kids have a set of dates, each equally meaningful to us and to our families, with certificates for proof— we're real-life Cabbage Patch Kids.

I don't think much about how differently my life could have turned out. When I was really young, my parents (both white, both from Michigan) did everything they could to make me experience my Korean roots. My parents would bring in foreign exchange students in an encouraging they're-Korean-you're-Korean-you-should-talk sort of way, someone to relate to. We read *The Korean Cinderella* book before bed. When I was seven, my parents took me to the Grand Rapids Food Festival, where I had my first taste of kimchi. I loved the flavor (the smell, not so much) and imagined how good it would be piled on top of a Quarter Pounder. This is, perhaps, one of my earliest memories of flavor. Later I realized that adding acid to something big and rich cuts through the fat. That might have been the first dish I built in my head. Like most cooks, I keep in my mind an ever-growing Rolodex of textures, colors, flavors, acidity, and even historical references and old menus. It turns and turns like a hamster wheel.

I'm told my love of knives started early. My mom would catch me cutting up carrots, cabbage, and whatever produce I could get my hands on. I always wanted to use the largest knife in the kitchen, zeroing in on our ten-inch chef's knife at the age of five. I would chop while cooking shows played on the small TV in the kitchen. I'm proud to tell you I grew up on home-cooked comfort foods, made with canned green beans, button mushrooms, and barbecue sauce from a jug—and even the occasional microwave dinner. These are the dishes that I still request whenever I visit: vegetable soup made with a base of V8; standard meat loaf, which my mom makes with oats—not bread crumbs—and serves with a healthy side of ketchup and a baked potato loaded with sour cream and dried chives; and slices of floured chicken breast, stewed with potatoes, chicken gravy, and green beans.

I grew up in a white suburb forty-five minutes from Lake Michigan. I was very fortunate to have two vacations per year, one American Girl doll, basketball camp, summer day camps, and a running-home-after-dark-with-scraped-knees sort of existence. But my absolute favorite thing, starting around the age of five, was watching Discovery Channel's *Great Chefs of the World*. Seeing Alain Passard make cassoulet, Raymond Blanc creating cakes and confectionaries, and Takashi Yagihashi working acrobatics (purpose, no wasted movement, efficiency) with his mind-bending noodles—

though I didn't know their names then, I was mesmerized by the mix of global chefs and of places I could only dream of visiting. A great calm washed over me while watching hands work so confidently with what seemed to me then to be innate skill. Seeing the chefs' agility in the kitchen, the buzz, whisk, stir, and pour, and the little pots was very soothing to me. It was the only time in the day I'd be completely focused. After dinner I would run into our yard to create my own kitchen from twigs, stones, and dirt. I'd collect dried leaves by the handful and sprinkle them onto my tennis racket—my pan. Pretending I was in whites, a little great chef, I would shake the tennis racket like I watched the great *sauciers* do. I imagined the sizzle and the smells.

As I got older, I stayed indoors and traded my tennis racket for an actual sauté pan, and leaves for vegetables and chicken breasts. Home alone, I would throw whatever I could find into the pan and cook the shit out of everything, until it was basically sawdust. I was going through the process of cooking long before I had a concept of what went together or how to properly execute it.

AT THE AGE OF THIRTEEN I was at Woodland Mall with my mom, at 5-7-9, your average Forever 21 tween shop, when a man approached me and asked if I had ever considered modeling. I convinced my mom it was what I wanted to do even though I had no clue what it actually meant. My very first casting? A Paul Mitchell Hair runway show! But when they told me I would have to shimmy down the runway like Christie Brinkley (instead of just walking normally), I turned a thousand shades of red and refused.

I was devastated, cried for days. After that, modeling jobs, not

surprisingly, came few and far between, the biggest being for a profile of local designer's dresses in the *Grand Rapids Press*. When I was eighteen, despite having zero success with modeling to that point, the agent there suggested I sign with Elite, an international agency with offices around the world. Ford and Elite, I was told, were the biggest names. I didn't know anything about them; all I needed to hear was that they were the best. And so, after my senior year of high school, I hopped a train to Chicago and met with Elite. I shot a portfolio, a calling card for future potential clients who might want to book me. A highlight was the mandate to grow out my eyebrows: they wanted me to change my appearance, which made me even more insecure than before. It was a sign that modeling wasn't for me, and so I quit, again, at least temporarily.

The next couple years were a dark time in my life, one that is still not easy for me to focus on. But it *is* when I really got into cooking.

In 2002, I went to college for international business and hated it. I did it simply because it's what I assumed I was supposed to do. I thought it would provide the level of success that I believed I should be chasing, that my friends in high school were pursuing: power suit, mortgage, kids, all of it. I hated everything about the college experience. I didn't do well in school, nor did I feel I fit in socially. I wasn't comfortable with who I was, what I was doing, my sexuality, or what I wanted for my future. My mom could tell I was unhappy and thought speaking with a professional might help. But in therapy, I lied the entire time. I would only hint at the truth in the occasional session to make it seem *just* realistic enough, like I was making progress, but not enough that my therapist could catch onto me. I wasn't open to anyone.

That summer I decided not to go back to college, and my mom and dad, to their credit, suggested I go to the Cordon Bleu culinary school in Chicago instead. After suiting up with the requisite luggage of knives and far too many tools and gadgets—many more than one needs—I was underway. I doubled up on classes, often starting at 6 a.m. and not finishing until 6 p.m. From the moment I set foot in culinary school, I realized that I had never felt as confident as when I was learning in a kitchen. I loved it. Cooking school provided me with purpose. It didn't come easy, but it definitely came naturally. I felt happy, which is to say I didn't feel defeated every second of the day, which is how I often felt previously in school. The real world, however, remained a place where I had yet to learn how to be myself.

When I graduated in 2004, I started working a couple gigs in Chicago. I put in time at a private club in the city where I learned a lot. But I started drinking, doing a lot of drugs. I convinced a restaurant owner to hire me *while I was high*. Booze and drugs gave me the confidence I needed to get my foot in the door. I remember many instances of staff not being paid, purveyors not being paid. I quit and was without work for months. When not at a bar, I could be found in my apartment, wanting to be by myself, depressed, ashamed of who I was and what I felt I was becoming. I felt unworthy of such a nice apartment that my mom and dad paid for. Eventually, in 2006, at my parents' urging, I moved back to their house in Michigan as they no longer would support an unmotivated, nonworking child. They had a point.

After finding some form of balance at home and a dose of reality (including deciding to quit using drugs as a crutch), I decided to move to Boston, a city, but one that still seemed somehow manageable. It felt familiar, perhaps because I had visited it as a kid. I rented a single room and was offered a line cook position in a restaurant at the top of one of the tallest building in the city. Within the first year I was scouted again for modeling. I was feeling low—unaccomplished and several steps behind where I should be professionally—and the validation felt good, so I went back into it. I was placed in a Converse ad, had a couple spreads in local magazines, did some runway shows, and was nominated as "Model Boston." At the same time, I was double-shifting as a line cook in a place that did nearly five hundred covers a night. I learned speed, efficiency, and how to cook as a team. It was my first experience cooking on the line.

A year or so later, I was hired as an executive chef—at the age of twenty-four. I knew then that this was a bad sign but it was an offer I couldn't refuse. It was a shiny new title and incredibly validating— just too early. Yet again the checks bounced, and I was in a déjà vu scenario, just like in Chicago. After realizing it was time to start at the bottom and find patience in learning the craft the honest way, I applied for a position with Guy Martin, the French chef from the legendary Le Grand Véfour in Paris.

Guy had come to Boston to open Sensing at the Fairmont Battery Wharf hotel. In my universe, this was huge. It was also a possibility to phase out modeling. I finally felt like I was at a restaurant with credentials that made me proud to work there. I had found the right fit. Gérard Barbin was the chef de cuisine under Guy, and he turned out to be my first mentor. He was professional, confident, and honest, and spoke through his actions. In 2008 he made a banana cake *with seared foie gras and green tea*. I am not embarrassed to tell you that this blew my mind. Care and creativity and thought went into each dish. It was an open kitchen: quiet, focused, and immaculate, very European. The kind words of Gérard and Guy definitely guided me forward. As Sensing came to its natural end, so did the relationship with my boyfriend at the time. And perhaps my romantic relationships with all men, really.

Next, I toyed with moving to Dubai or London until my best friend, Stephanie Cmar, suggested I check out where she was working: Stir, an intimate (max ten people per night) dining room/demo kitchen. I would have kept running away when things got hard if it weren't for Stephanie's persistence that I give Boston and this job a year of my time. So I stayed. Owned by Boston's cooking doyenne Barbara Lynch, Stir had a rep for building great cooks. I applied and was accepted. How does Stir work? Well, in the space of an evening, the chef in charge is expected to prep and execute a multicourse meal, smile, clean pots and pans, and chat—an intimate dinner-party setting of sorts—all while teaching guests the hows and the whys of what they're making. It's a dance I loved then and still love now.

Not only was Stir a great podium to show Barbara what I could do and to give her a reason to trust me to cook for her company, it was a way for me to find my own style. I was fortunate to have a great mix of both freedom and her creative influence. She would tell me, "You already know how to do this, so stop thinking so hard about it!"

She was right. The less time I had to think about how and what to cook, the more my true cook came out. This was just what I needed to gain confidence and to find and trust my own vision.

One evening Barbara was set to come to Stir for the night for us to cook together. The theme was Birds & Burgundy. This was my moment: the first time I tried tweaking a technique for finishing a sauce. Instead of whisking butter into a reduced game-bird stock, I opted for a rich creamy cheese to make a flavorful sauce for a guinea hen dish. Service started and built and built, with great admiration from diners. Midway through, Barbara stopped and said, "This is so good, I can't take credit for it. This is all Kristen." And from there I began creating my own menus with more confidence and building my own following among Boston's diners.

The next year, Barbara was asked to be a guest chef on *Top Chef*. After that show wrapped, the producers asked her to suggest names for *Top Chef Seattle* for the following season. She put my name forward, telling the Bravo network and later the *New York Times*, "She is the rare female chef who has both the culinary chops and the telegenic appeal to suit the extraordinary demands of both professional settings."

Let me just say that being a TV game-show contestant is a superweird experience. But as you may have surmised so far, I wasn't the casting dream. (Friends with Padma Lakshmi, yes. Glamourous or even charismatic like Padma, no.) And being on TV was never my

intention. It was Barbara Lynch who mentored me and pushed me and gave me the confidence. She made me do it. And so I agreed to audition for season ten of *Top Chef* in the summer of 2013.

I arrived in Vegas to start filming the first segment at Emeril Lagasse's Table 10 restaurant. The setup for the show is that you don't have to worry about a goddamn thing other than cooking. No wallets, no books, no music, no phones—just your knives. That's all you're allowed to bring. In Vegas, we were five chefs vying to get a spot in Seattle.

We were mic'ed and, as soon as we walked in, it just started. Emeril introduced himself to each of the five contestants. The first challenge was to make a soup, any soup you wanted, in thirty minutes. You're in a brand-new kitchen and you don't know where anything is; you don't even know where the ingredients are, let alone what they are, and you are right away going to be judged on that dish! I made an English pea soup with scallops and apples. I would like to tell you it was an informed decision and break down my thought process, but these were simply the ingredients that came across my eyes first. I had to make a quick decision. Emeril told me it was one of the best soups he had had in a long time. As a result, I made it to *Top Chef Seattle*.

After that stint in Vegas, I went back to Boston for three weeks. During that time, I was allowed to tell only Barbara what I was up to. The confidentiality and contracts were airtight. I told my mom and dad that I'd be going away and we couldn't speak for six weeks. My long-running struggles with anxiety and depression simmered just below the surface. This would be a big test for me. When the wheels

touched down on the runway in Seattle, my heart was pounding. I was taken to a hotel to settle in and sign paperwork, have my chef coat fitted, and mentally prepare before the actual competition and the cameras. We were eighteen people including me all in twin beds and sharing rooms. Everything in our bags was checked for drugs, contraband fruit, excess knives—whatever.

The first day we were herded like cattle into tents and then walked into the studio. From that moment, the cameras were on. As a coping strategy, I immediately started stripping people down in my mind, thinking, "She's not going to make it past day one." I don't know that I always believed it, but I needed to do something. Padma came out and greeted us and delivered the quick-fire challenge: Pacific Northwest shellfish. And we were off!

We filmed every day, double-digit hours. We had very little freedom and even less privacy. I'm talking asking for permission to go to the bathroom. That said, I don't want to come across as melodramatic, and do want to emphasize that it was an incredibly fortunate life experience. I'm not saying I was in the trenches. *I was a cooking competition reality-show contestant.*

Throughout the season, I was winning individual challenges, surprisingly. My first win came from re-creating 1950s dishes. I was one of the last to pick something from the menu and chose two sides— french-fried onion rings and button mushrooms. I double-cooked the mushrooms—one of my favorite techniques to this day (see page 71)—and caramelized them with garlic, shallots, white wine, vermouth, butter, and parsley to make a classic steakhouse side.

The season began to air months later. As the weeks went by, people began recognizing me on the streets. Publishers, agents, and bad food companies hawking microwave dinners began contacting me. I was eliminated in the second half of the season, and while on the one hand I felt a huge sense of relief, it was tempered by my competitive nature—I still wanted to win.

I knew I'd get my shot on the *Last Chance Kitchen* (where eliminated contestants go head-to-head for a chance to return to the show). I won two cook-offs in Seattle and two more in Alaska and then was flown to Los Angeles to tape the final two episodes. At this point I already had four comeback wins under my belt by taking a one-day-at-a-time approach. All of a sudden, I had won those final two cook-offs and was back on *Top Chef* as one of the three finalists. Tom Colicchio walked me from *Last Chance Kitchen* over to the main set for the next challenge, to whittle us down from three to two finalists.

We had to run a service of our own food at Tom Colicchio's restaurant Craft in Los Angeles, with Tom expediting at the pass, coordinating the tables' orders between the kitchen and front of the house. Remember, I'd been working in a demo kitchen and hadn't worked anything like a traditional service in years. So now, nine months after that first Vegas shoot, I'm in the *Top Chef* finale. The episode was shot in an LA studio with 150 or so "diners" (along with my dad, brother, and best friend, Stephanie, among those eating). It was the calmest I had felt throughout the entire *Top Chef* experience. The challenge was simple: five courses head-to-head, the best three out of five wins, and I was up against Brooke Williamson, a tough competitor and LA native. It was a complete blur. We had very little time to think. So I relied heavily on what I knew—technique—to get me through. They declared me the winner after the fourth course. This fact didn't set in for months, which is good because I had to keep quiet about everything for weeks until the show aired.

I went back to Stir, and while I was relieved to be off camera, I did miss the adrenaline. I felt bored, which forced me to realize I was capable of doing more, of packing more into my day, and that I craved adventure and wanted a new challenge. Within six months, Barbara promoted me to chef de cuisine at Menton, the only Relais & Châteaux property in Boston. I was eager, excited, and ready to learn. I was in training for nearly three months before I touched the menu and made it mine. I loved the service, the kitchen, the process of how that restaurant runs. Menton turned into a lesson in what I wanted and who I wanted to be.

Now let me be clear: I believe it's important for a cook to stay at a job for at least a year to fully get a sense of the place. It's a display of character, discipline, integrity, and responsibility that every older and wiser chef looks for on a CV when hiring. However, in this case, I decided to leave after only nine months. Why? Suddenly, I felt I was cooking for the wrong reasons. Here I was with a coveted restaurant job, having just won a TV show, the restaurant was packed with people wanting to try my food—there was nothing not to love! I was comfortable running a kitchen, but cooking at Menton only magnified that I was not yet comfortable with myself.

By the time I left Menton, I'd been working in kitchens on and off for twelve years. Like most cooks, I visited my apartment only to sleep, and my home kitchen had rarely been touched. Truth be told, I feel most relaxed when I'm prepping food in a professional kitchen. I didn't know how to cook at home. Essentially, I didn't know how to slow down and take care of myself.

I love the meditative quality of rolling out pasta for hours on end, preparing canapés for a busy service, squeezing custard into countless *petits éclairs*, the "oh, shit, I'm in the weeds" moments . . . and, of course, using a knife constantly. And so, after the whirlwind, I realized I had to learn how to relax and cook for myself again. No walk-in refrigerator stocked to the gills, no team help, no adrenaline rush.

I also wanted to cook for my girlfriend at the time. Yes, I said *girlfriend*. I know for most of you this isn't that saloon moment where I bust through the swinging doors and the piano player stops. This isn't a shocking revelation now. But at the time, this was a big deal for me.

I've probably always known I was gay, but accepting it was another story. It wasn't until after *Top Chef* and Menton that, at the age of twenty-eight, I openly had my first girlfriend. I grew up in a very loving and accepting home, but I was still scared to be myself. I came to a point where I needed, wanted, and no longer could hide my love for another person. I remember lying face up in bed, staring at the ceiling in my apartment with my phone in my hand. I called my parents and scooted around the subject for a good twenty minutes. Finally, I said, "I'm dating someone and we are coming to Michigan," and then slyly dropped a "she" in somewhere. My mother paused for what felt like eternity and then responded with "Well, I think we already knew." They asked if I was happy, and I said yes, and that was that. I didn't publically come out until months later, when I posted a photo on social media of my then girlfriend and myself, not as a statement, just sharing a moment as we all do. The next day an article came out in the *New York Times* maga-zine that, in addition to talking about how a women's place is running the kitchen (the title of the article, actually), casually mentioned my girlfriend. It made a bigger splash than I had ever imagined, and the flood of messages and notes of support were overwhelming.

And just like that, my truth was out, and so was I.

When you are able to live your life as who you are—and not half-truths—every aspect, including your career, will have more room to flourish.

This is a cookbook of recipes from my life, from my beginnings as an adoptee in Seoul, South Korea, to my upbringing in the Midwest, years of cooking under Barbara Lynch, ultimately winning *Top Chef,* and to how I cook today. But how useful is that to a home cook?

My life has shaped my taste buds. My pro-fessional cooking career has focused on clas-sic techniques learned in culinary school and restaurants. Once you know the basics, from braising to pickling, smoking to searing, you can bend them to your will. For example, I love to build complex-tasting sauces by making a flavorful stock and then finishing it by melting stinky cheeses into the hot broth (like the recipe for rabbit loin with Époisses de Bourgogne cheese, mustard, and carrot on page 205). The idea is based on a technique called emulsification, where a fat is incorporated into a liquid in order to add richness, volume, and, in the case of Époisses, a hit of funk.

Take the two together—my taste buds and technique—and you have the essence of my cooking. Once you know basic cooking methods, you can also use them to translate your life and your taste buds into your cooking.

At its core, my food combines a reverence for the 101s with the beautiful mess that has been my life so far. I hope to continue telling my story through my recipes—and that you'll cook along with me, learn and hone some great techniques, and in turn be able to better express yourself through your cooking and your recipes.

A WORD ON PLATING AND PRESENTATION

I am particular regarding the kind of plates I use. Each one needs to
make sense for the dish at hand. For this book, I actually worked with
Jeremy Ogusky, a Boston potter, and created a few of my own original
pieces (see pages 6, 125, and 226). And because we all appreciate a
beautifully presented dish at a restaurant—I really believe it does
make great food taste even better—I am particular about how I put
food on each plate. As a result, some of the recipe photographs in this
book show smaller, tasting portions instead of the full dish described
in the text.

TECHNIQUES AND TERMS

My cooking is not rooted in a place or a region of the world: the core, the very root of my cooking, is technique. I'm all about properly searing and seasoning, the importance of knife skills, and understanding how things cook. And so I'm going to direct you, the reader, as I would instruct fresh cooks in my kitchen. I'm giving you some professional tips to add to your cooking arsenal.

The following classic techniques and terminology appear often in the book. That's because I consider them essential and use them often. Master them and any recipe, anywhere, will immediately reveal itself to you. I recommend giving this section a once-over before you begin cooking. I've also highlighted in each recipe the techniques employed so you will see examples of them in use. You can always come back here to refresh your memory on any method.

PRIMARY TECHNIQUES

BLANCHING: quickly parcooking an ingredient in boiling salted water. I use this method with all sorts of foods, including to make peeling pearl onions easier, to set the vibrant color of peas and other veggies, and even for sweetbreads. The water should taste salty so that the ingredient picks up that seasoning. The desired blanching time, once you have a boil going, is usually 1 to 2 minutes. Once blanched, the ingredient should be plunged into a big bowl of ice water. The point here is to stop the cooking process quickly. Drain the ingredient well before proceeding.

BRAISING: a method of cooking that combines dry heat, simmering, and poaching all in one. Braised meats, such as coq au vin and beef bourguignon, are perhaps the most popular examples of this technique. But I also love to braise vegetables, like radishes, leeks, and beets. The point is to slow-cook tougher cuts of meats (or heartier vegetables) at a low temperature to break them down and yield a luscious texture. Braising can be done either on the stovetop or in the oven, and it's almost always done with a cover on the pan to retain moisture. It is important that there is enough liquid to come roughly halfway up the piece of meat or vegetables. You don't want to drown your food, but you need to maintain enough liquid during a long cooking time so food doesn't burn, and you need to develop enough steam in order to properly braise. Timing cues? A beef bourguignon, for example, takes upward of 4 to 4½ hours, whereas medium-size vegetables can be done in as few as 40 minutes. I almost always sear a cut of meat (see page 27) before I braise it to maximize flavor.

BRINING: preserving and flavoring with salted water. A brine lets you season an ingredient in its entirety as opposed to just seasoning the outside with salt. Brining is ideal for large pieces of lean meat, especially whole poultry. It adds flavor and ensures a moist end result. Think of your holiday bird: you brine it to season the meat of the bird from the inside. As the bird sits in the brine, the salt pulls out moisture from the meat. As it continues to sit, the bird will end up drinking up the flavored brine to equal the water weight lost.

CURING: preserving and flavoring with salt. Curing originated hundreds and hundreds of years ago in order to preserve items to extend their shelf life. I do it to season, draw out moisture, and concentrate an ingredient's texture. In this book I cure fish, squab legs, and duck legs before cooking or smoking.

EMULSIFYING: combining two or more liquids or fats together to create one smooth, consistent sauce. Aioli, butter sauces, cheese sauces, and vinaigrettes are all examples. Personally, I like to fortify stocks with butter or cheese, another example of an emulsification. A properly emulsified sauce is glossy and smooth; a sauce that looks separated, with liquid pooling around curds of solids, has broken. We also emulsify when we're combining a cold fat into a hot liquid. When emulsifying, a whisk, a hand blender, or a blender is essential. You are looking to incorporate fat into liquid, which is not a natural pairing, so the quick movement of the whisk (or blender blade) is important. Adding the fat little by little is imperative; if you were to dump it all in at one time, the sauce would be more likely to break. The temperature of the ingredients can also play a role. Often a cold fat is whisked bit by bit into a hot liquid. When an emulsion breaks, it can be hard to resuscitate. Sometimes a little hot water can help bring a mayonnaise back together, but more often it is just easier to start over, adding the fat more slowly.

FRYING: cooking an ingredient in hot fat until crisp. If done correctly and in a well-ventilated kitchen, you can fry up some great crunchy, delicious foods. In this book I either shallow-fry or deep-fry. With shallow frying, when the ingredient isn't completely submerged in the oil, I'll use grapeseed or another neutral oil, such as canola or vegetable—anything that is essentially flavorless. More and more, I use coconut oil in recipes where I'm not going to mind picking up the flavor from the coconut.

Whenever I fry garlic or shallots, I always start them in cold oil. Bringing the temperature of the ingredient up slowly aids in cooking out any of the pungent onion flavor. The taste becomes less that of a fried onion and more intensely golden and rich. I also find the onion or garlic gets crisper, too, this way.

With a deep fry, where you need a lot of oil to cover the food completely, I use a cheaper neutral oil, usually canola.

There are two important rules about frying:

1. Make sure the oil is hot enough that a bit of food or batter sizzles away as soon as it's dropped into the oil. If it's not hot enough, whatever you're frying will simply act as a sponge and soak up the oil before the crust starts to form, if it ever does, which isn't pleasant.
2. Always wear pants.

MAKING CONFIT: cooking and preserving meat in fat. Traditionally used for meat, such as duck legs cooked in duck fat, this method can be used for vegetables, too, and oil or clarified butter can take the place of animal fat. For example, I make tomato confit using olive oil with herbs and seasoning. Both the slow-cooking method and the fat are incredibly gentle, rendering ingredients soft, rich in flavor, and unctuous once cooked.

MAKING CUSTARD: the process of emulsifying egg yolks and hot liquid and cooking them until slightly thickened. The ice cream recipes in this book all begin with the base of a stirred custard, or crème anglaise: egg yolks are whisked with sugar, and hot milk and cream are added slowly to temper the yolks; the mixture is then stirred over low heat until it coats the back of a spoon (the nappe stage). This process needs attention. Too fast and too hot will scramble your eggs as opposed to creating a silky smooth, creamy custard. The cooked, stirred custard is then chilled, and you have an ice cream base. But that's where the standard method stops. I play around with the types of sweeteners, including sugar, honey, and corn syrup. I also experiment with adding cornstarch, and adjusting the ratios of whole eggs to yolks and of milk and cream. Depending on what the ice cream is paired with, I balance all of these factors appropriately. That said, each ice cream also can be made and eaten on its own.

MAKING FRESH PASTA: mixing flour and eggs makes dough. Making fresh pasta is meditative for me and something I recommend that anyone who loves to cook try at least once. Start with my Basic Pasta Dough (page 158) and roll it to the thickness you desire. For ravioli, I like it so thin that I can see my hand through it. Cut as desired for the recipe at hand.

Here are some tips:

- When rolling pasta dough, use just enough flour to prevent sticking—not so much that you end up with a tough, dry dough.
- Filled pastas need to be sealed. The most efficient way is to grab a small spray bottle and fill it with water. It's fast, and this way you keep your fingers dry for pressing the edges together. I prefer plain water as opposed to an egg wash.
- When cooking pasta, make sure your pot is large and you have more water than you need. Pasta water should taste like the sea. Salt the water aggressively so that the pasta is seasoned as it cooks. For 1 gallon of water, I recommend ½ cup of kosher salt. You can't really ever fix underseasoned pasta once it's done cooking. Add the pasta little by little to the boiling water, keeping a rolling simmer; if you get your batch of pasta all in within 10 seconds, you can be assured that it will all cook evenly. Otherwise, pasta can sink to the bottom and become a gluey mess.
- When the pasta is cooked, avoid violently dumping all those lovingly crafted dumplings or noodles right into a colander with a torrent of hot cooking water gushing over them. Instead, when the pasta is al dente, remove it from the water in batches using a slotted spoon or a spider. Much more civilized.

MAKING MERINGUE: whipping egg whites with sugar until the mixture is glossy and beautifully white. There are several versions of meringue, some made from cooked sugar and others from raw sugar. Whichever version you are preparing, I recommend using a stand mixer as the process takes a bit of time. Meringue is often whipped to soft, medium, or stiff peaks. This is where you hold up the whisk and the meringue will curl over on itself (soft, see below) or stick straight up (stiff). Room-temperature eggs whip up best. Make sure the bowl is impeccably clean and that no bits of yolk make it into the whites, or they will not whip to their fullest. Cream of tartar is often added as a stabilizer. Keep soft uncooked meringue at room temperature until ready to use and make it as close as possible to the time you want to use it. Cooked meringue needs to be kept in a cool, dry place to avoid becoming chewy and soft.

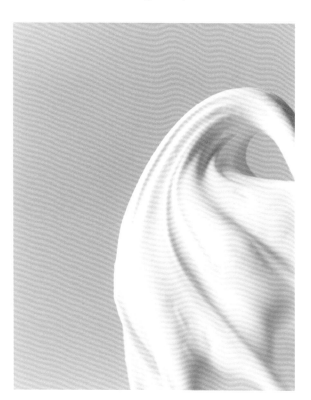

PICKLING: preserving and flavoring with acid and salt. Pickling incorporates acid and tang, and so I like adding pickled components to rich dishes to help cut through the fat. There are many ways to pickle. In this book you will see various pickled items using the vinegar method: pouring vinegar, hot or cold, over an ingredient and letting it marinate. Hot vinegar will soften an ingredient a touch, and the flavor will be stronger; cold vinegar will keep things crisper and lighter. Fermented pickles are also amazing but do not make an appearance in this book.

The traditional rule of thumb for pickling is 3:2:1—that is, 3 parts water, 2 parts vinegar, and 1 part sugar (by volume), with the sugar dissolved in the boiling water and vinegar. You can play around with this formula using different herbs and spices, more or less sugar, and different vinegars. The solution can also be used hot or cold, depending on the pickle you want.

POACHING: lightly and slowly cooking something in a flavorful liquid. A stage below a simmer, poaching involves submerging an ingredient in liquid and cooking it very gently until tender. It keeps even lean foods like chicken breasts moist.

REDUCING: to cook a liquid down over time, thus minimizing the quantity, thickening the texture, and intensifying the flavor. Reducing should be done over medium heat in as wide a pan as possible to reduce the cooking time; liquid should boil in the pan. Pan juices and braising and poaching liquids can make flavorful sauces on their own once reduced.

RENDERING: to melt and cook the fat out of an ingredient, typically meat. This technique is often used to cook meat in its own fat, while crisping the skin. Duck skin, for example, has quite a bit of fat to render before the skin will crisp. The rendered fat can then be used to make a confit (see page 24) or to roast potatoes.

ROASTING: to cook using high and dry heat in the oven. This is the number one way of browning and bringing out the natural sugars of an ingredient—or crisping its fat—without adding any additional liquids. A key to roasting is not to overcrowd the pan, as doing so will increase moisture and provide steam, the enemies of dry heat. Another tip: don't line your trays with foil; that creates steam as well! Cut vegetables that are the same size so they cook evenly. And separate different types of vegetables, which might not cook at the same rate.

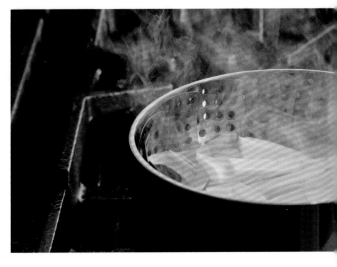

SEARING: applying high heat to caramelize the exterior of an ingredient. The myth of "it seals in the juices" is something I never bought in to. It sounds nice, but caramelizing meat on the outside does not scientifically create such a barrier. I do it purely for flavor. Searing, or browning, is basically cooking over very high heat with a bit of fat just *briefly* to brown and color. The meat or vegetables may or may not need additional cooking to cook the inside, but the sear is referring to just the outside. When you place a sirloin in a hot pan, preferably cast-iron, and you see the meat immediately beginning to contort or seize—that's a good sear. A pan that's not hot enough means the meat kind of stews and simmers, giving off liquid and not browning. Avoid that sad fate for your steak at all costs!

SMOKING: flavoring and cooking with wood smoke. Smoking can be done either hot or cold. For the latter, the smoke is purely a flavoring and does not cook the food at all. In this book, I smoke using only the hot method, primarily on the stovetop, to incorporate a beautiful smoked flavor into a dish. Smoking at home is easy with an outdoor grill or smoker—or in a well-ventilated kitchen. Here's how I do it indoors: Soak the wood chips in water for 45 minutes; drain. Put the chips in a small cast-iron pan and ignite them with a kitchen torch. You will begin to notice steam, and then the white smoke will start. When you see the smoke, you're in business. Lay the ingredient on a small, sturdy wire rack or in a perforated pan. Set over the burning chips in the cast-iron pan. Wrap the setup tightly with aluminum foil to prevent smoke from escaping. Smoke over low heat on your stovetop for as few as 20 minutes or as long as 1½ hours, until the ingredients are to your desired smoky taste. When you're checking for doneness, be careful when lifting the lid: smoke inhalation is real. If you're indoors, you might want to step outside for this part!

STEAMING: cooking with indirect moist heat. This method of cooking over—but not touching—simmering liquid keeps foods moist and retains their delicate flavor and texture.

SWEATING: cooking without coloring, usually to remove pungency and soften ingredients such as onions or garlic. Here you're looking to take out some moisture from an ingredient, not brown it, though the heat should still be in the medium range. Adding a pinch of salt at the beginning helps draw out the moisture to ensure no color or caramelization forms. An average sweat time is 8 to 10 minutes.

ADDITIONAL TECHNIQUES

COOKING MUSHROOMS: heating mushrooms so that they release their liquid and caramelize. The majority of mushrooms carry significant moisture, so I like to double-cook them: the first cooking pulls out excess water, and

the second cooking caramelizes them and lets you incorporate flavorings, such as shallot, garlic, herbs, or wine. Without the first step, mushrooms tend to steam and simmer in unflavored liquid, and it can be difficult to get a nice caramelized exterior.

This is how I do it: Cut the mushrooms into sizable pieces—leave the smallest mushrooms whole, halve the medium ones, and quarter the largest ones. Keep in mind that the mushroom pieces will shrink by a third or so during the cooking process. In a large sauté pan, heat oil over medium-high heat until it begins to shimmer. Add a portion of the mushrooms, being careful not to overcrowd the pan, and a pinch of salt. Sweat the mushrooms over medium-high heat until the liquid begins to cook out and the mushrooms are tender. Transfer to a colander set over a bowl to drain them. Once all of the mushrooms have been cooked, repeat the process, adding more oil to the pan and letting it get hot before cooking each batch of mushrooms until caramelized.

COOKING SOUS VIDE: slow-cooking a vacuum-sealed ingredient with flavorings (fat and herbs) in a temperature-controlled water bath. Cooking sous vide keeps an even cooking temperature during the entire process without anything burning off or evaporating. It's a way of making sure the outside doesn't cook before the inside, while retaining moisture and imparting flavor. In the past I've rigged my own setup at home using plastic wrap and a pot of water whose temperature I monitored with a probe thermometer.

DEGLAZING: adding a liquid after a fond (caramelized bits stuck to the pan) has formed and cooking it until the liquid has fully evaporated. Pour a small amount of liquid (stock, water, wine) into a pan that's been used for sautéing and bring the liquid to a boil, scraping the bottom of the pan to dissolve the pan sediment and juices. Add additional liquid to make a pan sauce.

SOUS VIDE

GLAZING VEGETABLES: coating them in an emulsion of a fat and liquid. This is usually done to cooked vegetables to add flavor and fat and a glossy sheen. The vegetable is rolled in butter or oil and water or stock in a sauté pan over medium heat until the liquid evaporates and the fat coats the vegetable. Seasonings can include, but are not limited to, herbs, salt, or honey.

MAKING CARAMEL: cooking sugar until liquid and amber in color. This is a simple way of elevating ice cream or adding sweetness to a sauce. Caramelized sugar is nutty with a slight bitterness, depending on how far you take the sugar. I use the sugar and water method, mixing the two together and simmering them until the water evaporates and the sugar can begin to color. (It's a bit more error proof than starting with dry sugar in a dry pan.)

Here are some tips:

· Brush down the sides of the pan with a little water, as any loose sugar crystals climbing up the sides can crystalize your entire sauce.

· Don't agitate the pot. Once the sugar is damp and it's cooking, avoid touching or stirring it.

· Adding an invert sugar (e.g., corn syrup) can act as extra insurance against crystallization.

· Be careful when adding cream to the sauce. The sugar is insanely hot and can burn you terribly. Room-temperature cream or even warm cream won't bubble up as much as cold cream. Either way, go little by little, and make sure your pot is large enough for the cream to temporarily bubble up and double in size.

· Don't try to taste the hot sugar or sauce or dip your finger in it before it has a chance to cool. Cooked sugar is HOT. Have patience.

· Keeping caramel sauce in the refrigerator to use later is great, but as it cools, it will thicken. Just warm it back up in a microwave or double boiler, or add more liquid so it can remain loose while cold.

MAKING CLASSIC SAUCES: preparing the five classic sauces in French cooking, known as the "mother sauces:" velouté, béchamel, espagnole, tomato sauce, and hollandaise. Three of these five use a roux (see page 30). Velouté begins with a light roux and traditionally a light stock made without browning any of the ingredients. It's the starting point for a gravy, for example. Béchamel begins with a light roux and an added dairy (think mac and cheese or lasagna); if you add Gruyère, you've got a Mornay sauce. Espagnole uses a dark roux to thicken a dark beef or veal stock, which is usually flavored with a browned mirepoix (a mix of carrots, celery, and onions). In a diner or on the streets of New York, you'll hear it referred to as "brown sauce." Dressed up, it could be a bordelaise, which has the addition of red wine and when completed often accompanies a great steak. Tomato sauce veers into the Italian with a host of pastas and pizzas. For those two items, you skip the roux;

it's just pure tomatoes and herbs. Hollandaise is an emulsion of egg yolks and clarified butter and usually a hit of acid. On its own, it reigns with asparagus or over eggs Benedict. Add shallots, champagne vinegar, and tarragon and you have another steak and french fry accomplice: béarnaise sauce. An aioli is just like a cold version of hollandaise, if you think about it. Once you know the basics, you can start tweaking them. Think of these sauces as the ultimate building blocks to your cooking repertoire.

MAKING COOKIE DOUGHS AND CAKE BATTERS: combining butter, sugar, flour, and eggs properly. Start with room-temperature butter and eggs, unless your recipe states otherwise. Creaming, or mixing the butter and sugar together until light and fluffy, is one of the first steps in making a dough. Scrape down the sides and the bottom of the mixing bowl often. When you add the eggs, do so slowly, one at a time, scraping down the sides as needed; otherwise your eggs won't fully incorporate, and you will end up with lumps and pockets of butter in your batter (in essence, a broken emulsion). If you have wet and dry ingredients, it's best to alternately add each to the creamed mixture. Once you add the flour, the key is to not overmix. Why? Because overmixing creates a tough dough instead of a tender final product.

MAKING POTATO PURÉES: cooking potatoes and then mashing them. I love country-style mashed potatoes: skin-on, lumpy, and satisfying. But there is also something about a perfectly silken and rich fancy restaurant–quality potato purée. I cook my potatoes one of two ways: baked skin-on or simmered in salty water skin-on until tender when pierced with a knife. I highly suggest the water is perfumed with bay leaves, whole garlic cloves, and thyme.

I peel the potatoes with a small knife while they are as hot as I can carefully handle; the skin will come right off. To yield the smoothest texture, I pass them through a few vessels. First through a ricer, and you could certainly stop here if you wanted. In a restaurant, I continue. I scrape the riced potatoes through a *tamis* (a round sieve of sorts). From there, I begin to emulsify my fat and/or liquids into them. Finally, the potatoes get pushed through a *chinois* (a fine-meshed conical sieve) with the back of a ladle to ensure the smoothest of smooth purées.

MAKING A ROUX: a great thickening agent that also adds flavor (depending on how much you toast the flour) and richness via the fat. A roux is equal parts of fat and flour mixed together and cooked over low heat, usually between 8 and 18 minutes (unless you are making a gumbo, which is a whole other story). The more you toast the flour in the fat, the darker the roux, but the less the thickening power. There are four varieties of roux: white, blond, brown, and dark brown. White is cooked for the shortest time, while dark brown cooks the longest. In the recipes herein, I use only white or blond roux. Usually used to thicken sauces, soups, and chowders, this is a building block for the classic sauces. (See also Making Classic Sauces, page 29)

TEMPERING: to gradually increase temperatures of delicate ingredients like eggs or chocolate without altering them. Most people know that if you pour a hot liquid over an egg and try to mix the two, the egg will scramble. When cooking a custard, for example, you want to add the hot liquid very slowly, whisking constantly, to gradually increase the eggs' temperature before proceeding. Tempering meat, on the other hand, means taking the chill off of thick cuts by letting them sit at room temperature for 20 minutes before cooking.

WHIPPING: incorporating air to yield a fluffy, light, voluminous result. Your whipper can be a whisk, elbow grease, an electric mixer, or even a whipping canister. When whipping cream, peaks will form a bit quicker if the cream is cold. When whipping egg whites, the opposite is true: room-temperature whites whip to the fluffiest peaks. Make sure no fat has been introduced to the whites; even a spot of egg yolk can slow down or inhibit your whites. So make sure your bowl is clean, too. I am a big fan of an iSi canister fitted with a nitrous oxide cartridge. (The same canister can be fitted with a carbon dioxide, or CO_2, cartridge that also adds air, but in the form of carbonation typically used for making sodas.) You can aerate more than cream or egg whites in an iSi, such as a sauce or a purée. The sauce must be completely smooth, and some may need gelatin or another type of stabilizer to help keep its form once released from the canister. Science and a bit of experimentation and trial and error are helpful when playing around with different liquids in the canister.

WORKING WITH GELATIN: using a gelling agent to set liquids. There are two kinds of gelatin: powdered and sheet. I prefer the latter. Sheets will yield a clearer gel compared to powdered; that's why they are used more commonly in professional kitchens. One envelope equals 3½ (silver; see below) sheets. Gelatin, whether powdered or in sheets, must be bloomed, or soaked, in cold water for 5 to 15 minutes, until soft. Sheet gelatin should be squeezed out in your hands before using. Gelatin will dissolve into your mixture at 80°F to 100°F and will set once chilled. Boiling gelatin inhibits its setting power. Be sure to leave a minimum of 6 to 8 hours for it to firm up.

In most kitchens we use silver-strength gelatin sheets. There are also bronze and gold sheets; the grades refer to the gelling power of the sheet. Silver grade is the most common because it can be adapted to many recipes without much adjustment.

WORKING WITH YEAST: using a leavening agent to add air, texture, and flavor. The most basic example of yeast in this book is in brioche dough (see page 45). I find myself using active-dry yeast that you can find in any grocery store, usually in the little packets. I follow two rules when it comes to yeast:

1. The temperature of the liquid mixed with the yeast cannot be too hot; it will kill the yeast, and you will not get that rise you want. Aim for 5 to 10 degrees above body temperature. There's no need to measure it using a thermometer; if the liquid feels like a warm bath on your hand, you're in the right area.
2. Add salt after you add either all or some of the flour, as direct exposure to the salt can retard yeast's ability to rise.

Your yeast should bubble and foam a few minutes after the warm water and a pinch of flour or sugar is added. If it does not, throw it out and buy fresher yeast.

COOKING TERMS

BRUNOISE

ONION BRÛLÉE

QUENELLE

AU SEC: to cook a deglazing liquid until *au sec* ("nearly dry"), simmering it until it has completely evaporated.

BÂTON: an ingredient, often a vegetable, but also bacon and chives, that's been cut into thin, even-length sticks.

BRUNOISE: vegetables (e.g., carrots, onion, celery) cut into a minuscule ⅛-inch dice.

CARTOUCHE: a circular piece of parchment paper used to cover the surface of a simmering liquid, acting as a lid. This helps keep food submerged and reduces evaporation, while not preventing it completely.

EGG WASH: a mixture of beaten eggs or eggs beaten with milk, water, or cream that is brushed on to the surface of raw dough or pastry prior to baking. It adds to the browning and shine of the finished baked good. I prefer to use just one whole egg, beaten until smooth.

ICE BATH: a combination of ice and cold water in a bowl, generally two handfuls of ice in a large bowl filled with water until half full. An ice bath is used to quickly stop the cooking process when you've boiled or blanched something (e.g., vegetables, gnocchi, sweetbreads) as well as to stop the cooking of a custard, such as an ice cream base.

JULIENNE: vegetables (and other foods) cut into thin sticks or bâtons, generally 1⁄16 inch thick.

MIREPOIX: a mixture of diced carrots, onion, and celery, typically used to enhance the flavor of a sauce or stock.

MONTER AU BEURRE: the act of whisking cold butter into a sauce to make it creamier and more luscious.

NAPPE: to coat with a sauce. This term is used to refer to the consistency or thickness of a sauce. Dip a spoon into the sauce, then lift it and run a finger along the back of the spoon to expose the metal or wood. The consistency is correct if the sauce does not re-cover that exposed portion of the spoon. If it's still too runny, keep reducing the sauce.

ONION BRÛLÉE: a burnt onion, used as a flavor and color enhancer in stocks. Line a large sauté pan (or more than one if you have many onion halves) with three layers of aluminum foil, place onion halves (that have been cut across their equators) cut-side down in the pan, and set the pan over high heat, simply letting the

SUPRÊME

TURNED VEGETABLES

onions be. Once the onion faces start to blacken, reduce the heat to medium-high and let them sit for 35 to 40 minutes. You want to burn those onion faces completely for best color and flavor before adding them to stock.

PIPING BAG: a tool used to accurately press custards or creams (or even potato purée) through a narrow tube when precision is necessary and a spoonful or dollop won't do. I love and recommend disposable plastic piping bags, but failing that, zip-top plastic bags work great. Just cut off one of the corners to mimic the diameter of a piping tip and start piping!

QUENELLE: a food mixture (e.g., ice cream, vegetable purée, mayonnaise-bound meat or fish) that's been shaped into an oval or football shape using two dessert spoons with deep bowls (the kind of vintage spoons your grand-

mother might have had lying around). To make a quenelle, wet two spoons in hot water and put one in each hand. Scoop up a portion of the mixture you're shaping with one spoon, and use the second spoon to scoop the mixture from the first spoon, smoothing it in the process. Hold the spoons horizontally and give the empty spoon a quarter turn each time you scoop. Repeat a few times until you have a neat oval shape. (For ice cream, just use one spoon to scoop a neat quenelle.)

SABAYON: a foamy, frothy sauce made from wine, sugar (or honey), and egg yolks and whisked continuously over steaming water.

SOUBISE: a sauce made from cooked onion purée.

SUPRÊME: a segment of citrus fruit that is free of any skin, pith, membranes, and seeds. To make

citrus suprêmes, use a very sharp knife to cut off the bottom and top of the fruit. Stand the fruit on one of its truncated ends and, following the contours of the fruit, carve off the skin and pith to expose the bright flesh underneath. Next, holding the fruit in one hand and a sharp paring knife in the other, and working over a bowl to catch the juices, free the wedges of fruit from the membranes that surround them.

TURNED VEGETABLES: vegetables cut into little football shapes for easier cooking and attractive presentation. Cut the vegetable into even lengths, then, using a small paring knife, trim a thin curved layer off each length. Turn the vegetable slightly and repeat the trimming gesture; repeat until you have an oblong elegant shape.

SNACKS

ROASTED GARLIC SCAPES
LEMON AIOLI, CRISPY SOPPRESSATA

BRAISED ENDIVE
GRUYÈRE, 'NDUJA, PARSLEY

DEAD-OF-WINTER VEGETABLE RÖSTI
SAFFRON AIOLI

POTATO AND MUSHROOM TOAST
POTATO BRIOCHE

CHICKPEA-BATTERED BROCCOLI
LOMO, MORNAY

BAKED POTATO PURÉE
CRISPY CHICKEN, CAVIAR

BRAISED BABY POTATOES
PANCETTA, COMTÉ, SAGE

SEARED AVOCADO SALAD
PICKLED SHRIMP, PUFFED RICE
CRACKER, CILANTRO

BEET AND POTATO CHIPS
PARSNIP, CARAMELIZED ONION, MIZUNA

HAM AND COMTÉ
SEEDED CRACKER, SHALLOT

PUFFED RICE CRACKER
SESAME SEED, HONEY, PEANUT

SPRING PEA TOAST
RADISH, LEMON, CHILE FLAKE

ROASTED GARLIC SCAPES

LEMON AIOLI, CRISPY SOPPRESSATA

SERVES 4 TO 6

I've been roasting these tasty tendrils for over a decade; they make the perfect summer starter with a crisp rosé. Scapes are the stalks that grow from the bulbs of garlic plants. But unlike the bulb's, the flavor is mellow with a slight sweet bite. I love to buy these by the wild and unruly bundle at the farmer's market. If you can't get your hands on scapes, scallions are a good option. Basically, any allium is delicious when dragged into this dip. The whole combination is also a great topping for cheeseburgers!

MAKE THE AIOLI: Combine the egg yolks, zest, lemon juice, and garlic in a blender. Pulse for 10 seconds. Switch to medium speed and very slowly begin to stream in the oils. You're doing a dance here: you don't want the mixture to break, but you want to incorporate all of the oil, both olive and canola. If it's too thick to blend properly, slowly add water, a teaspoon at a time. Add a pinch of salt, taste, and adjust the seasoning accordingly.

If not using right away, refrigerate the aioli with plastic wrap pressed against the surface so a skin doesn't form.

ROAST THE SCAPES: Preheat the oven to 425°F.

In a bowl, toss the garlic scapes with 3 tablespoons of the grapeseed oil and season with salt. Spread the scapes evenly on a sheet pan lined with parchment paper. You don't want the scapes piled too closely onto one another, so if another pan is needed, go ahead and use one.

Put the pan on the middle rack in the oven and roast just until the ends of the scapes begin to char, about 8 minutes.

In the meantime, in a medium sauté pan, toss the soppressata with the remaining 1 tablespoon oil over medium heat and render until crispy, 12 to 15 minutes.

TO SERVE: Remove the scapes from the oven and pile them on a serving dish or cutting board. Serve the aioli into a small bowl and scatter the soppresatta on top of the aioli, spooning the cooking oil along with it.

EMULSIFYING
ROASTING

AIOLI

3 large egg yolks

Grated zest of 1 lemon

1 tablespoon fresh lemon juice

1 garlic clove

½ cup plus 1 tablespoon extra-virgin olive oil

½ cup canola oil

Kosher salt

SCAPES

1 pound garlic scapes, stem ends trimmed

4 tablespoons grapeseed or other neutral oil

Kosher salt

½ pound soppressata, cut into ¼-inch cubes

NOTE
The aioli recipe yields 1 cup and can be made a day in advance. Everyone has their own preference when it comes to making aioli, be it elbow grease and a whisk, or the addition of potatoes, but I prefer a blender to make the emulsion.

BRAISED ENDIVE

GRUYÈRE, 'NDUJA, PARSLEY

SERVES 4 TO 6

BRAISING

NOTE
The endives need to be salted and refrigerated for 2 hours prior to cooking.

ENDIVE

3 large heads Belgian endive

¼ cup kosher salt

1 to 2 cups vegetable stock, homemade (page 89) or store bought

6 fresh thyme sprigs

2 teaspoons honey

3 tablespoons unsalted butter

1 teaspoon sherry vinegar

2 tablespoons olive oil

Freshly ground black pepper

GARNISH

1½ cups panko bread crumbs

6 ounces 'nduja sausage

6 ounces Gruyère cheese, grated

2 teaspoons grapeseed or other neutral oil

Kosher salt and freshly ground black pepper

20 to 30 small fresh flat-leaf parsley leaves

I love hearty French country cooking. A case in point is this vegetable gratin, which features cheesy, crunchy, creamy endive with 'nduja, a spreadable form of Calabrian sausage. This is a flavorful way to kick-start a dinner on a chilly night. My go-to for 'nduja and other charcuterie is Olympia Provisions (www.olympiaprovisions.com) or Formaggio Kitchen in Cambridge, Massachusetts.

PREP THE ENDIVE: Cut each endive in half lengthwise and lay them in a single layer cut-side up on a sheet pan or plate. Sprinkle the salt evenly over the endive. Refrigerate for 2 hours; the salt helps to draw out some of the bitterness of the endive.

Preheat the oven to 325°F.

Rinse the endive thoroughly and place them, cut-side down, on a paper towel to drain; pat dry. In a baking dish, arrange the endive, cut-side up, in a single layer. Add just enough vegetable stock to come halfway up the endive. Add the thyme, honey, butter, sherry vinegar, olive oil, and black pepper to taste. Cover with foil and braise until al dente, 45 to 50 minutes.

Using a slotted spoon, transfer the endive, cut-side down, to a towel to drain off any excess liquid. Pat them dry and transfer them to a small sheet pan or clean baking dish, cut-side up.

Preheat the broiler to high.

MIX THE GARNISH: In a medium bowl, combine the panko, 'nduja, cheese, and grapeseed oil, and season with salt and pepper. Mix into a thick paste using your hands.

Crumble the 'nduja mix over the endive. Broil, rotating the pan to ensure even coloring and cooking, until golden and bubbling, 6 to 8 minutes.

TO SERVE: Serve family-style on a platter. Sprinkle liberally with the parsley.

DEAD-OF-WINTER VEGETABLE RÖSTI

SAFFRON AIOLI

SERVES 6 TO 8

The idea for this came to me when my coauthor, Meredith, and I were in Montreal late one February, working on the cookbook. It was eighteen degrees below zero, and my ambitious plans of running the famed stairs at the L'Oratoire Saint-Joseph quickly degenerated into eating and drinking the best of what this city has to offer. Which is a lot. And all I could think about eating was rösti, a crisp potato pancake—a hash brown, if you will. Using winter root vegetables brings a depth of flavors and textures. This is perfect for lunch or dinner in an igloo.

Preheat the oven to 400°F.

In a medium bowl, combine the potatoes, beet, rutabaga, squash, cheese, drained raisins, caraway, rosemary, cornstarch, and egg. Season with salt and pepper.

Heat a large cast-iron or heavy-bottomed ovenproof sauté pan over high heat. Add a dash of the olive oil and a little butter: I recommend you fry a spoonful of the mix to test for the balance of seasonings and adjust your overall mixture accordingly. Now get the full amount of olive oil and butter sizzling. The hotter the fat is, the less soggy the finished rösti will be—and know this: the crust is the most important part.

Add the vegetable mix to the pan, spreading it out to form a large, thin pancake. Let it sit on high heat until it just starts to brown around the edges, 3 to 4 minutes. Transfer the pan to the oven and bake for 10 to 12 minutes.

TO SERVE: I like to serve the rösti presentation-side up—that is, the side you browned first. Cut it into wedges and serve with a big dollop of aioli and the sunny-side eggs, if using.

FRYING

1 pound Idaho or russet potatoes, peeled and grated on the large holes of a box grater

1 medium red beet, peeled and grated on the large holes of a box grater

8 ounces rutabaga, peeled and grated (2 cups)

8 ounces butternut squash, peeled and grated (2 cups)

½ cup grated Gruyère cheese

¼ cup golden raisins, plumped in warm water and then drained

2 teaspoons caraway seeds, toasted and finely ground

1 teaspoon chopped fresh rosemary

3 tablespoons cornstarch

1 large egg

Kosher salt and freshly ground black pepper

2 tablespoons olive oil

3 tablespoons unsalted butter

Aioli (see page 37), made with half the garlic and 1 teaspoon saffron soaked in 1 teaspoon water

6 to 8 eggs, cooked sunny-side up (optional)

POTATO AND MUSHROOM TOAST

POTATO BRIOCHE

SERVES 6

BLANCHING

PICKLING

NOTES

The dough will need to rise for 2 hours, chill for 8 hours or overnight, then proof for another 2 hours the next day.

You will need a potato ricer and an 8½ × 4½-inch loaf pan for this recipe.

I love baking bread at home, and aside from focaccia, potato brioche is the easiest bread recipe I know.

Using the potato flour here gives you a hint of a different flavor, but I really like it for the texture; it adds density while still keeping the dough light. I also find that the brioche holds its crumb better; once toasted, brioche can often be too dry.

The active cooking time here is nothing—under an hour. The most time-consuming part is proofing and chilling the bread dough (see Notes). The brioche, the potato purée, and the pickled onions are all great additions to your arsenal on their own. For the purée, for example, if you add flour and eggs you can proceed to a variation of the Baked Potato Purée (page 49). Or you can whisk it into a Roasted Chicken Stock (page 206) and build a potato soup.

Akin to a tartine, or open-faced sandwich, this is best served with a frisée salad.

PICKLED ONIONS

¾ cup white vinegar

¼ cup water

1 tablespoon sugar

2 teaspoons kosher salt

5 pearl onions, blanched (see page 23), shocked, and peeled

PICKLE THE ONIONS: In a small saucepan, combine the vinegar, water, sugar, and salt; bring to a simmer over medium heat, and cook until the sugar and salt have dissolved. Add the pearl onions and simmer until al dente, 4 to 5 minutes. Transfer the onions and pickling juice to a small nonreactive bowl or container and refrigerate. The longer the onions sit in the juice, the more picking liquid they absorb. Once cooled, cut them into small onion coins, separating the rings from each other to resemble miniature onion rings. The pickling liquid can be used to pickle other vegetables in the future; it will keep covered in the fridge for up to 3 days.

POTATO PURÉE

1 pound Idaho or russet potatoes, unpeeled

Kosher salt

1 teaspoon black peppercorns

2 tablespoons unsalted butter, melted

½ cup crème fraîche

¼ cup heavy cream

Freshly ground black pepper

MAKE THE POTATO PURÉE: Put the whole, unpeeled potatoes in a medium pot and add enough water to cover by 2 inches. Season the water with 1 tablespoon salt and the peppercorns. Bring to a boil and cook until tender, about 25 minutes. Remove the potatoes from the heat and drain.

After they have cooled enough to handle, approximately 10 minutes, peel the potatoes using a paring knife. Push them through a potato ricer into a bowl, and then, using the back of a large spoon, pass the purée through a fine-mesh sieve into another

recipe continues

bowl. Add the melted butter, crème fraîche, and heavy cream. Whisk well and season with salt and pepper to taste. Keep warm in a double boiler.

MUSHROOMS

6 tablespoons grapeseed or other neutral oil

5 ounces maitake mushrooms

6 garlic cloves, smashed

9 fresh thyme sprigs

Kosher salt and freshly ground black pepper

12 tablespoons (1½ sticks) unsalted butter

Sherry vinegar

2 tablespoons chopped fresh flat-leaf parsley leaves

5 ounces oyster mushrooms

5 ounces chanterelles

GARNISH

8 tablespoons (1 stick) unsalted butter

6 (½-inch-thick) slices Potato Brioche (recipe follows)

Kosher salt

15 fresh flat-leaf parsley leaves

2 frisée lettuces, hearts only

Fresh lemon juice

Extra-virgin olive oil

2 tablespoons finely sliced fresh chives

COOK THE MUSHROOMS: Into a large cast-iron skillet set over high heat, pour 2 tablespoons of the oil to coat the bottom of the pan. When it just begins to smoke, add the maitake mushrooms in one layer without overcrowding the pan. Resist the urge to move the mushrooms around in the pan—let them begin to brown, 3 to 5 minutes. You'll be able to smell them caramelizing. Next add 2 garlic cloves and 3 thyme sprigs, stirring the mushrooms slightly and seasoning them with salt and pepper. Once the mushrooms are just about browned all over and slightly crisped around the edges, add 4 tablespoons of the butter, letting it foam and bubble for 2 minutes. Add a splash of vinegar, just to add a little tang to the mushrooms' umami. Sprinkle in one-third of the chopped parsley. Mix well and transfer the contents of the pan to a large plate lined with paper towels. Repeat this entire procedure twice more, wiping your pan before you start afresh, first with the oyster mushrooms and then with the chanterelles. Mix the different mushrooms together.

TO SERVE: Preheat the oven to 400°F. Transfer the mushrooms to a parchment-lined sheet pan and heat in the oven for 5 minutes. Butter each side of the brioche slices and season with salt. Working in batches, toast the bread in a sauté pan over medium-high heat until each side is deep brown and looking slightly fried around the edges.

Toss the parsley, frisée, lemon juice, and olive oil in a bowl and season with salt. Spread roughly ¼ cup of the warm potato purée on each slice of brioche. Now pile on one-sixth of the mushrooms. Garnish with the frisée salad, a few rings of pickled onion, and the sliced chives.

POTATO BRIOCHE

MAKES ONE 8½ × 4½-INCH LOAF

In the bowl of a stand mixer, combine the milk, sugar, and yeast and let it sit for about 6 minutes, until the yeast is activated and the mixture starts to foam.

Combine the all-purpose flour and potato flour in a small mixing bowl. With your stand mixer running on medium speed and the dough hook attachment in place, add half the flour mixture gradually. Stir in the kosher salt. Add 3 eggs, one at a time. Add the remaining flour mixture. Once the dough starts to pull away from the sides of the bowl and looks smooth, incorporate the cubed butter gradually. Once all of the butter has been added, mix until the dough looks glossy, another 3 minutes. Remove the bowl from the machine and cover it with plastic wrap. Allow it to sit in a semi-warm place for 1 hour.

Put the bowl in the refrigerator and let the dough chill and rest for 8 hours or overnight.

Generously butter an 8½ × 4½-inch loaf pan. Punch the dough down and form it into a cylinder shape to fit the pan. Lightly pinch together the bottom seams of the dough. Put the bread into the pan, seam-side down, and allow it to rise, uncovered, until the dough has doubled in volume, about 2 hours.

Preheat the oven to 375°F. In a small bowl, beat the remaining egg with a fork and brush the dough with this egg wash, sprinkle with fleur de sel, and bake until the loaf has risen, is golden brown, and a cake tester inserted into the center comes out clean, 40 to 50 minutes. Allow to cool completely in the pan.

¼ cup lukewarm milk

1½ tablespoons sugar

1 teaspoon active-dry yeast

1½ cups all-purpose flour

½ cup potato flour

1 teaspoon kosher salt

4 large eggs

8 tablespoons (1 stick) unsalted butter, cut into ½-inch cubes, at room temperature, plus more for the pan

Fleur de sel, for sprinkling

NOTES

You will have leftover Potato Brioche; use it for the Lobster (page 111).

Also, when making the brioche dough for this recipe or the Egg Pudding (page 91), make sure you save 2 ounces of raw dough to make brioche sauce (page 111).

CHICKPEA-BATTERED BROCCOLI

LOMO, MORNAY

SERVES 4 TO 6

The oddly orangey-yellow broccoli cheddar soup I had as a kid is the inspiration for this dish. But here, I've taken those original flavors and added *lomo,* a cured Spanish pork tenderloin. And instead of making a soup, I fry the broccoli in a chickpea-flour tempura; the chickpeas lend a gritty texture that holds the Mornay sauce, which is a béchamel sauce (milk, flour, butter) with Gruyère cheese added. A legit Velveeta, if you will.

MAKE THE SAUCE: Melt the butter with the flour in a medium saucepan over medium heat, whisking until it becomes a paste (or roux). Cook gently so that the roux does not brown. Slowly whisk in the warm milk, avoiding lumps if possible (the sauce can be strained if you end up with lots of lumps), and bring the mixture to a simmer. Heat, whisking, until the flour is cooked and the mixture has begun to thicken, 3 to 4 minutes. Add the cheese in three batches, whisking well after each addition. Cook until the cheese is completely melted, 2 to 3 minutes. Season with salt and pepper, and set aside over very low heat or keep warm in a double boiler.

BROCCOLI: In a heavy high-sided pot, heat the canola oil to 350°F. Line a sheet pan with paper towels for the broccoli to drain on after it comes out of the oil.

To make the tempura batter, whisk together the chickpea flour and 1 cup of the rice flour in a medium bowl, add the ice, and whisk in the soda water, blending well but not whisking too much: you want to keep the bubbles in the soda water! Season with salt. The mixture should resemble a runny pancake batter.

Lightly dust the broccoli florets with the remaining ½ cup rice flour. Shake off any extra flour from each broccoli floret and then dip the floret into the batter, letting the excess drip off for a few seconds. Add florets to the hot oil in batches of 6 or 7. Do not overcrowd the pot. Fry until crisp (rice flour doesn't ever really get brown), 4 to 5 minutes. Transfer to the paper towel–lined sheet pan to drain.

EMULSIFYING

FRYING

MORNAY SAUCE

2 tablespoons unsalted butter

2 tablespoons all-purpose flour

2 cups whole milk, warmed

3 ounces Gruyère cheese, grated

Kosher salt and freshly ground black pepper

BROCCOLI

2 quarts canola oil, for frying

2 cups chickpea flour

1½ cups rice flour

1 cup ice cubes

3 cups soda water

Kosher salt

4 cups broccoli florets (ping-pong ball size), each with 2 inches of the stem

recipe continues

Immediately season with salt while still piping hot. This ensures the seasoning will stick. Continue cooking the rest of the broccoli in batches.

GARNISH

4 ounces finely sliced *lomo* or prosciutto

TO SERVE: I like to serve this family-style. (If your broccoli has cooled off too much, you can place it in a 300°F oven to bring back up to temperature.) Coat the bottom of your serving plate with the Mornay sauce, pile the crunchy broccoli on top, and drape the finely sliced *lomo* over that. Forks optional.

BAKED POTATO PURÉE
CRISPY CHICKEN, CAVIAR

SERVES 6

The brininess of the caviar, fat of the crispy chicken skin, and the starch from the potatoes make this the new expression of umami: the Big Mac 2.0, if you will. This is an indulgent starter or side, or even a festive main with the caviar piled high, perfect for Christmas or a luxe weekend brunch, à la Russ & Daughters, the famed New York City Jewish appetizing shop. I like Snake River Royal White Sturgeon caviar, but use whatever your pocketbook allows. Caviar of any kind is a state of mind as much as a delicacy.

COOK THE POTATOES: Put the potatoes in a medium pot and add enough water to cover by 2 inches. Season the water with 1 tablespoon salt and the peppercorns. Bring to a boil and cook until tender, about 25 minutes. Remove the pot from the heat and drain the potatoes.

PREP THE GARNISH: Preheat the oven to 350°F.

Line a sheet pan with parchment paper and spray it with cooking spray. Lay the chicken skins flat, but try not to overlap them. Season with salt and freshly ground black pepper. Then lay a sheet of parchment paper over the skins. Put another sheet pan over top, to act as a weight and ensure the chicken skins will crisp flat. If in doubt, add a cast-iron pan on top as an additional weight. Bake for 8 minutes.

Increase the oven temperature to 400°F. Bake until the skin is a deep golden color and the fat has rendered, an additional 20 minutes. Remove from the oven and transfer the chicken skins to a paper towel–lined plate. Strain and reserve the rendered chicken fat—the schmaltz—for future use; once cool, cover it and refrigerate or freeze. Keep the oven on.

PURÉE THE POTATOES: Once the potatoes are cooked, remove the potatoes from the heat and drain. After they have cooled enough to handle, approximately 10 minutes, peel the potatoes using a paring knife. Push them through a potato ricer into a bowl, and then, using the back of a large spoon, pass the purée through a fine-mesh sieve into a large bowl.

RENDERING

NOTE

You will need a potato ricer for this recipe.

POTATOES

3 pounds Idaho or russet potatoes, unpeeled

Kosher salt

1 teaspoon black peppercorns

4 tablespoons (½ stick) unsalted butter, melted

2 large eggs

2 large egg yolks

¾ cup crème fraîche

1 cup heavy cream

4 tablespoons all-purpose flour

Freshly ground black pepper

GARNISH

Nonstick cooking spray

6 ounces raw chicken skin (ask your butcher; you'll need enough for 12 crispy chips)

Kosher salt and freshly ground black pepper

2 ounces caviar

3 tablespoons finely sliced fresh chives

¼ cup crème fraîche

recipe continues

Add the melted butter, eggs, yolks, crème fraîche, and heavy cream to the bowl. Whisk to combine. Sprinkle the flour over the potato mixture and gently whisk again until the flour has been incorporated. Season with salt and freshly ground black pepper to taste.

Set 6 ramekins on a sheet pan. Portion the mixture into the ramekins, filling each three-fourths of the way. Transfer to the oven and bake until golden brown, like a baked potato skin, 16 to 20 minutes.

TO SERVE: Spoon a dollop of caviar atop each ramekin, scoop some crème fraiche next to the caviar, sprinkle with the chives, then plunge a couple of chicken-skin chips into each purée.

BRAISED BABY POTATOES

PANCETTA, COMTÉ, SAGE

SERVES 4

I'm always looking for new ways to cook potatoes, those favorite little sponges for flavor and salt. We fry, mash, sauté, purée, roast—so why not braise? Surround them with a flavorful liquid and let them drink it up. The skins hold on to that wonderfully salty liquid, and the meat of the potato remains light, soft, and creamy.

In a wide saucepan—you want the potatoes to lie in one layer—heat 1 tablespoon of the oil over medium heat. Add the pancetta and cook until it begins to crisp, 6 to 8 minutes. Add the butter and heat until it melts and begins to sizzle. Continue to fry the pancetta in the fat for 2 minutes.

Add the potatoes and, when they begin to brown on one side, roll them in the fat to brown as much of the outside as possible. Season with salt but be careful: potatoes need a fair amount of seasoning, but the pancetta is salty. Grind in some black pepper; I like a lot for this dish. Push the thyme and sage into the bottom of the pan in between the potatoes to brown and crisp these up, too. Once everything is beautiful and golden, add just enough vegetable stock to come halfway to three-fourths of the way up the potatoes. Cover and simmer over medium heat for 15 minutes.

Remove the lid and allow the liquid to boil and evaporate until the fat is left and you hear a sizzling sound; this signals everything is re-crisping. Cook until crisp and golden, which could take 12 to 15 minutes.

Meanwhile, dress the watercress with the remaining 2 teaspoons olive oil and the vinegar; season with salt.

TO SERVE: Spoon the potatoes onto a platter, sprinkle the cheese on top, and garnish with the watercress salad.

BRAISING

1 tablespoon plus 2 teaspoons olive oil

4 ounces pancetta, cut into a small dice

2 tablespoons unsalted butter

2 pounds small new potatoes

Kosher salt and freshly ground black pepper

3 fresh thyme sprigs

8 fresh sage leaves

2 cups vegetable stock, homemade (page 89) or store-bought

3 ounces watercress

2 teaspoons white vinegar

3 ounces Comté cheese, finely grated

SEARED AVOCADO SALAD

PICKLED SHRIMP, PUFFED RICE CRACKER, CILANTRO

SERVES 4

PICKLING
SEARING

Pickled shrimp salad is a Southern thing. I had my first pickled shrimp at the Ordinary in Charleston. I've added some traditional shrimp-go-with suspects to this recipe, including avocado and cilantro. I like to dip the rice crackers into the salad or just crumble them on top. This dish is like shrimp toast and avocado toast had a baby, and it's a very tasty one.

PICKLED SHRIMP

1 pound peeled and deveined 16/20 shrimp, cut into bite-size pieces

2 cups white vinegar

1 cup water

1 tablespoon kosher salt

1 tablespoon sugar

2 bay leaves

1 teaspoon coriander seeds

2 teaspoons peeled and coarsely chopped fresh ginger

PICKLE THE SHRIMP: Put the shrimp in a medium nonreactive, heat-proof bowl. In a small nonreactive saucepan, bring the vinegar, water, salt, sugar, bay leaves, coriander seeds, and ginger to a boil, and boil for 2 minutes. Immediately pour this liquid over the shrimp and let it sit at room temperature for 15 minutes. Place the bowl in an ice bath, cover, then refrigerate for at least 45 minutes, until chilled, or up to 2 hours.

SHRIMP SALAD

Grated zest of 1 lemon

1 tablespoon fresh lemon juice

2 tablespoons chopped fresh cilantro

¼ small red onion, finely sliced, soaked (see Note), and drained

¼ cup English cucumber, peeled, seeded, and cut into brunoise (see page 32)

1 teaspoon finely minced jalapeño pepper (remove the seeds if you like less heat)

3 tablespoons extra-virgin olive oil

Kosher salt

MAKE THE SHRIMP SALAD: Drain the liquid from the shrimp and wipe off the coriander seeds. Toss the shrimp with the lemon zest, lemon juice, chopped cilantro, onion, cucumber, jalapeño pepper, olive oil, and salt to taste.

NOTE
To take the bite out of raw onion in a salad, soak it in cold water for 3 minutes, drain, and rinse. Repeat three times more. Drain and refrigerate until ready to use.

SEAR THE AVOCADO: Halve the avocadoes lengthwise and then pit and peel them. Cut each piece again in half lengthwise, parallel to the original cut. Slice a little off the two rounded pieces so they lie flat. Sprinkle the avocado pieces with the lime juice and salt on both sides. Heat the grapeseed oil in a sauté pan over high heat. Just as it begins to smoke, add the avocado pieces and lower the heat to medium-high. Sear the first side until nicely browned, about 2 minutes. Gently turn over and repeat on the other side.

TO SERVE: Put one avocado piece on each plate and arrange the shrimp salad around the outline of the avocado, garnishing with the cilantro leaves, scallion greens, and shards of puffed rice cracker.

SEARED AVOCADO

1 just-ripe avocado

2 teaspoons fresh lime juice

Kosher salt

1 tablespoon grapeseed or other neutral oil

GARNISH

12 cilantro leaves

5 scallions, dark green part only, finely sliced on the bias

Rice Crackers (page 63)

BEET AND POTATO CHIPS

PARSNIP, CARAMELIZED ONION, MIZUNA

SERVES 6 TO 8

This recipe and the following one are a one-two punch of approachable and tasty hors d'oeuvres. I made this dish the second time I cooked at the James Beard House in New York City. I wanted to do something nostalgic, because of the Beard house space—with its flat brick facade, multiple levels, and outdoor garden reception area tucked away on West 12th Street. It's such an iconic place in American culinary history. So I honored it by updating another American classic: chips and dip. I grew up on Lay's potato chips and packaged onion dip. My grandma taught me to get the crumbs at the bottom of the bag by sticking my spoon in dip and using it to lure the little pieces into my mouth. You'll crave this grown-up version just as much.

ROAST THE PARSNIPS: Preheat the oven to 400°F.

Toss the parsnips in 2 tablespoons grapeseed oil and season with salt. Roast in the oven until very tender, 20 to 25 minutes. Remove from the oven and set aside to cool a little.

Meanwhile, caramelize the onions. In a large skillet, heat 1 to 2 tablespoons grapeseed oil over medium-high heat until it begins to shimmer. Add the onions and a pinch of salt. Sweat the onions until the liquid begins to cook out and the onions are tender. Reduce the heat to low and slowly caramelize, stirring occasionally, until dark amber in color, 45 minutes to 1 hour. Transfer the onions to a colander set over a bowl to drain. Once the onions have cooled, transfer them to a cutting board and chop them until you have ½ cup.

While the parsnips are still warm (but not hot), transfer them to a blender with the mascarpone and blend on high until smooth. You're looking for medium to stiff peaks here, and if you have to add 1 tablespoon water or so to achieve that, then so be it.

Scoop the mixture into a bowl, and fold in the onions, crème fraîche, lemon zest, chives, and mustard. Season with salt and pepper. Cover with plastic wrap and chill in the refrigerator until ready to use, at least 1 hour or up to 2 days.

FRYING

ROASTING

SWEATING

NOTE
You will need a mandoline for this recipe. It's mandatory.

PARSNIP DIP

2 large parsnips, peeled, and cut into a large dice

Grapeseed or other neutral oil

Kosher salt and freshly ground black pepper

2 large yellow onions, halved and sliced

⅓ cup mascarpone cheese

¼ cup crème fraîche

Grated zest of 1 lemon

1 tablespoon finely sliced fresh chives

1 tablespoon whole-grain mustard

recipe continues

BEET AND POTATO CHIPS

Canola oil, for frying

1 large Idaho or russet potato, unpeeled and sliced ⅛ inch thick on a mandoline

Kosher salt

1 large red beet, peeled and sliced ⅛ inch thick on a mandoline

GARNISH

25 mizuna leaves (optional)

¼ cup malt vinegar

FRY THE CHIPS: In a large pot, heat 3 to 4 inches of canola oil to 350°F. Line a sheet pan with paper towels.

Working in batches, fry the potatoes until golden brown, 3 to 4 minutes. After each batch of potatoes comes out of the oil, put them on the paper towel–lined pan and season immediately with salt. Salt won't stick to chips that have cooled. Next fry the beets in batches until the edges curl and crisp, 3 to 4 minutes. These will be a bit more difficult to tell because the golden brown will be harder to see through the deep red color. Remove each batch to the paper towels to drain and salt them.

TO SERVE: On a medium round white plate, pipe a 3- to 4-inch ring of dip in the center. Create a good ¾-inch-high wall of the dip. Stick the beets and potatoes in the ring, alternating the two and creating a wreath of chips. Lay the mizuna leaves, if using, in one layer on the plate. Put the vinegar in a spray bottle (a great way to disperse liquid over leaves without adding too much and wilting them), if you have one, and gently mist the leaves; alternatively, drizzle a little vinegar over them. You will not use all the vinegar. Stick clumps of mizuna leaves in between sections of the chips.

HAM AND COMTÉ

SEEDED CRACKER, SHALLOT

SERVES 4 TO 6

Hip-hop musician Questlove's food salons in New York City are casual parties he hosts every few months, inviting different chefs each time to prepare individual courses for the evening. Each chef takes a turn in his kitchen to dole out a dish. For a recent edition, I was asked to provide the opening salvo, while Edouardo Jordan (Salare, Seattle) followed with a great octopus dish, Andy Ricker (Pok Pok, Portland, Oregon) made a tasty ramen, and Jennifer Yee (Lafayette, New York City) whipped up homemade push-pops and a sundae "dip" station for dessert. *So why not start with some kind of a dip and finger food to get the party going,* I thought? Deviled ham and pimento cheese hors d'oeuvres in all their delightful tackiness were my inspiration. I prepped all the crackers the night before in an NYC apartment and made a quick day-of run to Eataly for the Comté and country ham. This is a make-ahead gem.

MAKE THE DIP: Fold together the ham, crème fraîche, mascarpone, mustard, lemon zest, lemon juice, Sriracha, fried shallots, salt to taste, and the pepper. Refrigerate for at least 1 hour and up to 2 days.

MAKE THE CHEESE SAUCE: Close to serving time, bring the heavy cream to a light simmer in a medium saucepan over medium heat, then whisk in one-third of the cheese at a time, until all the cheese is incorporated. Allow it to simmer until the mixture thickens slightly and makes a runny cheese sauce that's slightly thicker than heavy cream. Season to taste with salt.

TO SERVE: Make quenelles of about 3 heaping tablespoons each of the ham mixture and set one in the center of each plate. Spoon some of the cheese sauce over each quenelle, letting it spill onto the plate. Sprinkle the fried shallots over the ham dip. Garnish with the scallions and some baby arugula. Break off large shards of crackers—roughly 3 pieces per portion—and stand them upright in the ham dip.

EMULSIFYING
FRYING

HAM DIP

7 ounces finely sliced jambon de Paris (French ham) or country ham, finely minced

½ cup crème fraîche

½ cup mascarpone cheese

1 tablespoon whole-grain mustard

Grated zest of 1 lemon

1 teaspoon fresh lemon juice

2 teaspoons Sriracha or other hot sauce

2 tablespoons fried shallots (see page 82)

Kosher salt

1 teaspoon freshly ground black pepper

CHEESE SAUCE

1 cup heavy cream

4 ounces Comté cheese, finely grated

Kosher salt

GARNISH

2 tablespoons fried shallots (see page 82)

3 scallions, green part only, finely sliced on the bias

15 to 20 baby arugula leaves

Kosher salt

Seeded Crackers (recipe follows)

recipe continues

SEEDED CRACKERS

MAKES 4 LARGE CRACKER SHEETS

In a medium bowl using a spoon, mix together the semolina, all-purpose flour, olive oil, water, and kosher salt into a dough. Transfer the dough to a countertop and knead it for 5 to 6 minutes; when you're done, it should feel like Play-Doh. Set the dough on a lightly floured surface and cover with a kitchen towel. Let it rest for 20 to 30 minutes.

Preheat the oven to 450°F.

Cut the dough into quarters. Using a lightly floured rolling pin, roll out a quarter of the dough at a time until the dough is thin enough that you can see the outline of your hand through it.

Sprinkle a little semolina flour on a sheet pan and transfer the rolled-out dough to the pan. Sprinkle the top of the dough evenly with a quarter of the poppy and sesame seeds and with Maldon salt and some pepper. Use your palms to press the seasonings lightly into the dough to make sure they adhere. If you have a second sheet pan available, repeat the procedure with another quarter of the dough.

Bake until the cracker starts to bubble and turn golden brown, 4 to 6 minutes. Remove the pan from the oven and transfer the cracker to a wire rack or balance it on top of 4 glasses, anything to keep it from sitting directly on top of a flat surface and steaming itself into softness. This way the cracker will harden as it cools.

Repeat the procedure with the remaining quarters of dough.

1 cup semolina flour, plus more for the pan

1 cup all-purpose flour, plus more for rolling

¼ cup olive oil

¼ cup warm water

1 teaspoon kosher salt

1 tablespoon poppy seeds

2 tablespoons white sesame seeds

Maldon salt

Freshly ground black pepper

NOTE

The crackers can be made up to 5 days ahead of time and stored in an airtight container in a cool, dry place.

PUFFED RICE CRACKER

SESAME SEED, HONEY, PEANUT

SERVES 8 TO 10

FRYING

I turned an Asian peanut bar snack into a dip after appreciating the sticky, candied nuts plus nori combo at a karaoke bar in Gowanus, Brooklyn, with my friend Stacy. You never know where inspiration will strike! The rice cracker is a neutral crisp vehicle to get that shit in your mouth. (It also reminds me of my favorite chip, Munchos, which are puffy.) It's best to make the rice cracker with leftover cooked rice. Actually, scratch that, it's best to make the cracker with the overcooked rice that you botched during last night's dinner (admittedly this happens to me often), so let's consider this recipe not just tasty but also an opportunity to correct any rice mistakes!

1 tablespoon honey

¼ cup toasted skin-on peanuts, coarsely chopped, plus 1 tablespoon for grating

½ teaspoon unsalted butter

2 tablespoons white sesame seeds

1 teaspoon Aleppo pepper or ½ teaspoon crushed red pepper flakes

Fleur de sel and freshly ground black pepper

Rice Crackers (recipe follows)

In a small sauté pan over medium heat, bring the honey to a simmer for 2 minutes. Stir in the ¼ cup peanuts and the butter and continue simmering for 2 additional minutes. Remove from the heat, add the sesame seeds, Aleppo pepper, and fleur de sel and black pepper to taste. Spread on a parchment-lined sheet pan to cool completely.

TO SERVE: Place a pile of large shards of the puffed crackers on a flat platter and drizzle with the peanut-honey mixture. Finely grate a tablespoon of peanuts over the top of the crackers. (Eat fast or the crackers get mushy.)

RICE CRACKERS

MAKES ABOUT 20 MEDIUM CRACKERS

Preheat the oven to 225°F.

In a high-speed blender, blend the rice into a smooth paste, adding a little water if necessary to get it going. Spread the rice paste very thinly onto a sheet pan lined with a silicone baking mat or parchment paper. Dehydrate in the oven for 3 to 4 hours, until crisp but still pale. Break into large shards or desired size.

To fry and "puff" the crackers, in a high-sided medium pot, heat the oil to 425°F, until just smoking. Fry the crackers in batches for 5 to 8 seconds, until the cracker puffs and curls. This puffing and curling will happen almost instantly. Drain on paper towels, seasoning with salt immediately. Repeat the process until all your crackers are fried. Store them in a cool, dry place; if your crackers pick up any humidity, they can be refried briefly to crisp them back up.

¾ cup overcooked white rice

¼ cup water, or as needed

2 cups canola oil, for frying

Kosher salt

SPRING PEA TOAST

RADISH, LEMON, CHILE FLAKE

SERVES 4

Avocado toast is delicious and I will continue to eat it long after other chefs and restaurants have moved on. But, for me, avocado has more texture than flavor, so I like to re-create its creamy, fatty, unctuous mouthfeel with the more flavorful English pea. I pair this green spread with butter-fried seeded bread and top it with a little radish and a sprinkling of chile flakes.

In a bowl, mash together the peas, lemon zest, olive oil, and salt to taste with a fork until it looks like lumpy mashed potatoes. Take 2 tablespoons of the peas and pack it onto each slice of bread, creating a mound on top of the bread. In a large skillet over medium-high heat, melt half of the butter. Once it begins to bubble slightly, add 1 garlic clove and 2 thyme sprigs. Add half the bread slices, pea-side up. You are shallow-frying the toast in an aromatic butter. Once the bread is a nice golden brown, 2 to 4 minutes, remove it from the pan and put the toasts on a paper towel to absorb any excess fat. Dump out the used butter, wipe the pan clean, and repeat with the remaining 4 toasts.

TO SERVE: Arrange the toasts on a platter, season with salt, if necessary, and sprinkle with the red pepper flakes. Scatter the radish and the pea tendrils on top, if desired, and finish with a few turns of black pepper and a squeeze of lemon juice.

BLANCHING

FRYING

1 cup English peas, blanched (see page 23)

Grated zest of 1 lemon

3 tablespoons olive oil

Kosher salt

8 (1-inch-thick) slices ficelle bread (see Note)

8 tablespoons (1 stick) unsalted butter

2 garlic cloves, smashed

4 fresh thyme sprigs

GARNISH

½ teaspoon crushed red pepper flakes, or to taste

2 red radishes, cut into julienne

12 to 15 pea tendrils (optional)

Freshly ground black pepper

1 lemon wedge

NOTE
A ficelle is a thinner, smaller version of a baguette.

BEGINNINGS

MELTED LEEKS
MOREL MUSHROOM CREAM

SQUASH AND COCONUT MILK CUSTARD

ROASTED WHOLE HEN-OF-THE-WOODS
PANCETTA PARMESAN BROTH, WILD RICE

TOMATO SALAD
WILD POPPY VINEGAR, ORANGE OIL,
GARLIC CARAMEL

DUCK CONFIT SALAD
ROASTED SHALLOT, MUSTARD, ALMOND

CHARRED BEAN SALAD
VINEGAR, SHALLOT

ASPARAGUS SALAD
SMOKED AVOCADO, GRAPEFRUIT, SABAYON

BEET AND NECTARINE
CRUNCHY SEEDS, BAYRISCHER BLUE CHEESE

EGG PUDDING
BROWN BUTTER, CAVIAR, BRIOCHE

KATAIFI-WRAPPED BURRATA
DATE SYRUP, RADISH SALAD

SMOKED VEGETABLE SALAD
BANYULS VINEGAR, LETTUCES, MARCONA
ALMONDS

CHICKEN LIVER MOUSSE
PICKLES, PEANUT, CILANTRO

MELTED LEEKS

MOREL MUSHROOM CREAM

SERVES 4

BRAISING

LEEKS

4 medium leeks, dark green part removed (save for stocks or sauces), trimmed to 4 to 5 inches in length

2 cups Roasted Chicken Stock (page 206) or store-bought low-sodium stock

3 fresh thyme sprigs

2 fresh flat-leaf parsley sprigs

2 strips lemon zest

2 garlic cloves, smashed

1 teaspoon honey

1 tablespoon sherry vinegar

2 tablespoons olive oil

3 tablespoons unsalted butter

Kosher salt and freshly ground black pepper

I buy morels from Oregon during peak season, from April to the end of June. Cooking them whole and as simply as possible is ideal. Braising leeks is one of my favorite techniques. I love the texture and the flavor that braised vegetables pick up over time. They remind me of the mushy carrots and celery from a pot roast in the most appealing way.

Leeks are very dirty; they grow vertically up through the soil, and that's how the dirt gets stuck deep within their layers. To clean them but keep them whole, I prefer this method: Remove the hearty outer layer of the leek. Lay the leek on your cutting board. Insert the tip of your knife 1 inch from the top and slice almost to the bottom of the leek, stopping 1 inch short of the root end. Roll the leek one quarter turn and repeat once more. You are essentially cutting a long + sign down most of the leek while the ends will hold it together. Soak the leeks in cool water for 15 minutes or so, agitating them and running the water into the slits in between soakings. Do this a couple times until the water is clean and free of any particles.

Morels are even dirtier! There's nothing more satisfying than air-gun-cleaning morels—kind of like taking a can of compressed air to your keyboard or power-washing your car—before service in a restaurant, but yes, I realize that probably isn't going to happen at home. So water and patience will have to do, because there's nothing worse than a gritty mushroom. Soak them thoroughly in water, rinse, and repeat a few times until there's no more grit at the bottom of the bowl. Bite into a mushroom to make sure they are clean.

BRAISE THE LEEKS: Preheat the oven to 350°F.

Nestle the leeks in a small rectangular roasting dish. Slowly add the chicken stock, stopping short of covering the leeks (about three-fourths of the way). Scatter the thyme sprigs, parsley, lemon zest, and garlic cloves around the leeks. Drizzle the honey, vinegar, and olive oil over top. Dot with the butter. Season with salt and pepper. Cover with aluminum foil or a lid. Bake until the leeks are fork-tender, 1 to 1½ hours. Reserve 1 cup of the cooking liquid to use with the mushrooms.

MEANWHILE, START THE MUSHROOM SAUCE: I like to double-cook mushrooms, once to remove any excess water (water = no flavor) and the second time to caramelize them. Set up a colander or strainer over a bowl next to your stovetop. In a large sauté pan, over medium-high heat, bring 1 tablespoon of the grapeseed oil to a shimmer. Sauté the mushrooms (do this in two batches if your pan feels too small), seasoning with a little salt. Keep stirring them; you'll begin to notice mushroom water accumulating. Once the mushrooms have purged that initial liquid and before the liquid evaporates, after 3 to 5 minutes, dump the mushrooms and liquid into the strainer. Allow the mushrooms to drain for 15 minutes or so; you'll be surprised to see how much water was in them.

Wipe out the pan and add the remaining tablespoon grapeseed oil to it. Heat on high until the oil shimmers. Add the mushrooms and spread them out, allowing them to sear and caramelize for 1 to 2 minutes. Don't touch them! Once you begin to see and smell the browning, sprinkle the shallot, garlic, and thyme over them. Cook, stirring once or twice, until the aromatics have begun to brown, about 3 minutes.

Deglaze the pan with the sherry and cook until au sec (the sherry has evaporated). Add the reserved leek braising liquid and the heavy cream, and reduce over medium heat until the sauce coats the back of a spoon. Turn off the heat and slowly whisk in the cold butter. Add the parsley and the lemon juice, and season to taste with salt and pepper.

TO SERVE: Spoon roughly ¼ cup of warm mushroom sauce onto the center of each plate. Set a leek off to one side of the sauce on each plate. Toss the frisée and chives with the lemon juice and olive oil. Finish each plate with a little bundle of chives and frisée salad on the other side of the sauce. Sprinkle with fleur de sel and pepper.

MUSHROOM SAUCE

2 tablespoons grapeseed or other neutral oil

1 pound morel mushrooms, trimmed, rinsed, and dried, halved only if very large

Kosher salt

1 tablespoon minced shallot

1 garlic clove, minced

½ teaspoon chopped fresh thyme

2 tablespoons dry sherry

1 cup reserved leek braising liquid

½ cup heavy cream

2 tablespoons (¼ stick) cold unsalted butter, cubed

2 teaspoons finely chopped fresh flat-leaf parsley leaves

1 teaspoon fresh lemon juice

Freshly ground black pepper

GARNISH

3 ounces frisée hearts

2 tablespoons finely sliced fresh chives

1 teaspoon fresh lemon juice

1 teaspoon olive oil

Fleur de sel and freshly ground black pepper

SQUASH AND COCONUT MILK CUSTARD

SERVES 4

MAKING CUSTARD
ROASTING

Here half a roasted squash is filled with coconut milk that's cooked into a savory crème brûlée of sorts. Delightfully jiggly. I like to serve it as a starter or as a side with roasted chicken; the coconut flavor gives the squash that sweet-savory mix. It's a great autumn dish that would make a nice veggie option at Thanksgiving.

This dish is inspired by my days at Sensing restaurant.

SQUASH

2 acorn squashes, halved from tip to stem, seeds scooped out

2 tablespoons olive oil

Kosher salt

6 fresh sage leaves

ROAST THE SQUASH: Preheat the oven to 400°F.

Trim a small sliver off the skin side of each squash half to create a flat surface so the squash halves sit evenly, like bowls. Transfer to a parchment-lined sheet pan.

Next drizzle ½ tablespoon of the olive oil over each half and season with salt. Tear the sage and sprinkle it over the squash. Roast the squash for about 25 minutes, or until just over halfway cooked.

CUSTARD

2 cups canned coconut milk

1 cup heavy cream

6 large egg yolks

2 tablespoons sugar

Grated zest of ½ orange

2 teaspoons freshly ground black pepper

Fleur de sel

MAKE THE CUSTARD: While the squash is roasting, in a large bowl, whisk together the coconut milk, cream, egg yolks, sugar, orange zest, pepper, and fleur de sel to taste. Remove the squash from the oven and reduce the oven temperature to 350°F.

Wrap the outside of each squash half tightly with foil, in anticipation of the impending water bath. Transfer the squash to a baking dish or roasting pan. Pour the coconut custard into the well of each squash, allowing it to seep in and fill up. Next, add hot water from the tap to the baking dish until it reaches halfway up the sides of the squash halves. Bake until the custard begins to set, 1 hour to 1 hour 15 minutes. When you move the squash to test the custard, it should jiggle a bit like gelatin. As it cools slightly, it will set up further. I like to serve this at room temperature, but it's also good piping hot.

GARNISH

3 tablespoons Brown Butter (page 92)

¼ cup coarsely chopped walnuts, toasted

TO SERVE: Serve family-style on a small platter in halves, as roasted, or quartered. Drizzle brown butter over the top of each squash half and sprinkle with the toasted walnuts.

ROASTED WHOLE HEN-OF-THE-WOODS
PANCETTA PARMESAN BROTH, WILD RICE

SERVES 4

Hen-of-the-woods mushrooms (also known as maitake) are made for roasting: the edges get crispy in texture and the flavor is meaty and full of umami, reminiscent of bacon. Because of their low moisture content, they are easy to crisp up—whereas many mushrooms have a tendency to steam. They are beautiful when kept whole. The rich Parmesan broth, crispy-salty pancetta, and chewy wild rice add up to an incredible balance of flavors and textures.

EMULSIFYING
ROASTING

Preheat the oven to 400°F.

First start cooking the wild rice. In a small saucepan, combine the rice with 1½ cups water, and season with salt to taste. Bring the water to a boil over high heat, cover the pan, and reduce the heat. Simmer until tender, 35 to 45 minutes.

While the rice is cooking, in a medium saucepan, heat the olive oil over medium-high heat and cook the pancetta until crisp, about 10 minutes. Scoop out the pancetta and drain on paper towels. Drain and discard the fat from the pan, and add the chicken stock and Parmesan rind. Bring to a boil over high heat, then lower the heat to medium and simmer until the stock has reduced by one-fourth to about 3 cups, about 20 minutes.

Lay the mushrooms on a parchment-lined sheet pan. Drizzle with the grapeseed oil and tuck 1 thyme sprig into the folds of each mushroom cluster. Roast until the mushrooms begin to crisp around the edges and their core is just tender, 10 to 15 minutes. Season with salt as soon as you remove the pan from the oven. Discard the thyme.

Discard the Parmesan rind. Add the butter and vinegar to the hot stock and, using a hand blender or a whisk, emulsify the mixture. Season with salt to taste.

½ cup wild rice

Kosher salt

1 tablespoon olive oil

4 ounces pancetta, cut into a small dice

1 quart Roasted Chicken Stock (page 206) or store-bought low-sodium stock

1 (4 × 4-inch) Parmesan cheese rind

12 ounces hen-of-the-woods mushrooms, broken into 4 clusters

2 tablespoons grapeseed or other neutral oil

4 fresh thyme sprigs

3 tablespoons unsalted butter

1 teaspoon sherry vinegar

TO SERVE: Divide the wild rice among four deep but narrow bowls. Place a mushroom cluster on top of each portion of rice. Sprinkle Parmesan evenly on top. Ladle ⅔ cup of broth into each bowl. Garnish with the crispy pancetta bits.

8 teaspoons freshly grated Parmesan cheese

TOMATO SALAD

WILD POPPY VINEGAR, ORANGE OIL, GARLIC CARAMEL

SERVES 4 TO 6

NOTE

If you can't find wild poppy vinegar at a specialty store, you can buy it online from Oliviers & Company (www.oliviersandco .com). Or you can substitute your favorite vinegar, such as white balsamic, red wine vinegar, or another interesting flavored vinegar.

1 whole head of garlic

1 teaspoon olive oil

1 pound ripe heirloom tomatoes, preferably a mix of colors, shapes, and textures

3 tablespoons wild poppy vinegar (see Note)

3 tablespoons grapeseed or other neutral oil

2 tablespoons grated orange zest

3 tablespoons sugar

2 teaspoons water

3 tablespoons heavy cream

When I was working at Sensing in Boston in my early twenties, Gérard Barbin, the chef de cuisine, turned me on to wild poppy vinegar. He made a tomato salad, and the vinegar, which smells like flowers and ripe fruit, was the perfect seasoning. Gérard would bring in half a dozen new ingredients a week. As a young cook, I loved being introduced to so many new flavors.

Tomato seeds are full of umami, and I love how the slightly bitter yet sweet caramel here balances their natural acidity. The combo makes my mouth water.

Preheat the oven to 400°F.

Rub the garlic bulb with the olive oil, wrap it inside a pocket of foil, and place it on a sheet pan. Roast until the garlic is very soft, 25 to 30 minutes. Remove from the oven, open the foil, and set aside until the garlic is cool enough to handle. Slice the cooled bulb crosswise and squeeze out the roasted garlic pulp from each half, reserving it in a small bowl. Discard the skins.

Cut the tomatoes into random shapes: wedges, slices, oblong . . . whatever. The more shapes and sizes there are, the more pockets and wells for the oil and vinegar to seep into. It also makes for a more visually interesting salad. Combine the tomato pieces in a bowl with the vinegar and allow them to sit at room temperature as you prepare the other ingredients.

Warm the grapeseed oil and orange zest in a very small saucepan over medium-low heat, just until the zest begins to sizzle, 8 to 10 minutes. Remove from the heat and allow it to sit for 30 minutes. Strain and reserve the oil.

recipe continues

Next start the caramel for the garlic sauce: Combine the sugar and water in a small saucepan and cook over medium-high heat until the syrup turns dark amber in color, 8 to 10 minutes. Lower the heat before you carefully pour in the heavy cream: it will sizzle wildly! Whisk over low heat to dissolve the caramel into the cream. Add the roasted garlic, lightly mashing it with the whisk as you stir. Remove from the heat and pass through a small strainer to remove any large pieces of garlic. Keep the caramel at room temperature.

GARNISH

Fleur de sel and freshly ground black pepper

15 purple basil leaves

2 teaspoons poppy seeds, toasted

TO SERVE: Season the tomatoes with fleur de sel and pepper, then add the orange oil to the bowl and toss gently. Spoon 2 teaspoons of the garlic caramel into the bottom of each deep bowl. Divide the tomatoes on top and spoon 2 tablespoons of the juices in the bowl over each portion. Garnish each bowl with basil leaves, a pinch of poppy seeds, fleur de sel, and pepper.

DUCK CONFIT SALAD

ROASTED SHALLOT, MUSTARD, ALMOND

SERVES 4 TO 6

This dish is inspired by my time as a culinary student in Chicago. My favorite little bistro there, Bijan's, still serves my favorite roast chicken salad, packed with romaine, almonds, and goat cheese, and tossed with a mustard vinaigrette. I would sit at the bar or just get it to go after school. Here is my grown-up version of the salad that got me through school, with the same satisfying textures and rich and highly seasoned duck confit standing in for the chicken.

MAKE THE DUCK CONFIT: Sprinkle about half the salt, half the rosemary, 3 of the parsley sprigs, 3 of the thyme sprigs, and the pink peppercorns in a baking dish just large enough to hold the legs in a single layer. Put the duck legs on top, skin-side down, then sprinkle the remaining salt and aromatics over the duck. Tuck the garlic between the legs. Cover with plastic wrap and refrigerate for 24 to 36 hours.

When ready to cook the duck, preheat the oven to 220°F.

In a medium saucepan, melt the duck fat over medium heat.

Remove the duck from the fridge and rinse the salt and aromatics off under running cold water; pat dry. Wipe out the baking dish and return the duck to the pan. Pour the melted fat into the pot to cover the duck. Cover with foil or a tight-fitting lid. Transfer to the oven and cook for 6 to 7 hours, until the meat is fork-tender. Remove from the oven and transfer the duck legs to a wire rack set over a sheet pan to cool. Pick the duck meat off the bones in large pieces. Discard the bones and skin.

Increase the oven temperature to 400°F.

PREP THE GARNISH: Toss the shallots with the olive oil and thyme sprigs and season with salt and pepper to taste. Spread out the shallots on a parchment-lined sheet pan and roast until golden and tender, 15 to 18 minutes. Remove from the oven and set aside to cool. When the shallots are cool enough to handle, peel off individual shallot petals.

CURING

EMULSIFYING

MAKING CONFIT

DUCK CONFIT

¼ cup plus 2 tablespoons kosher salt

5 fresh rosemary sprigs, leaves only

5 fresh flat-leaf parsley sprigs

5 fresh thyme sprigs

1 tablespoon pink peppercorns, crushed

4 duck legs

2 garlic cloves, finely sliced

5 to 6 cups rendered duck fat, as needed

NOTE

The duck needs to cure for 24 to 36 hours before being cooked in its own fat for 6 to 7 hours. Once cooked, the duck can also be reserved for at least a week in the fridge in its fat. Plan accordingly.

GARNISH

6 shallots, halved lengthwise

3 tablespoons olive oil

4 fresh thyme sprigs

Kosher salt and freshly ground black pepper

¼ cup Marcona almonds, toasted and quartered lengthwise

recipe continues

MAKE THE SALAD DRESSING: Combine the egg yolks, mustard, vinegar, and honey in a blender (or in a tall jar if you plan on using a hand blender). Start blending on low speed, then gradually increase the speed and slowly stream in both of the oils, creating an emulsion. Season the dressing with salt and pepper to taste.

In a large bowl, combine the different lettuces. Add 3 tablespoons of the dressing and very gently toss the lettuces to coat; add more dressing as desired. Taste and adjust the seasoning.

TO SERVE: Place a mound of lettuce in the center of each plate—I like a shallow, wide bowl. Next gently toss the duck pieces and petals of roasted shallot in the same bowl you used for the lettuce. Top the salad with duck pieces and shallot petals. Sprinkle each plate with Marcona almonds.

SALAD

2 large egg yolks

2 tablespoons whole-grain mustard

3 tablespoons sherry vinegar

2 teaspoons honey

¼ cup olive oil

¼ cup grapeseed or other neutral oil

Kosher salt and freshly ground black pepper

3 heads frisée, white hearts only

4 ounces baby spinach

3 ounces purple mustard greens

CHARRED BEAN SALAD

VINEGAR, SHALLOT

SERVES 4 TO 6

FRYING

Sweet three-bean salad was a Michigan summer picnic staple, along with grilled chicken with barbecue sauce, potato salad, and spaghetti salad (my mom's version: cooked spaghetti, Italian dressing, salad seasoning mix, chopped scallions, diced celery, diced bell pepper, and halved cherry tomatoes). I use whatever beans look best at the market.

Grapeseed or other neutral oil

¼ pound wax beans, trimmed

½ pound haricots verts, trimmed

½ pound purple French beans, trimmed

¼ pound dragon tongue beans, trimmed

¼ pound romano beans, trimmed

1 teaspoon chopped garlic

1 tablespoon chopped fresh oregano

2 teaspoons chopped fresh thyme

¼ cup apple cider vinegar

2 tablespoons olive oil

2 tablespoons sugar

1 teaspoon whole-grain mustard

Kosher salt and freshly ground black pepper

2 large shallots, finely sliced on a mandoline

Heat a large heavy-bottomed skillet over high heat, and coat the bottom lightly with grapeseed oil. Make sure you turn your fan or vent on, open a window, disable your smoke detector, or warn your neighbors that you aren't burning the place down. Once your oil is smoking, throw in a layer of beans. Press them down firmly using a spatula, until a nice char develops on parts of the beans. Once that happens, sauté the beans until they become as soft or as crisp as you like them (I prefer crisp and slightly undercooked, 4 to 5 minutes total). Transfer the beans to a paper towel and allow them to cool. Repeat the procedure with the rest of the beans, using more grapeseed oil as needed. Combine all the charred beans in a large bowl.

In a small sauté pan over medium-low heat, cook the garlic gently in a little grapeseed oil with the oregano and thyme until fragrant and golden, 2 to 3 minutes. Add this to the beans, along with the vinegar, olive oil, sugar, mustard, and salt and pepper to taste. Toss together. Cover and refrigerate for at least 1 hour and up to 2 days. The longer the beans sit, the more the flavors will develop.

In a small saucepan, combine the shallots and enough grapeseed oil to deep-fry them, about 1 cup. Over medium to medium-high heat, slowly stir the shallots using a wooden chopstick or spoon that won't conduct heat up to your fingers. Because these are very delicate rings of shallot, you want to start them in cold oil (see page 82). The deep-frying process will take 15 to 20 minutes. Have patience: you will eventually see the shallots begin to color. Once they turn a light golden brown, fish them out and transfer them to a paper towel. Season with salt.

TO SERVE: Plate up the salad in portions or serve family-style on a platter, and sprinkle the fried shallots over the top.

ASPARAGUS SALAD

SMOKED AVOCADO, GRAPEFRUIT, SABAYON

SERVES 4 TO 6

I love asparagus when the jumbo stalks are in season or when I find white asparagus. I grew up on the pencil-thin stalks, and while I don't dislike them, I really prefer my vegetables hearty. White asparagus and pink grapefruit pair beautifully in terms of flavor, but I also love the pink fruit against the almost iridescent white vegetable. The sabayon and avocado add the creamy factor.

BLANCH THE ASPARAGUS: Bring a medium pot of water to a boil, add a generous amount of salt to it, then blanch the asparagus until just tender, 2 to 3 minutes (I prefer mine on the crisp side, but it's up to you—just don't cook it to death). Strain and shock in an ice bath immediately. Allow the asparagus to cool completely, remove them from the ice bath, and drain on paper towels.

SMOKE THE AVOCADO: Halve, pit, and peel the avocados. Gently toss the avocado halves in a bowl with the lemon juice, then strain off and reserve the juice. Smoke the avocado over the applewood chips (see page 27) for 25 minutes.

Using a blender, purée the smoked avocado with 2 teaspoons of the reserved lemon juice until very smooth and season with salt to taste. Set it aside in a bowl, pressing plastic wrap directly onto the surface to prevent a skin from forming.

COOK THE SABAYON: Bring a large pot of water to a boil. Turn the heat to low. Whisk together the egg yolks, wine, honey, and grapefruit juice in a stainless steel bowl. Place the bowl over the pot of simmering water (making sure the bowl doesn't touch the water) and whisk the sabayon continuously until the sauce is super light, airy, and fluffy, about 20 minutes. Don't overcook it, however, or it will go from a lovely velvety texture to scrambled eggs. Season with salt to taste.

BLANCHING
EMULSIFYING
SMOKING

ASPARAGUS

Kosher salt

12 jumbo asparagus stalks (white or green), trimmed (optional; see Note)

2 teaspoons olive oil

1 teaspoon sesame oil

3 tablespoons benne seeds or toasted white sesame seeds

SMOKED AVOCADO

2 ripe avocados

Juice of 1 lemon

½ cup applewood chips, soaked in cold water for 45 minutes and drained

Kosher salt

SABAYON

2 large egg yolks

1 tablespoon dry white wine (Grüner Veltliner is ideal)

1 teaspoon honey

3 tablespoons grapefruit juice (reserved from making suprêmes)

Kosher salt

recipe continues

1 small grapefruit, cut into suprêmes (see page 33) and each suprême cut into 5 to 6 mini triangles

NOTE

I like trimming my asparagus into the shape you see in the photo (page 84) for aesthetic reasons. You don't have to, but I find it a soothing activity, especially when I can do it at home and am not racing against the prep clock for service. A few inches from the tip, lightly score the asparagus using a paring knife. Using a vegetable peeler, peel the stalk from the scored section down the stem. Using the paring knife, lightly shave the ½ inch of stem, moving your knife toward the score to create a little ledge.

FINISH THE ASPARAGUS: Mix the olive oil and sesame oil together. Lay the asparagus on a sheet pan and brush with the oil mixture. Season with salt to taste. Sprinkle the benne seeds evenly over the asparagus.

TO SERVE: In the center of each round plate, create a small circle with a couple of tablespoons of the warm sabayon. Stagger 2 or 3 pieces of asparagus over the top. Lay small quenelles of the avocado purée around and over the asparagus on each plate. Garnish with the grapefruit triangles.

BEET AND NECTARINE

CRUNCHY SEEDS, BAYRISCHER BLUE CHEESE

SERVES 4 TO 6

Beets and blue cheese are a classic combination. The dense, earthy beets are practically crying out for fat—and I'd say specifically for this cheese. Bayrischer Blauschimmelkäse, a Bavarian blue cheese (see note), is often referred to as "blue butter." It's so creamy and rich with just enough tang—but not too much. Adding a bit of fruit and some crunchy seeds elevates this beloved pairing.

BAKE THE NECTARINES: Preheat the oven to 250°F. Line a sheet pan with a silicone baking mat or parchment paper and spray with non-stick cooking spray. Lay the nectarine wedges on the pan. Bake just until they begin to dehydrate, 1 to 1½ hours. Their texture should feel like that of a soft fruit gummy candy. Set aside to cool.

Increase the oven temperature to 300°F.

TOAST THE SEEDS: In a small bowl, toss the various seeds with the olive oil, honey, and salt to taste. Spread out in a single layer on a small parchment-lined rimmed sheet pan. Bake until just toasted, 8 to 10 minutes. Set aside to cool.

Increase the oven temperature to 375°F.

ROAST THE BEETS: Arrange the beets in a roasting pan. (If using different sizes or colors of beets, roast them in separate pans; cooking times vary depending on size, and red beets will turn your yellow or candy-striped beets reddish.) Sprinkle the thyme, honey, black peppercorns, coriander, and 2 tablespoons salt over the beets. Pour the stock into the pan until the liquid comes one-fourth to halfway up the beets. Cover the pan with aluminum foil and roast in the oven until tender, approximately 35 to 40 minutes for smaller beets and 1 hour for larger ones. Transfer the beets to a cutting board and set aside until cool enough to handle. Wipe off the skins using a paper towel. Cut into desired shapes and sizes.

BRAISING

NECTARINES AND BEETS

Nonstick cooking spray

2 medium nectarines, cut into 8 wedges

2 pounds assorted beets (I like to use both baby and regular), stems trimmed

3 fresh thyme sprigs

1 teaspoon honey

1 teaspoon black peppercorns

1 teaspoon coriander seeds

Kosher salt

2 cups Vegetable Stock (recipe follows), or enough to submerge the beets halfway

2 teaspoons fresh lemon juice

1 tablespoon olive oil

SEEDS

2 tablespoons pepitas (pumpkin seeds)

1 teaspoon white sesame seeds

1 teaspoon flaxseeds

2 tablespoons sunflower seeds

½ teaspoon olive oil

1 teaspoon honey

Kosher salt

recipe continues

In a bowl, toss the beets and nectarines with the lemon juice, olive oil, and salt to taste. Let sit for 15 to 30 minutes to marinate.

TO SERVE: Arrange the beets and nectarines in your preferred serving bowl or on a platter. Crumble the blue cheese over the beets and nectarines and liberally sprinkle the seed mixture on top. In a small bowl, toss the parsley leaves with lemon juice and olive oil to coat. Garnish with the parsley leaves.

GARNISH

9 ounces Bayrischer Blauschimmelkäse (see Note)

20 fresh flat-leaf parsley leaves, or micro parsley if you can get it

1 teaspoon fresh lemon juice

2 teaspoons olive oil

Fleur de sel

NOTE

If you can't find Bayrischer Blauschimmelkäse, look out for Bleu de Bresse, a French cheese, or substitute any good blue cheese that's flavorful but not overly assertive.

VEGETABLE STOCK

MAKES 5½ QUARTS

For this delicate, lightly colored all-purpose stock, I like a classic mirepoix balanced with herbaceous notes from fennel, parsley, and thyme, and a bit of tang and sweetness from orange and apple. David Chang introduced me to the method of grinding the vegetables and steeping them in water for the best and freshest flavor.

In a large stockpot, combine the water, onions, oranges, apples, peppercorns, and coriander seeds. Bring to a boil over high heat and cook for 5 minutes. Turn the heat to medium and simmer, periodically skimming the surface of foam and any impurities, for 20 minutes.

Meanwhile, grind the carrot, celery, and fennel in a food processor. Add to the pot along with the thyme and parsley stems. Turn off the heat, cover the pot, and steep for as few as 15 minutes, or up to 40 minutes for a stronger flavor. Strain through a fine-mesh sieve, let cool completely, and then cover and refrigerate for up to 4 days or freeze for up to a month.

6 quarts water

2 yellow onions, quartered

2 oranges, zest and pith removed, quartered

2 Granny Smith apples, quartered and cored

1 tablespoon whole black peppercorns

1 teaspoon coriander seeds

4 large carrots

6 celery stalks, peeled

1 fennel bulb

5 fresh thyme sprigs

20 fresh parsley stems

EGG PUDDING

BROWN BUTTER, CAVIAR, BRIOCHE

SERVES 4

Let's be completely honest: "egg pudding" is just a more elegant name for soft scrambled eggs, which is how I love my eggs. Scrambled eggs shouldn't be just for breakfast—though this recipe would make for a very sexy, romantic, and indulgent one of those, too. This makes an elegant starter, especially when paired with a little caviar. I love Snake River Royal White Sturgeon caviar, but any sustainable option is good.

Using a rolling pin, flatten each slice of brioche to ⅛-inch thickness, then use a 3½-inch round cutter to cut out 4 brioche circles. Melt 4 tablespoons of the butter in a large sauté pan over medium-high heat. Add the brioche circles just as the butter begins to sizzle. Let the bread fry on one side until crisp and browned, about 3 minutes. Flip the brioche circles over and repeat on the other side. Once the bread is crisped, transfer it to paper towels. Immediately season with salt and pepper on both sides.

Using a fork or a whisk, whip the eggs in a mixing bowl until they are completely fluid—that is, the whites and yolks have mingled completely. In a cast-iron or very well-seasoned pan set over medium-low heat, melt the remaining 3 tablespoons butter. As the butter starts to melt, add the eggs. Using a rubber spatula, stir the eggs very slowly and keep stirring. You do not want big curds or clumps. Be patient. Season with salt as you go, and after 6 to 8 minutes, when the mixture starts to thicken, incorporate the crème fraîche. The eggs are ready when everything looks like a perfectly runny risotto or a loose pudding. Check the seasoning one final time.

TO SERVE: Divide the eggs among four small bowls (I like to use bowls whose diameter is not much larger than that of the brioche). Drizzle ½ teaspoon brown butter and lemon juice over each portion of eggs, then top with the brioche rounds. Set a quenelle of caviar onto one side of the brioche and evenly sprinkle the chives over the remaining section of brioche. Serve right away.

NOTE

You'll need a 3½-inch round cutter.

4 (½-inch-thick) slices of brioche, homemade (page 45) or store-bought, crusts removed

10 tablespoons (1¼ sticks) unsalted butter

Kosher salt and freshly ground black pepper

8 large eggs

¼ cup crème fraîche

GARNISH

2 teaspoons Brown Butter (recipe follows), melted

1 teaspoon lemon juice

3½ ounces caviar

2 tablespoons finely sliced fresh chives

recipe continues

BROWN BUTTER

MAKES 1 CUP

Brown butter (*beurre noisette* in French) can be made quickly, on an ad hoc basis, for a specific recipe. It also can be made ahead of time in larger quantities and refrigerated or frozen until needed. In addition to using brown butter in Egg Pudding (page 91), it's an ingredient in my Almond Brown Butter Cake (page 278) and Crab Faraglioni (page 173). It's also great for searing steaks, finishing sauces, spreading on your morning toast, or drizzling over hot oatmeal—basically anywhere butter or oil is called for and you want to add some richness and a nutty flavor.

16 tablespoons (2 sticks) unsalted butter

In a small saucepan or sauté pan (either stainless steel or with a light-colored bottom, so you can gauge browning as it happens) set over medium heat, melt the butter. The butter will initially foam, the water content of the butter will evaporate, and the remaining butterfat will slowly start to brown, turning from light golden to the color of toasted nuts, 10 to 15 minutes. You'll also notice a toasted hazelnut (*noisette*) aroma—hence its French name.

Strain the butter through a fine-mesh sieve or cheesecloth to remove the burnt milk particles and dark specks. It's now ready to use. It can be kept, covered and refrigerated for later use, for up to 2 weeks.

KATAIFI-WRAPPED BURRATA

DATE SYRUP, RADISH SALAD

SERVES 4

Don't let the veneer of cook and food sophisticate fool you: next to chicken fingers, mozzarella sticks were pretty high on the list of things I loved eating as a child. So here's a gussied-up version to hit that sweet spot: I've added date syrup and a radish salad to validate it as "adult." Somewhat. At home I'll eat this as a snack; if I'm cooking for others, I like to serve this as a starter or cheese course.

MAKE THE DATE SYRUP: In a small saucepan, combine the dates, honey, and water and bring to simmer over medium-high heat. Lower the heat and simmer gently until the dates have softened, about 15 minutes. Transfer to a blender. Blend on high, then strain through a fine-mesh sieve. Thin out with additional water, as needed, if the simmering caused the syrup to overreduce; it should be the consistency of warm maple syrup. Season with salt and a few drops of lemon juice. You're looking for a nice balance of sweet, with a touch of salty. Once cool, the date syrup can be covered and refrigerated for up to 3 days. Serve at room temperature.

PREP THE SALAD INGREDIENTS: Thinly slice the radishes on a mandoline. Thinly slice the scallion greens on the bias. Put each in separate bowls, cover with cold water, and refrigerate.

FRYING

DATE SYRUP

5 pitted dates, coarsely chopped

1 teaspoon honey

1 cup water

Kosher salt

Fresh lemon juice

RADISH SALAD

3 red radishes, stems on

2 scallions, green part only

10 mizuna leaves

6 radish green leaves

6 small fresh mint leaves

Fresh lemon juice

Olive oil

Kosher salt and freshly ground black pepper

NOTE

Kataifi is shredded phyllo dough, which is perhaps best known as the pastry used in baklava. Look for it in the freezer section of Middle Eastern food shops or well-stocked markets, or online.

recipe continues

FRY THE BURRATA: Drain the burrata on a towel to remove any moisture. Using a brush, lightly coat one ball of burrata with the egg wash, then sprinkle half of the nigella seeds on it and season with kosher salt and pepper.

On a sheet pan, lay out a large "blanket" of the kataifi. Set a ball of burrata on one far end and roll it around, being sure to surround the cheese completely with the kataifi. Don't worry too much about it looking like a perfect ball yet; just try to keep track of where the seam is. Repeat the entire procedure with the second ball of burrata.

The process of frying the burrata may take a few practice rounds, but it gets easier—I promise!

In a small sauté pan, heat ¼ inch of grapeseed oil over medium-high heat until the oil begins to shimmer. Now you need to work quickly: as soon as you put a coated burrata in the pan, seam-side down, you need to roll it around to get oil on all of it to soften the kataifi. If you don't work fast enough, the kataifi will begin to crisp up, and you won't be able to achieve that perfectly round final shape (though the end result will still taste great). Once you have maneuvered the ball around the oil, and it is nearly a perfect sphere, take your time and brown all of it evenly. Keep moving it around in the pan on all sides, while basting it with hot oil from the pan. Once you have gotten that perfect golden sphere of crunchiness, about 4 to 5 minutes total, add ½ tablespoon butter and let it foam up in the pan. Baste the kataifi a few times before removing it, draining it on paper towels, and seasoning it with salt. Repeat with the second ball of burrata.

ASSEMBLE THE SALAD: Drain the radishes and scallion greens. Toss them in a bowl with the mizuna, radish greens, mint, lemon juice, olive oil, and kosher salt and black pepper to taste.

TO SERVE: Serve the burrata on a platter with the date syrup, a sprinkling of fleur de sel, and the salad arranged around.

BURRATA

2 (8-ounce) balls of burrata

1 large egg beaten with 1 teaspoon water

1 teaspoon nigella seeds, toasted

Kosher salt and freshly ground black pepper

1 (16-ounce) package kataifi (see Note), defrosted, covered with a damp tea towel

Grapeseed or other neutral oil, for frying

1 tablespoon unsalted butter

Fleur de sel

SMOKED VEGETABLE SALAD

BANYULS VINEGAR, LETTUCES, MARCONA ALMONDS

SERVES 4 TO 6

EMULSIFYING

SMOKING

NOTE
I like to buy 3 or 4 loose lettuces to create my own mix, like baby spinach, baby kale, red romaine, and mizuna.

1 large carrot, cut into
1/16-inch-thick coins

1 turnip, peeled and sliced
1/16-inch thick

1 parsnip, cut into
1/16-inch-thick coins

1/2 cup applewood chips, soaked in cold water for 45 minutes and drained

1 large egg yolk

1 1/2 teaspoons whole-grain mustard

1/2 teaspoon honey

2 tablespoons Banyuls vinegar

1/4 cup plus 2 tablespoons canola oil

Kosher salt

12 ounces mixed greens
(see Note)

1 cup loosely packed fresh flat-leaf parsley leaves

GARNISH

4 to 6 fresh chervil sprigs, leaves only

4 to 6 fresh chives, cut into
1/2-inch bâtons

1/4 cup Marcona almonds, toasted and coarsely chopped

I am a fan of salads with more stuff than lettuce. You know—a fucking SALAD, not a *salad*. This salad brings the element of smoke to raw vegetables for richness of flavor, and the thick, emulsified vinaigrette is creamy and sweet-tart from the vinegar. The smoked veggies are the star here and easier than you think to achieve at home, even if you lack an outdoor grill. And once you master this technique, you'll be wondering what else you can smoke this way!

Smoke the carrots, turnips, and parsnips over applewood chips for 40 to 45 minutes (see page 27).

In a medium bowl, whisk together the egg yolk, mustard, honey, and vinegar. Still whisking, stream in the oil, little by little, until all of it has been incorporated. Season with salt. Cover and refrigerate until ready to use, up to 2 days.

TO SERVE: Toss the greens and parsley with a few tablespoons of the vinaigrette. Add a little at a time—don't overdress. Season with salt to taste. In a separate bowl, toss the smoked vegetables with a few tablespoons of the vinaigrette; season with salt to taste. Mixing the vegetables separately from the greens keeps the smoke flavor from transferring to the lettuces; also, your vegetables and greens will be easier to portion evenly (mixed together, the vegetables have a tendency to sink to the bottom of the bowl).

Arrange a few rounds of each vegetable in each shallow bowl or plate. Pile a small mound of greens on top, and repeat with another layer of vegetables and greens. Garnish each with 1 chervil leaf, 1 chive bâton, and some Marcona almonds.

CHICKEN LIVER MOUSSE

PICKLES, PEANUT, CILANTRO

SERVES 4 TO 6

In July 2015, I was invited to the White House to attend President Obama's address during LGBTQ month. I was honored and super excited—and, of course, I took the opportunity to navigate the city through my stomach. And so I went to Rose's Luxury, which remains a favorite restaurant to this day. Among the many amazing dishes that chef Aaron Silverman made, there was an incredible chicken liver mousse set in a bowl, piled with whole leaves of cilantro and Thai basil, and assorted pickles, which inspired my own version. Here, the pickles and peanuts remind me of the flavors in a Vietnamese *bánh mì* sandwich. I love this as an appetizer.

MAKE THE CHICKEN LIVER MOUSSE: Lightly coat the bottom of a sauté pan with grapeseed oil and set over medium-high heat. Add the shallot and sweat for 1 minute. Add the thyme sprigs and cook for 30 seconds or so, until aromatic.

Next add the chicken livers and season with pepper. Cook the livers, turning once, until medium rare, 4 to 5 minutes. Deglaze with the brandy and cook until the liquid has evaporated (au sec), 1 to 2 minutes.

Discard the thyme sprigs and transfer the livers and shallots, while still hot, directly to a high-speed blender or food processor. Add a small pinch of pink curing salt, if using, and a generous pinch of kosher salt. If using a food processor, I would recommend passing the blended mixture through a fine-mesh sieve just to make sure the texture is as velvety as possible. Start to blend and gradually increase the speed to medium-high, then add the cubes of cold butter little by little—you will need to use the plunger from your blender or a spatula to help the blending along (if using a spatula, be sure to stop the blending before mixing things up with the spatula!). If the mixture seems too thick and, even after you add the butter, it won't blend while on high speed, add a splash of heavy cream. Adjust the seasoning to taste; keep in mind that, when seasoning something that is to be served cold, you will need a bit more salt than what you think tastes best when testing it warm.

EMULSIFYING

PICKLING

NOTE
The chicken liver mousse can be made 1 to 2 days ahead, and the cucumbers can be pickled up to a day ahead.

CHICKEN LIVER MOUSSE

Grapeseed or other neutral oil

1 tablespoon minced shallot

2 fresh thyme sprigs

6 ounces chicken livers, cleaned, rinsed, and patted dry

Kosher salt and freshly ground black pepper

1 tablespoon brandy

Pink curing salt (optional)

8 tablespoons (1 stick) cold unsalted butter, cubed

Heavy cream, if needed

recipe continues

Meanwhile, prepare an ice bath.

Transfer the mousse while still warm to an airtight vessel to prevent oxidation: I use a plastic takeout quart container and press a layer of plastic wrap directly on top of the mousse. Put the container in the ice bath to chill the mixture as quickly as possible, then refrigerate.

PICKLES

2 Kirby cucumbers

1 cup rice vinegar

¼ cup water

2 tablespoons sugar

1 fresh Thai chile, halved lengthwise, seeds and ribs removed

1 teaspoon kosher salt

Peanut Shortbread (recipe follows)

GARNISH

8 to 12 fresh cilantro sprigs

8 to 12 small fresh Thai basil leaves

Fleur de sel

4 roasted unsalted peanuts

MAKE THE PICKLES: Slice the cucumbers on a mandoline, to no thicker than a nickel (⅛ inch). Transfer to a heatproof container. In a small nonreactive saucepan, combine the vinegar, water, sugar, chile, and salt. Over medium heat, bring to a simmer and cook until the sugar and salt have fully dissolved, 3 to 5 minutes. Allow to cool slightly for 5 minutes, then pour the mixture over the cucumbers, making sure they are submerged. Cover and refrigerate for at least an hour or overnight. Keep chilled until ready to use.

TO SERVE: For each portion, use a large serving spoon (roughly 2 to 3 tablespoons) to make a nice quenelle of chicken liver mousse straight from the container and set it onto a round medium plate, laying the quenelle off-center to the left. Arrange a small stack of 6 to 8 pickles in a pile at the bottom right of each plate. Shingle 4 to 5 peanut shortbread cookies above the pickles. Drape 2 cilantro sprigs and a few Thai basil leaves over each plate. Finish with a sprinkle of fleur de sel on the mousse. Using a Microplane zester, grate some peanut over each quenelle.

PEANUT SHORTBREAD

MAKES 20 TO 25 COOKIES

Preheat the oven to 350°F.

In a food processor, combine the flour, peanuts, baking powder, salt, and sugar. Pulse until the mixture looks like coarse sand. Add the butter and pulse a few times more until the mixture has turned to the size of small peas. Add the egg yolk and pulse until the mixture looks like wet sand, adding a couple of drops of ice water as needed to help it clump. Turn the mixture out onto the counter or a board and gently shape into a flat disc. Wrap in plastic and refrigerate for 30 minutes to 1 hour.

Put the dough on a lightly floured surface and, using a lightly floured rolling pin, roll the dough into a large sheet approximately ¼ inch thick. Using a 2½-inch round cutter, cut out as many disks as you can; you should get 20 to 25. Transfer to a parchment-lined sheet pan, leaving ½ inch between each cookie. Brush a thin layer of the egg wash over each one, and sprinkle the white sesame seeds over the top. Bake until lightly golden, 7 to 9 minutes. Transfer to a rack to cool. Once cool, store in an airtight container for up to 4 days.

1½ cups all-purpose flour, plus more for rolling

¾ cup roasted unsalted peanuts

½ teaspoon baking powder

½ teaspoon kosher salt

1½ tablespoons sugar

8 tablespoons (1 stick) cold unsalted butter, cubed

1 large egg yolk

Ice water, as needed

1 large egg, lightly beaten

1 tablespoon white sesame seeds

NOTE
You will need a 2½-inch round cutter.

FROM THE SEA

POACHED BAY SCALLOPS
BABY TURNIP, UNI CREAM, SAFFRON

HAMACHI
SWEET ONION, BACON, MISO, POTATO

SALMON
ENGLISH PEA, ARTICHOKE, PANCETTA

LOBSTER
BRIOCHE SAUCE, LEMON, CELERY,
BLACK TRUFFLE

SEARED LOBSTER
FOIE GRAS SAUCE, TURNIP,
PICKLED RADISH

TUNA
CITRUS, LOBSTER SAUCE, CARROT SALAD

LANGOUSTINE
MUSHROOM BROTH, LEMON CUCUMBER,
BASIL

SEARED SCALLOP
PISTACHIO, MELON, LARDO

STEAMED RED SNAPPER
SORREL, CRISPY FISH SKIN, HAZELNUT OIL

BAY SCALLOP CRUDO
LABNEH, APPLE, CILANTRO

ARCTIC CHAR
ARTICHOKE, BLACK TRUFFLE,
ONION SAUCE

FLUKE
BROWN BUTTER, TEMPURA PARSLEY,
CAULIFLOWER

COBIA
POTATO CHIPS, LEEK, BLACK TRUFFLE

HALIBUT
SMOKED HAM HOCK, FENNEL,
PEAS, AND RADISH

OCTOPUS
CHORIZO PURÉE, CELERY SALAD

SMOKED FISH SALAD
CRUDITÉS

SMOKED COD RILLETTES
CRÈME FRAÎCHE, DILL, ORANGE,
CUCUMBER

POACHED BAY SCALLOPS

BABY TURNIP, UNI CREAM, SAFFRON

SERVES 4

EMULSIFYING
POACHING

This combo of ingredients tastes like the ocean in the sexiest way. Bay scallops come and go so fast; buy them when you see them! I especially love them raw or barely cooked, as here. This dish is silky, luscious, creamy, and rich, and during white truffle season, it only gets better.

POACHED SCALLOPS

3 cups Lobster Stock (page 117)

½ cup heavy cream

1 teaspoon saffron strands

6 pieces uni, preferably from Santa Barbara

2 tablespoons cold unsalted butter, cut into pieces

½ teaspoon sherry vinegar

Fleur de sel

20 bay scallops

In a medium saucepan, bring the lobster stock to a boil over medium-high heat, then reduce the heat and simmer until the stock has reduced to 2½ cups. Whisk in the cream and saffron, and simmer over low heat for 10 minutes.

Using an immersion blender, emulsify the uni directly into the sauce. Pass it through a fine-mesh sieve into a medium saucepan. Next whisk the butter into the sauce until it becomes glossy—not a lot of elbow grease here, just some quick wrist action, about 30 seconds. Add the vinegar and fleur de sel to taste.

Over medium-low heat, add the scallops to the saucepan and poach until the scallops are just warmed through, 4 to 5 minutes. Do not boil.

GARNISH

2 teaspoons finely sliced fresh chives

2 baby turnips, root ends trimmed

Freshly shaved white truffle (optional)

Fleur de sel

TO SERVE: Scoop 5 bay scallops into each bowl, spooning ½ cup of the sauce around them and garnishing with the chives. Next, using a mandoline, shave 7 or 8 razor-thin slices of turnips and ½ ounce of white truffle, if desired, over each portion. Sprinkle with fleur de sel.

UNI CREAM

HAMACHI

SWEET ONION, BACON, MISO, POTATO

SERVES 4 TO 6

When I was in Oregon filming the *36 Hours* "Portland Cool" episode, Gregory Gourdet, runner-up on *Top Chef*'s season 11, took us clamming on the beach about an hour and a half outside the city. Kyle, my cohost, started a fire, we threw a grill grate and some cast-iron skillets on top, and Gregory and I each cooked up a dish using our clams and the produce we'd brought for dinner. I also like to make this with raw hamachi (Pacific yellowtail) and a little miso in place of the clams and broth.

Put the onion slices into a bowl with ice-cold water and refrigerate for 10 minutes. Drain the water and refill the bowl of onion with fresh ice water and return it to the refrigerator.

In a medium saucepan, combine the water and bacon. Bring to a boil over high heat, then reduce the heat so the water just simmers. Cook for 10 minutes. Remove the bacon with a slotted spoon, pat it dry, then cut the slices into ⅛-inch-thick bâtons. Add the kombu to the bacon-infused water and simmer gently for 4 to 5 minutes. Remove and discard the kombu. Next add the bonito flakes and turn off the heat. Allow the flakes to steep for 5 to 8 minutes.

Strain the broth through a fine-mesh sieve directly into a blender and add the miso; discard the bonito flakes. Blend on high speed until the bacon fat and miso have emulsified into a milky liquid.

Return the mixture to the saucepan, add the potato, and simmer over medium-low heat until just tender, 10 to 12 minutes. Keep warm.

While the potato is cooking, render the bacon bâtons in a small sauté pan over medium-high heat. You may need to add 1 to 2 teaspoons of grapeseed oil to your pan, depending on the fat content of your bacon. Cook until the bacon is crisp, 5 to 7 minutes. Drain on paper towels. Finely chop the bacon into bits. Take the onion slivers out of the refrigerator and drain them on a separate paper towel.

TO SERVE: Thinly slice the hamachi on the bias at a 45-degree angle. In high-sided bowls, fan the hamachi in a semicircle. Garnish with crispy bacon bits. Gently pour ¼ cup (or more, as desired) of the miso broth into each bowl, dividing the potatoes equally. Finish with fleur de sel and a heavy pinch of the iced onions.

RENDERING

¼ sweet onion, preferably Vidalia, sliced paper thin from tip to root

2¼ cups water

5 ounces thick-cut smoked bacon

3 ounces kombu (about 2 sheets), lightly rinsed

1½ cups loosely packed bonito flakes

1 tablespoon white miso

1 large Idaho or russet potato, peeled and cut into ¼-inch dice

1 to 2 teaspoons grapeseed or other neutral oil, as needed

1 pound hamachi loin

Fleur de sel

NOTE

If the hamachi isn't top-notch at your market, you can substitute steamed clams, sliced raw salmon, or even a cooked piece of your favorite fish. To make lovely thin slices of fish, use a very sharp long knife, and do not saw through the fish; instead, use one long swooping slicing motion to carve one smooth and pristine-looking slice at a time.

SALMON

ENGLISH PEA, ARTICHOKE, PANCETTA

SERVES 4

BLANCHING

SEARING

In spring, I can't get enough of the seasonal produce, and English peas are a favorite: mashed, puréed, lightly buttered, or just raw. The salmon-cooking technique here is completely lifted from Thomas Keller: low and slow on the skin side (as opposed to high-heat searing), followed by 20 seconds only on the flesh side. This ensures the interior of the salmon is the most delicate, perfect light-orange hue of medium-rare. If TK loves it low and slow, so do I!

2 cups dry white wine

1 cup olive oil

6 fresh thyme sprigs

3 strips lemon zest

¼ cup fresh lemon juice

1 tablespoon pink peppercorns

Kosher salt

12 baby artichokes, cleaned and trimmed

½ cup shelled fresh English peas (save the pea pods to make broth, see Note, page 110)

4 tablespoons (½ stick) unsalted butter

Grapeseed or other neutral oil

4 ounces pancetta, cut into a small dice

4 (4-ounce) portions of skin-on, center-cut wild salmon, each ideally 2½ inches thick

2 lemon wedges

In a large saucepan, combine the wine, olive oil, thyme, lemon zest, lemon juice, peppercorns, and salt to taste. Add the artichokes. Fashion a lid for the saucepan out of a round of parchment paper (a cartouche) and lay it over the artichokes. Bring to a boil over medium-high heat, reduce the heat to medium, and simmer until the artichokes are almost tender when pierced with a knife, 20 to 25 minutes. Turn off the heat and let the artichokes sit in the broth; they'll keep cooking and absorbing the flavors of the broth.

Put a small saucepan of salted water (or the juice from the pea pods plus a little water; see Note) with a dash of salt on to boil over high heat.

In the meantime, transfer the artichokes to a cutting board and coarsely chop them into bite-size pieces. Discard the cooking liquid.

Prepare an ice bath.

Blanch the peas until tender, 3 to 4 minutes. Transfer the peas to a blender, reserving the cooking liquid—you may need it for blending. Purée the peas on high speed until you have a silky-smooth purée (it should hold its shape on the plate), adding a splash of reserved cooking liquid as necessary. With the blender still running, add 1 tablespoon of the butter and season with salt. Transfer to a small stainless steel bowl and set it in the ice bath. You want the purée to cool as quickly as possible to preserve its lovely color. Press plastic wrap directly on the surface of the purée to prevent a skin from forming, and refrigerate it until ready to use.

Add a splash of grapeseed oil to a small sauté pan set over medium heat and render the fat out of the pancetta until the meat turns crispy, 8 to 10 minutes. Transfer to paper towels to drain.

recipe continues

If you have a juicer, the discarded pea pods can—and should—be juiced for a cooking broth. Poaching vegetables in their juice keeps the flavors vibrant and intense. Everything from beets to carrots to celery can be juiced and used as a cooking liquid. You only need to be aware that this method is not made for long cooking processes or very large quantities. Take a small saucepan, add 2 to 3 tablespoons of juice, toss in a couple teaspoons of peas, lightly simmer them for 2 minutes, throw in a knob of butter, season with salt and, voilà, a beautifully rich, flavorful sauce.

GARNISH

12 to 15 pea tendril tips

Coat the bottom of a large cast-iron pan with grapeseed oil. Season the salmon on both sides with salt. Before you turn on the heat, place the salmon in the pan, skin-side down: the oil, the pan, and the salmon will all come up to temperature together. Now turn the heat to medium-high. Let the fish be; don't touch it! Let it cook for 3 to 4 minutes. Listen to it searing. You have my permission to gently lift up an edge to see how it's doing after those 3 to 4 minutes. If the skin smells like it's burning, or if your fillets are just sitting there doing nothing, adjust the heat accordingly.

Once the skin is evenly crisped, after 5 to 6 minutes total time, use a spoon to baste the fish with the hot fat repeatedly so that it starts to cook the top of the salmon. I recommend a medium-rare interior: if you gently squeeze the sides, it gives slightly. You can also use a cake tester to test for doneness: it should resist a little upon entry, and if you place the cake tester to your lip after taking it out of the fish, it should feel warm, just above body temperature.

Right before removing the salmon from the pan, add 2 tablespoons of the butter, turn over the fish, and baste the skin side with the now foaming butter four or five times. Remove the salmon from the pan.

Warm the pea purée in a small saucepan over medium-low heat.

In a small sauté pan, combine the remaining 1 tablespoon butter with the pancetta and artichokes, and sauté gently until warmed through. Season with salt and a squeeze or two of lemon juice.

TO SERVE: On large round plates, spoon a couple of tablespoons of the warm pea purée, using the back of the spoon to smooth it out and make a small circle. Next spoon a few tablespoons of the artichoke and pancetta hash onto each plate. Nestle the fish on top and garnish with 3 to 5 pea tendril tips per plate.

LOBSTER

BRIOCHE SAUCE, LEMON, CELERY, BLACK TRUFFLE

SERVES 4 TO 6

This dish originated in my pure love for warmed lobster with butter, lemon, and celery salt on a toasty split-top roll. The bread sauce
idea came to me straight from Barbara Lynch, who admittedly eyed
it in Pascal Barbot's cookbook, which details the recipes from his
Michelin-starred Parisian restaurant, L'Astrance. Once when Barbara
came to Menton for dinner, I served her a scallop, with the bread
sauce in question, chanterelles, and black truffles as part of the tasting menu. I asked the server to tell her that I wouldn't forget where
the sauce came from. It's in my arsenal always.

MAKE THE SAUCE: In a small saucepan over medium heat, combine
the brioche dough with the butter. As it begins to brown, stir and
break up the dough so it starts to crisp—it should end up looking
like buttery toasted bread crumbs. Next add the vegetable stock and
milk. Simmer until 5 to 6 minutes. Transfer the mixture to a blender
and blend until smooth. Pass it through a fine-mesh sieve back
into the saucepan and season with salt to taste. Place a cartouche
or plastic wrap directly onto the surface to prevent a skin from
forming. Keep warm.

MAKE THE SALAD: Cut the celery lengthwise in half, then into 2½-inch
pieces, and then thinly slice those pieces on the bias into both short
and long pieces. Combine with the celery heart leaves, truffle, lemon
juice, olive oil, and salt and pepper to taste in a bowl.

SEARING

NOTE

*You may be asking, Is it okay just to
buy brioche and tear up the pieces?*
Nope. Sorry. The sauce is best
because the dough is fried when
raw and there is a specific flavor
that develops in the pan. No
shortcuts here, unfortunately!

BRIOCHE SAUCE

2 ounces (about ¼ cup) raw
Potato Brioche dough (page 45)

2 tablespoons unsalted butter

1 cup vegetable stock,
homemade (page 89)
or store-bought

½ cup whole milk

Kosher salt

CELERY-TRUFFLE SALAD

2 stalks from the celery heart,
peeled to remove any stringy
fibers

Leaves from the celery heart

1 small black truffle, finely sliced
and then cut into julienne

2 teaspoons fresh lemon juice

2 teaspoons olive oil

Kosher salt and freshly ground
black pepper

recipe continues

LOBSTER

4 tablespoons (½ stick) unsalted butter

2 (1¼-pound) live lobsters, prepped and parcooked (see page 118)

Fleur de sel

COOK THE LOBSTER: In a sauté pan, warm the butter over medium heat. Gently cook the lobster tail and claw meat until slightly firm and warmed through, 2 to 3 minutes. Turn the heat up to medium-high and begin to sear the lobster ever so slightly: the butter will bubble and begin to brown, and that's a good thing. Remove the lobster from the pan.

TO SERVE: Slice the lobster tail lengthwise. Trim the knuckle meat to the desired size. Each portion should be half a tail, one knuckle, and one claw. Sprinkle with fleur de sel. Spoon a couple of tablespoons of the brioche sauce into the center of each plate. Arrange the lobster over the sauce and top with the celery-truffle salad.

SEARED LOBSTER

FOIE GRAS SAUCE, TURNIP, PICKLED RADISH

SERVES 4

This was one of my favorite dishes on my tasting menu at Menton. The sauce came to me first as a way to use the trimmed ends of foie gras once the lobes were portioned for the seared foie gras course (see page 189). The pickled radish was next, to add some balance to the rich sauce. Perhaps surprisingly, the lobster came last, but you'd never know it from the way it goes so well.

START THE SAUCE: Pour the lobster stock into a small saucepan and reduce it over medium-high heat, skimming it of foam and any impurities as it reduces, until it coats the back of a spoon. You should have about 1 cup of reduced stock.

Using a small food processor, make the foie gras butter by puréeing the butter with the foie gras until fully incorporated. Wrap tightly in plastic wrap or scoop into an airtight container and refrigerate until firm, or for up to 1 day.

PICKLE THE RADISHES: Put the radish slices in a vacuum sealer (see Note, page 116) with the vinegar, water, sugar, and thyme. Seal the bag airtight and refrigerate for 1 hour. Remove the radishes from the liquid, pat dry, and refrigerate until ready to serve.

FINISH THE SAUCE: Reduce the heat under the saucepan to medium. Cut the cold foie gras butter into pieces and then whisk it into the stock. Season with salt and sherry vinegar to taste. Cover and remove from the heat.

GLAZE THE TURNIPS: Into a small sauté pan over medium-high heat, pour just enough grapeseed oil to coat the bottom of the pan. Sear the turned turnips until lightly golden brown, about 2 minutes. Turn over the turnips and add the vegetable stock and butter. You want the liquid to reduce, glazing the turnips. Swirl the pan over the heat to keep the turnips moving, thereby basting them as the liquid reduces, 2 to 3 minutes. Remove from the heat and keep warm.

EMULSIFYING
PICKLING
SEARING

FOIE GRAS SAUCE

1 quart Lobster Stock (recipe follows)

3 tablespoons unsalted butter, at room temperature

3 tablespoons foie gras trimmings (ask your butcher for a 2-ounce portion or any trimmings they might have on hand)

Kosher salt

Sherry vinegar

PICKLED RADISHES

2 red radishes, sliced ¼ inch thick, keeping ⅛ inch of the stems on top

3 tablespoons white vinegar

2 tablespoons water

Pinch of sugar

2 fresh thyme sprigs

GLACÉ TURNIPS

Grapeseed or other neutral oil

8 baby white turnips, turned (see page 33)

¼ cup vegetable stock, homemade (page 89) or store-bought

3 tablespoons unsalted butter

recipe continues

LOBSTER

2 (1-pound) live lobsters, prepped and parcooked (see page 118)

Kosher salt

Grapeseed or other neutral oil

2 tablespoons unsalted butter

GARNISH

10 to 15 pea tendrils

NOTE

If you don't have a vacuum sealer to compress the radishes, you can simply marinate the radish slices in the vinegar, water, sugar, and thyme.

FINISH THE LOBSTER: Season the parcooked lobster pieces with salt. In a large sauté pan over medium-high heat, pour in just enough grapeseed oil to coat the bottom of the pan. Sear the lobster tails on their rounded side for 2 to 3 minutes, then turn the pieces over. Add the butter, let it melt and, using a spoon, baste the lobster with the butter for 1 to 2 minutes. Repeat with the claws and knuckles, which will take about half as much time to cook.

TO SERVE: On large round plates, spoon the foie gras sauce in a small circle in the center. Put the lobster on top of the sauce; I like to portion the lobster tails in half, serving a piece of the tail alongside a knuckle and a piece of claw. Arrange the turnips around the lobster and sauce. Lean 3 pickled radish slices in different places around each plate. Finish with 2 or 3 pea tendrils per person.

LOBSTER STOCK

MAKES 2 QUARTS

Prepare the lobster bodies by removing the top shell (carapace) and pinching out the little feathery gills. The shell has no flavor, and the gills make the stock muddy. Split the remaining lobster flesh and legs in half lengthwise. Pat dry with a paper towel.

Into a medium Dutch oven over high heat, pour just enough grapeseed oil to coat the bottom. Heat to the smoking point, then add the lobster bodies to the pot in one layer. Let them brown before flipping them, 3 to 5 minutes. Brown the other side, an additional 2 to 3 minutes. Transfer the lobster bodies to a bowl.

Reduce the heat under the pot to medium-high, add a bit more oil, if necessary, and sauté the onion, celery, and fennel. Once the edges of the vegetables begin to brown, after 8 to 10 minutes, stir and caramelize for an additional 2 to 3 minutes. Add the herbs and the tomato paste, and cook for 1 to 2 minutes. This helps cook out any metallic flavor in the paste and sweetens it a bit. Deglaze with the white wine and cook until the liquid has evaporated (au sec), 2 to 3 minutes.

Add the lobster bodies, any additional liquid that drained into the bowl, and the tomato to the sautéed vegetables. Fill the pot with enough water to cover the lobster. Bring to a boil over high heat, then reduce the heat to medium-low to achieve a light simmer. Cook, uncovered, periodically skimming the surface of foam and any impurities, until all the flavors have had time to meld together, 40 to 45 minutes. Taste it; if you get the intensity of the ingredients, then you are good to go.

Strain the lobster stock through a fine-mesh sieve. Use immediately, or let cool, cover, and refrigerate for up to 2 days or freeze in 1-cup portions for up to 3 weeks.

2 to 4 lobster bodies (including heads and legs)

Grapeseed or other neutral oil

1 large yellow onion, cut into large chunks

2 stalks celery, cut into large chunks

1 fennel bulb, cut into large chunks

5 fresh thyme sprigs

5 fresh flat-leaf or curly parsley sprigs

5 fresh tarragon sprigs

¼ cup tomato paste

½ cup dry white wine

1 plum tomato, quartered

HOW TO PREP A LOBSTER

My method for cooking lobster is always the same.

Start by sticking a sharp knife through the head and right between the eyes to kill the lobster.

Next take the lobster apart. Start by twisting off the claws and knuckles. Now separate the body from the abdomen and tail.

Shake the tail so the tomalley (aka "the green stuff") falls out and doesn't stain the lobster meat. Discard the tomalley.

Free the outer shell (the carapace) from the body using your thumbs to open up the carapace. Discard the top shell. Look for the little feathery gills and pinch them to remove and discard them. The body and walking legs can now be frozen for future use, for example, for Lobster Stock (page 117).

Next, using twine, tie each lobster tail to another lobster tail—underbellies facing each other—to straighten them out; this will prevent the tail meat from tearing when you extract it from the shell after cooking. Put the tails and the claws in a large heatproof container or stockpot.

Prepare an ice bath.

In another large pot, bring a few quarts of water to a boil, enough to completely submerge the lobster. Add a very generous amount of kosher

salt to the water (2 tablespoons per quart)—it should taste like the ocean! Pour the salted boiling water over the lobster. Let the lobster sit: remove the tails after 1½ to 2 minutes; the claws and knuckles will need 2½ to 3 minutes, depending on how big the claws are. Immediately plunge the tails into the ice bath. Repeat with the claws. Allow them to cool. Untie the tails.

To get the lobster meat from the tail, hold the tail in the palm of your hand, underbelly facing you and tail fans pointing upward. Using kitchen scissors, cut through the shell alongside both edges of the belly all the way to the central tail fan. Lift and remove that part of the shell. Once the meat is exposed, ease it out of the tail, working it gently side to side without tearing it. Using a small knife and tweezers, pull out the digestive tract (even a New Englander would not eat that!). The lobster meat will still be raw, which is what you want.

Crack the claws and knuckles to expose the meat: you can use the back of a chef's knife, scissors, or whatever method you are comfortable with. Be sure to pull out the pieces of cartilage, or "feathers," from the claws. Discard the shells.

Cover and refrigerate the lobster meat until you're ready to proceed with any of the lobster recipes in this book.

TUNA

CITRUS, LOBSTER SAUCE, CARROT SALAD

SERVES 4 TO 6

SEARING

Tuna is a fish that for a long time I equated only with Asian flavors: tuna and soy, mirin, ponzu...delicious! But once I started my cooking career, I began to look at it differently. Here, I pair tuna with one of my absolute favorite sauces, which is made from discarded lobster bits. We should all be cooking regularly with lobster bodies; just like animal and fish bones, they provide incredible flavor. I'll let you in on a secret: lobster meat is not my favorite, even though I live where lobster rolls and steamed lobsters are king, but this lobster sauce absolutely is.

2 cups Lobster Stock (page 117)

½ cup heavy cream

Kosher salt

Grapeseed or other neutral oil

1 pound center-cut yellowfin or bluefin tuna, cut into 5 rectangular blocks, each about 1 inch thick

3 baby carrots, tops trimmed, or 1 large carrot, cut into ⅛-inch-thick rounds using a mandoline

1 tablespoon fresh lemon juice

1 tablespoon olive oil

⅛ teaspoon finely ground toasted caraway seeds

In a medium saucepan over medium heat, reduce the lobster stock until it is the consistency of a thin syrup, 20 to 25 minutes. Add the heavy cream and reduce the mixture until it coats the back of a spoon. Season with salt to taste, remove from the heat, and keep warm.

Coat the bottom of a large cast-iron or heavy-bottomed skillet with grapeseed oil and set over high heat. Season the tuna blocks with salt on all sides. Just as the oil begins to smoke, add the tuna, searing the pieces evenly on each side, approximately 10 seconds per side. The timing will vary depending on the thickness of the pieces of tuna: you want to cook the outsides but retain a cold center.

Slice the tuna into 1-inch cubes.

Toss the carrots in a small bowl with the lemon juice, olive oil, caraway seeds, and salt to taste.

GARNISH

Meyer lemons, cut into suprêmes (see page 33) and each suprême then cut into thirds

20 to 30 carrot fronds (optional)

TO SERVE: Spoon a couple of tablespoons of the lobster sauce into the bottom of each individual bowl. Next evenly portion the diced tuna into each one. Arrange 6 pieces of Meyer lemon around and on top of each portion of the tuna. Lay 6 to 8 carrot slices over the top, covering the surface of all the tuna. Finish each with 5 carrot fronds, if using.

LANGOUSTINE

MUSHROOM BROTH, LEMON CUCUMBER, BASIL

SERVES 4

Langoustines are slim, orange-pink Norwegian lobsters that have very delicate and deliciously sweet flesh. If you watched my *36 Hours* Barcelona episode, you saw me pull a langoustine from a vendor's ice plate, carefully dissect it, and feed it raw to my cohost (and former US professional soccer player), Kyle Martino. He seemed to like it—I think by this point on the show, he was used to me feeding him random things. I trusted him with sports and seedy bars, and he trusted me with food. We were a good team.

I love langoustines raw or barely cooked, as in this recipe, where they're paired with an earthy mushroom broth, thinly sliced lemon cucumber, and the tiniest basil leaves you can find.

To clean and prepare the langoustines, you will need small seafood scissors or a sharp paring knife. Carefully remove the head of each langoustine, twisting and pulling gently at the same time. Reserve the heads for the mushroom broth.

Next hold the tail, abdomen facing up, in one hand, and using the scissors or a knife, carefully cut along the shell on one side of the abdomen until you reach the center of the tail fan, then cut along the other side of the abdomen. Peel off (but reserve) the thin shell you just cut through. Repeat the procedure with the remaining langoustines.

Run your thumb between the outer shell (carapace) and the flesh—the nail of your thumb should be facing the flesh—to loosen the flesh from the shell. Once that is done, carefully tug at the base of the tail, shimmying the meat completely loose. Reserve the shell for the mushroom broth.

Look for the intestinal tract on the underside of the tail meat, by the tail-fan end. Carefully expose the tract with the tip of a paring knife, and use tweezers to pull it out in one motion. Discard. Repeat with the remaining langoustines. Lay the tails flat on a paper towel–lined plate, then cover, and refrigerate the meat.

Next pulse the dried mushrooms in a food processor to coarsely chop them.

SEARING

NOTES

Feel free to use any variety of dried mushrooms that you are able to source.

If you can't find langoustines (I get mine from Browne Trading Company in Maine), use large prawns, head on, preferably. Any delicate white fish would be beautiful, too.

12 langoustines

3 ounces dried porcini mushrooms

2 ounces dried shiitake mushrooms

2 ounces dried mousseron mushrooms

Olive oil

1 shallot, chopped

1 garlic clove, smashed and peeled

3 fresh thyme sprigs

1 quart water

2 tablespoons dark soy sauce

Kosher salt

12 very thin slices of lemon or English cucumber

Fleur de sel

12 to 16 small or micro basil leaves

recipe continues

Lightly coat the bottom of a large saucepan with 1 to 2 tablespoons olive oil. Over medium heat, sweat the shallot and garlic until just soft, 3 to 4 minutes. Add the reserved langoustine heads and shells, and cook until lightly toasted, 5 to 7 minutes. Add the thyme and cook for an additional 1 to 2 minutes. Next add the mushrooms, with a little splash of more olive oil, as needed. Cook the mushrooms for 5 minutes. Top with the water, cover, and simmer over medium heat, periodically skimming the surface of foam and any impurities, 20 to 25 minutes.

Using a fine-mesh sieve, strain the mushroom broth into a bowl. Use a ladle to press down on the mushrooms in the sieve until they are almost dry to get all the liquid through the sieve. Discard the mushrooms and aromatics. Line the sieve with cheesecloth and strain the broth once more into a clean saucepan. Set the pan over medium-high heat and reduce the broth to 2 cups. Add the soy sauce and season with kosher salt to taste. Keep warm.

Make one cut from the center of each cucumber slice to the edge of the slice, then overlap the two ends to create a cone.

Lightly coat the bottom of a medium sauté pan with olive oil and set it over medium heat. Season the langoustine tails with kosher salt. Once the oil begins to shimmer, put the langoustine tails in the pan, top-side down. Lightly sear them for less than a minute, until the flesh turns reddish pink. Turn the tails over and lightly cook the underside for 10 seconds more. Remove and cut them crosswise into bite-size pieces.

TO SERVE: Portion the langoustine meat into small bowls. Pour approximately ¼ cup of the mushroom broth into each bowl. Arrange the tip of 3 cucumber cones in the center of each bowl, their openings facing out toward the rim. Drizzle with a little olive oil, season with fleur de sel, and garnish each bowl with 3 or 4 micro basil leaves.

SEARED SCALLOP

PISTACHIO, MELON, LARDO

SERVES 4 (2 SCALLOPS PER PERSON)

After I came across a beautiful melon from a small farm that was so sweet and tasted exactly as I'd imagined the most perfect melon would, almost artificial in flavor—in the best way possible—I created this dish around that single bite of fruit. I use lardo (cured pork fatback) to provide a fat with a delicate flavor. Because lardo is not smoked and has subtle notes of spices, it is not overpowering. Scallops add a different kind of sweetness and a little salinity to round out the dish.

Put the pistachios in a high-speed blender or food processor and process, adding 1 teaspoon of the olive oil at a time to get the contents moving and using the plunger tool as needed. The pistachio purée should be thick enough to hold a line but not so thick that it is stiff; it should resemble a loose crunchy peanut butter. Season with kosher salt to taste. Transfer to a small squeeze bottle or bowl.

In a small bowl, gently toss the melon with the lemon zest and lemon juice. Depending on how sweet and ripe your melon is, you may have to add more lemon juice; you want a nice balance between sweet and sour. Let this sit at room temperature while you cook the scallops.

Heat pan over high heat and pour in just enough grapeseed oil to coat the bottom. Pat the scallops dry and season with kosher salt. Once the oil begins to give off slight wisps of smoke, carefully put the scallops in the pan, flattest side down. You don't want to overcrowd the scallops (again, for the sake of the sear), so you may have to cook them in batches. Do not touch the scallops once they are in the pan. Lower the heat to medium-high. After a minute or so, carefully lift a small edge of each scallop up with a spoon or a small offset spatula, one after the next. This is to ensure the entire presentation side of the scallop is hitting hot oil. You may have to tilt the pan slightly to move the oil around then pan. After 2 to 3 minutes on the first side, take a peek at the scallops: you want them to be a beautiful golden brown. Flip them over and sear the other side for 30 seconds. You won't achieve the same color, and that's okay. Add the butter to the pan, allowing it to foam and bubble before you start basting the

SEARING

¼ cup shelled pistachios, toasted and cooled

2 to 3 teaspoons olive oil, as needed

Kosher salt

1 cup ripe cantaloupe, cut into brunoise (see page 32)

1 teaspoon grated lemon zest

1 teaspoon fresh lemon juice, plus more to taste

Grapeseed or other neutral oil

8 U10 dry-packed sea scallops, small side muscle removed

2 to 3 tablespoons unsalted butter

12 to 16 small basil leaves

8 (6-inch-long) thin slices lardo

Fleur de sel

NOTE

When it comes to cooking scallops, I like to use a cast-iron or an extremely well-seasoned pan. I find the sear develops better and the pan applies a nice even coloring to the scallops. Pat your scallops dry: any excess water will hinder the formation of that crust, and your scallop may also end up sticking to the pan.

recipe continues

scallops with it using a spoon, ten to twelve times. I like my scallops medium-rare, about 3 minutes of total cooking time.

TO SERVE: Using a small spoon or a squeeze bottle, make a line of pistachio purée in the center of each plate. If desired, cut one of the scallops for each portion in half and then in quarters (I do this purely for aesthetics). Arrange the scallops on the line, dark-side up and leaving gaps in between each one. Spoon the melon into the gaps. Next place 2 small basil leaves along the line. Drape 2 strips of lardo over the scallops and melon. Finish with a sprinkle of fleur de sel and basil leaves.

STEAMED RED SNAPPER

SORREL, CRISPY FISH SKIN, HAZELNUT OIL

SERVES 4 TO 6

This is a very straight-up, simple fish dish. Because I love a crispy fish skin but I want to flavor the fish with aromatics by steaming it, I remove the fish skin and cook it separately. It's like fish chicharróns.

COOK THE FISH SKIN: Preheat the oven to 350°F.

Line a sheet pan with parchment paper, then spray the parchment with cooking spray. Using the back of a knife, scrape any errant meat from the fish skins, then place them on the prepared sheet pan. (Reserve the pieces of fish in the refrigerator.) Lay a second sheet of parchment on top (also sprayed with cooking spray on the side in contact with the fish skin) and top it with a second sheet pan; the weight of the top sheet pan will keep the skin flat as it cooks. Bake until the fish skin is completely crisped but not burned, 20 to 25 minutes.

In a shallow sauté pan, heat about ⅓ inch of oil until it reaches the smoking point. When the oil is shimmering and you see wisps of smoke, add the fish skin. It will now puff and curl in 10 seconds or less. Transfer the fish skin to a rack, season with kosher salt, and let cool. Don't worry if the skin seems soft when it's in the oil or as you remove it. The skin will crisp up again as it cools.

FRYING

STEAMING

FISH SKIN

Nonstick cooking spray

4 to 6 (4-ounce) pieces red snapper, skins removed

Grapeseed or other neutral oil

Kosher salt

NOTE
I always ask for center-cut pieces of fish, because the thin end pieces often disintegrate quickly. Pick what looks the best . . . and thickest.

recipe continues

SORREL SAUCE

½ cup whole milk

½ cup heavy cream

2 cups vegetable stock, homemade (page 89) or store-bought

2 strips orange zest

1 Granny Smith apple, peeled, cut into 6 wedges, and cored

1 fresh thyme sprig

1 teaspoon white peppercorns

1 shallot, finely sliced

2 teaspoons fennel seeds, toasted

¼ cup loosely packed fresh flat-leaf parsley leaves

¼ pound fresh sorrel leaves, thick stems removed

Kosher salt

2 tablespoons extra-virgin olive oil

FISH AND AROMATICS

3 stalks lemongrass, coarsely chopped

2 shallots, sliced

5 fresh flat-leaf parsley sprigs

4 fresh thyme sprigs

1 cup dry white wine, plus more (optional) as needed

Kosher salt

Unsalted butter, for the parchment paper

GARNISH

Hazelnut oil

Fleur de sel

2 ounces caviar, such as white sturgeon (optional)

MAKE THE SAUCE: Combine the milk, cream, vegetable stock, orange zest, apple, thyme, peppercorns, shallot, and fennel seeds in a medium saucepan. Bring to a boil over high heat, lower the heat to medium, and simmer to let the flavors begin to infuse while also reducing the liquid by a third to roughly 2 cups. Strain through a fine-mesh sieve into a blender. Run the blender, slowly increasing the speed, adding the parsley leaves and sorrel. Blend on high until fully incorporated, season with salt and add the olive oil. Return to the saucepan to keep warm until serving.

COOK THE FISH: Set your favorite steamer insert (bamboo, stainless steel) into a saucepan. To the saucepan, add the lemongrass, shallots, parsley, thyme, and wine. You'll want a couple of inches or so of liquid in your pan, so add more wine or water as required. Season the pieces of fish with kosher salt and place each one on top of a lightly buttered piece of parchment paper in the steamer basket—make sure the parchment is the same size as the fish, to leave room for the steam to enter the basket. Cover the pan and bring the aromatics to a boil over high heat. Lower the heat to medium-low and steam until the fish looks opaque and gives slightly if you gently press on it (like squeezing a firm marshmallow), 4 to 5 minutes.

TO SERVE: Put the fish in shallow bowls. Spoon about one-quarter of the sorrel sauce around the fish. Garnish with hazelnut oil, fleur de sel, and the puffed fish skin. Add a dollop of caviar, if using, to top each piece of snapper.

LABNEH

BAY SCALLOP CRUDO

LABNEH, APPLE, CILANTRO

SERVES 4 TO 6

My amazing traveling sous chef, former cook at Menton, and hopefully sous chef in some future restaurant venture, Robeisy Sanchez, is one of the greatest cooks I've ever worked with. She knows my cooking style and my palate far better than even I do. We came up with this amuse-bouche for a private dinner we cooked. It comes together quickly, and the flavors are surprising in concert: sweet briny scallops, creamy tangy labneh (like a thick yogurt), crunchy apple, and sweet-hot spice Urfa pepper. Great bay scallops are a must for this, especially because they're served raw—the best way to eat them, in my opinion.

In a small bowl, mix together the labneh, Urfa pepper, and the 1 teaspoon olive oil.

Toss the scallops with the remaining 2 tablespoons olive oil, the lemon juice, chives, and salt to taste.

TO SERVE: Scoop 2 tablespoons of the labneh in the center of each plate. Using the back of your spoon, spread the labneh out into a 5-inch circle. Evenly divide and arrange the scallops and then the apple julienne. Place the cilantro leaves on top.

¾ cup labneh

2 teaspoons Urfa pepper

2 tablespoons plus 1 teaspoon olive oil

1 pound bay scallops

1½ tablespoons fresh lemon juice

2 teaspoons finely sliced fresh chives

Kosher salt

1 Granny Smith apple, cored and cut into julienne

20 small cilantro leaves

ARCTIC CHAR

ARTICHOKE, BLACK TRUFFLE, ONION SAUCE

SERVES 4

SEARING
SWEATING

Arctic char, the love child of salmon and trout, is one of my favorite fish: I adore everything from cleaning and filleting it to cooking and finally eating it. The sauce comes from when I worked at Menton and needed to do something with the truffle ends that were left over each night once we had shaved the truffles over dishes. (A great problem to have!) The pairing of sweet onion with earthy truffle, bright artichokes, and the silky char really hits it home for me.

Olive oil, plus more if needed

2 tablespoons unsalted butter

1 large yellow onion, halved and finely sliced

1 shallot, finely sliced lengthwise

Kosher salt

1 garlic clove, minced

3 fresh thyme sprigs, leaves only

½ ounce black truffle pieces, finely chopped

½ cup whole milk

Grapeseed or other neutral oil

4 (4-ounce) skin-on arctic char fillets

5 baby artichokes, cleaned and trimmed

1 tablespoon fresh lemon juice

1 tablespoon porcini oil (or olive oil)

20 to 24 small fresh chervil leaves

Fleur de sel

Lightly coat the bottom of a medium saucepan with olive oil. Add 1 tablespoon of butter and, over medium heat, cook the onion and shallot. Add a pinch of kosher salt to help sweat the onion and to draw out the moisture. Gently cook, lowering the heat if necessary, as they begin to color, stirring regularly. Just as the onion begins to turn a light golden color, after 20 to 25 minutes, add the garlic and thyme. Reduce the heat to low and continue to cook until the onion reaches a dark amber color, 30 to 35 minutes. Add the truffle and sweat for 3 to 4 minutes. Pour in the milk, add the remaining tablespoon of butter, and simmer until perfumed, 8 to 10 minutes. Season to taste with kosher salt, transfer to a blender, and purée until smooth. Transfer to a clean saucepan and keep warm.

Lightly coat the bottom of a cast-iron pan with grapeseed oil. Bring the oil to a shimmer over medium-high heat. Season the fish with kosher salt on both sides and place the fillets in the pan, skin-side down. Do not move the fish for the first few minutes: you can lift up a corner to check the crispiness of the skin and to help the oil slide under to ensure even doneness. The fish will need 3 to 4 minutes to cook—and only on one side. Baste the flesh of the fish with the hot oil six to eight times until it turns opaque; it will be medium-rare inside. Remove the fish from the pan and let it rest, skin-side up, on a plate while you prepare the artichokes. Thinly slice the artichokes into a small bowl and combine with the lemon juice, porcini or olive oil, and kosher salt to taste.

TO SERVE: Spoon a few tablespoons of the sauce into the center of each plate. Set the fish on top. Arrange 6 to 8 slices of the artichokes. Garnish with 5 to 6 chervil leaves. Sprinkle with fleur de sel to taste.

FLUKE

BROWN BUTTER, TEMPURA PARSLEY, CAULIFLOWER

SERVES 4 TO 6

I fell back in love with steamed fish while I was filming *36 Hours* in Berlin, Germany. We were eating at a beautiful restaurant called Nobelhart & Schmutzig, one that opened my eyes to the modern Berlin food scene. One of our seven courses was a flaky white fish with spinach juice and potato purée. I translated that into classic meunière flavors: lemon, capers, brown butter, and parsley. It was clean, simple, perfectly executed, and inspiring. In this recipe I blend brown butter with cauliflower to bring that same fat and richness, and I fry the parsley for extra texture.

PREPARE THE TEMPURA PARSLEY: In a heavy, deep pot, heat 3 inches of oil to 375°F.

While the oil is heating, in a medium bowl whisk together the rice flour, all-purpose flour, and cornstarch. Slowly whisk in the vodka, soda water, and ice cubes until there are no lumps. The batter should have the consistency of a thin pancake batter. Submerge one sprig of parsley at a time in the batter, allowing the excess to run off for a few seconds before you put the sprig in the hot oil. Fry for 2 minutes, or until the batter has turned puffy and crunchy. It won't turn golden brown, so don't wait for it! Drain on paper towels, immediately seasoning with salt. Repeat with the remaining parsley sprigs.

MAKE THE CAULIFLOWER PURÉE: Simmer the cauliflower florets in salted water until tender, 15 to 18 minutes. Drain and transfer to a high-speed blender. Add the brown butter and blend on high until frothy and completely smooth. Keep the purée warm in a double boiler until ready to serve.

FRYING
STEAMING

TEMPURA PARSLEY

Canola oil for frying

¾ cup rice flour

¼ cup all-purpose flour

3 tablespoons cornstarch

¼ cup vodka

1½ cups soda water

Handful of ice cubes

8 to 12 fresh flat-leaf parsley sprigs, each with 2 or 3 small leaves attached

Kosher salt

CAULIFLOWER PURÉE

8 ounces cauliflower florets

Kosher salt

2½ tablespoons Brown Butter (page 92)

recipe continues

FISH

½ cup dry white wine

½ cup water

3 fresh thyme sprigs

3 fresh flat-leaf parsley sprigs

½ lemon

4 to 6 (3- to 4-ounce) pieces skinless fluke fillet or cod or halibut

Kosher salt

Unsalted butter, for the parchment paper

2 tablespoons extra-virgin olive oil

2 teaspoons fresh lemon juice

Fleur de sel

GARNISH

2 teaspoons olive oil

4 teaspoons brined capers, rinsed and drained

COOK THE FISH: Match your favorite steamer (bamboo, stainless steel) to a saucepan. In the saucepan, combine the white wine, water, thyme, and parsley, and squeeze the lemon juice directly into the pan, then throw in the squeezed lemon half as well. You'll want a couple of inches or so of liquid in your pan, so add more wine or water as needed. Season the pieces of fish with kosher salt and place each one on top of a lightly buttered piece of parchment paper in the steamer basket—make sure the parchment is the same size as the fish, to leave room for the steam to enter the basket. Cover the pan and bring the liquid to a boil over high heat. Lower the heat to medium-low and steam until the fish looks opaque and gives slightly if you gently press on it (like squeezing a firm marshmallow), 4 to 5 minutes. Remove from the heat, then drizzle the fish with the olive oil, lemon juice, and fleur de sel.

PREPARE THE GARNISH: Warm the olive oil in a very small saucepan over medium heat, then add the capers. Allow the capers to warm up and sizzle for 3 to 4 minutes.

TO SERVE: For each serving, dollop a couple of tablespoons cauliflower purée on a shallow, narrow plate. Place the fish portions on the plates. Spoon 1 teaspoon of the capers in olive oil on top of each. Garnish with tempura parsley.

COBIA

POTATO CHIPS, LEEK, BLACK TRUFFLE

SERVES 4

I love the texture of poached cobia; it's almost meaty. As such, I love it with traditional (French) sides to a good steak: soft leeks, creamy mashed potatoes, crisp potato chips for crunch, and a little bit of black truffle for earthiness.

FRYING

POACHING

Marinate the leeks in the white wine for 2 hours at room temperature. Drain and pat dry. Preheat the oven to 400°F.

Rinse the potatoes, place on a sheet pan, and bake until tender, 45 minutes to 1 hour, then halve the potatoes lengthwise and scoop out the inside. Pass the potato flesh through a ricer or a fine-mesh sieve into a bowl. While the potatoes are still hot, use a spatula to incorporate the heavy cream and 5 tablespoons of the butter, allowing each tablespoon to melt before adding the next. The final texture should be that of loose mashed potatoes. Season with kosher salt to taste. Keep warm in a double boiler.

Put each portion of fish into a small vacuum sealer, add 1 tablespoon olive oil and a thyme sprig, and season with ½ teaspoon fleur de sel per portion. Seal the bags airtight. Set up an immersion circulating water bath at 147°F. Submerge the bags of cobia in the water. Cook for 6 minutes. Remove the fish from the bags, pat dry, and slice into 5 to 6 pieces. (If you're searing the fish, season each portion with salt and sear in grapeseed oil in a pan over medium-high heat, 3 minutes on the first side, 1 minute on the second, until golden and firm to the touch.)

In a small sauté pan over medium heat, pour in just enough grapeseed oil to coat the bottom. Add the leeks and a pinch of kosher salt and begin to sweat them. Once the leeks begin to soften, about 4 minutes, cover with the vegetable stock. Simmer until the stock evaporates almost completely (au sec) and the leeks have completely softened, 8 to 10 minutes. Finish with the remaining 2 tablespoons butter, the sherry vinegar, and kosher salt to taste. Keep warm.

TO SERVE: Spoon some of the mashed potatoes in the center of each plate. Spoon the leeks across the potatoes. Put the fish on top and season with fleur de sel. Garnish with 6 or 7 potato chips and, using a Microplane, grate black truffle over the top, if using.

1 large leek, white and pale green parts only, halved lengthwise and cut into ¼-inch half-moons

½ cup dry white wine

2 medium Idaho or russet potatoes

½ cup heavy cream, warmed

7 tablespoons unsalted butter, cubed, at room temperature

Kosher salt

4 (4-ounce) cleaned cobia fillets

4 tablespoons olive oil

4 fresh thyme sprigs

Fleur de sel

Grapeseed or other neutral oil

1 cup vegetable stock, homemade (page 89) or store-bought

1 teaspoon sherry vinegar

Potato Chips (page 58)

Fresh black truffle (optional)

NOTE

I've tried to steer clear of cooking sous vide (see page 28) for this book, but this is a case when it yields a silky, velvety texture that melts into the potato purée and plays off the texture of the leeks, yet still stands up to the earthiness of the truffle. If you don't have a vacuum sealer, you can roast, sear, or steam the fish.

HALIBUT

SMOKED HAM HOCK, FENNEL, PEAS, AND RADISH

SERVES 4

BRINING
SEARING

The *Boston Globe* once asked me to put together a summer dinner party. I had an afternoon to prepare before that evening's dinner. This is what I served: tender fish fillets in a smoky-rich ham hock cream sauce, dotted with spring peas and crisp radishes. Roasted Garlic Scapes (page 37) was the appetizer, and Sponge Cake (page 246) was dessert.

BRINE

1 quart water

¼ cup kosher salt

3 fresh thyme sprigs

1 garlic clove, smashed

1 teaspoon black peppercorns

1 teaspoon fennel seeds

MAKE THE BRINE: In a medium saucepan, combine the water, salt, thyme sprigs, garlic, peppercorns, and fennel seeds. Bring to a boil over high heat, and cook for 2 to 3 minutes. Lower the heat and simmer for 5 minutes. Transfer the brine to a bowl and chill until cold, at least 1 hour.

Add the fish fillets to the brine (nuzzling them so they are all submerged) and refrigerate for 4 hours.

HALIBUT

4 (4-ounces) skinless halibut fillets (ask for the center of the halibut—the meatiest part)

2 tablespoons grapeseed or other neutral oil

2 fresh thyme sprigs

2 tablespoons unsalted butter

NOTE
The halibut needs to brine for 4 hours, and the stock for the sauce needs to simmer for the same amount of time. Keep this in mind when prepping this dinner.

recipe continues

HAM HOCK STOCK AND SAUCE

3 pounds smoked ham hocks

3 large fennel bulbs: 2 quartered and 1 finely sliced, fronds reserved for garnish

1 teaspoon fennel seeds, toasted

1 tablespoon grapeseed or other neutral oil

3 scallions: white parts, finely sliced; green tops, sliced, for garnish

1 large shallot, finely sliced

1 teaspoon chopped fresh thyme

2 tablespoons dry white wine

½ cup heavy cream

9 radishes, sliced

¾ cup shelled fresh peas or frozen (in a pinch)

1 teaspoon fresh lemon juice

1 teaspoon ground sumac

Kosher salt

GARNISH

Fleur de sel

4 teaspoons olive oil

4 lemon wedges

12 to 15 watercress or bitter green sprigs

3 scallions, dark green part only, finely sliced on a bias

MAKE THE SAUCE: In a large saucepan, combine the ham hocks, the quartered fennel, the toasted fennel seeds, and enough water to cover. Over medium-high heat, bring to a boil, then reduce the heat and simmer, partly covered, for 4 hours.

Strain the stock through a fine-mesh sieve and return it to the saucepan. Let the ham hocks cool. Return the stock to a boil, then simmer vigorously over medium heat, periodically skimming the surface of foam and any impurities, until reduced by half, 25 to 30 minutes. The goal here is to reduce the liquid to 2 cups.

Pour the grapeseed oil into a medium saucepan and, over medium-high heat, sweat the whites of the scallions, the shallot, fennel slices, and chopped thyme until the vegetables are translucent, 3 minutes. Add the white wine and cook until evaporated. Pour in the cream and reduced ham hock stock. Simmer over medium-high heat for 3 to 5 minutes. Add the radishes and the fresh peas. (If you're using frozen peas, add them later with the lemon juice and sumac.) Simmer the vegetables until tender, 4 to 5 minutes. Remove from the heat and add the lemon juice and sumac. Season with salt to taste.

COOK THE FISH: Remove the fish from the brine and pat the fillets dry with paper towels. Discard the brine. Heat a large cast-iron pan (my preference for searing fish) over high heat, and add the oil. As soon as it begins to smoke, bring the heat down to medium-high. Add the fish to the pan, skin-side down. Sear until golden brown, 3 to 4 minutes, then carefully flip. Cook for another 2 minutes. Add the thyme and butter; the butter should foam, and the thyme should crackle. Using a spoon, baste the fish with the fat about twelve times; the fish should give slightly to the touch.

TO SERVE: Spoon about ½ cup creamy ham hock sauce onto each plate, and top with a halibut fillet. Finish with fleur de sel, 1 teaspoon olive oil, a squeeze of the lemon wedge, and the scallion greens, and the watercress.

OCTOPUS

CHORIZO PURÉE, CELERY SALAD

SERVES 4 TO 6

Octopus is tasty and wonderfully tender when cooked long enough at a low temperature. In all honesty, without a good soak in a marinade and a long braise in flavors that completely permeate the meat, octopus is a bit bland. The classic Spanish pairing with chorizo, paprika, and potato is simple and delicious. This is my take on that combo.

MARINATE THE OCTOPUS: Pat the octopuses dry and put them in a medium bowl along with the parsley, rosemary, lemon zest, lemon juice, garlic, paprika, red pepper flakes, olive oil, 1 tablespoon salt, and ½ tablespoon black pepper. Massage the seasonings into the octopuses. Cover with plastic wrap pressed directly on top of the octopuses and marinate in the refrigerator for 24 hours.

Preheat the oven to 300°F.

Transfer the octopuses and their marinade to a medium baking dish. Cover with vegetable stock until just submerged. Wrap the dish tightly with foil and braise in the oven for 3 to 3½ hours, or until the octopus is tender.

IN THE MEANTIME, MAKE THE CHORIZO PURÉE: Coat the bottom of a medium saucepan with grapeseed oil. Over medium-low heat, sweat the shallot and garlic until translucent, 3 to 4 minutes.

Add the chorizo and cook for an additional 5 to 6 minutes. Pour in water to cover and simmer gently until softened, 8 to 10 minutes. Add the heavy cream and simmer for an additional 10 minutes. Transfer the chorizo and cream mixture to a blender and purée until very smooth. Add more water as needed; the final consistency of the

BRAISING

SEARING

NOTE

The octopuses need to marinate for 24 hours and braise for up to 3½ hours in the oven. Plan accordingly.

OCTOPUS

2½ pounds cleaned baby octopuses

¼ cup fresh flat-leaf parsley leaves, finely chopped

2 fresh rosemary sprigs, leaves finely chopped

Grated zest of 2 lemons

2 tablespoons fresh lemon juice

5 large garlic cloves, grated

1 tablespoons smoked paprika

1 teaspoon crushed red pepper flakes

1 cup olive oil

Kosher salt and freshly ground black pepper

2 cups vegetable stock, homemade (page 89) or store-bought, or water

Grapeseed or other neutral oil

CHORIZO PURÉE

Grapeseed or other neutral oil

1 shallot, minced

1 garlic clove, minced

8 ounces Spanish (cured) chorizo, small diced

1 cup heavy cream

Kosher salt

recipe continues

sauce should resemble that of a loose pancake batter. Season with salt to taste. Keep warm if you're close to mealtime, or refrigerate until later, heating it up in a saucepan before serving.

Transfer the octopuses to a cutting board and pat dry with paper towels.

Lightly coat a large cast-iron skillet with grapeseed oil and heat over high heat. Season the octopus with salt and black pepper. As the oil begins to smoke, sear the flat sides of the octopus, charring them just slightly, 3 to 4 minutes.

MAKE THE SALAD: In a bowl, toss the celery, sherry vinegar, lime juice, chives, and olive oil. Season with salt and black pepper to taste.

TO SERVE: Using wide, deep bowls, spoon 3 tablespoons of the chorizo sauce into each bowl. Arrange the octopus in the center and the salad to the side. Garnish with 4 or 5 celery leaves on the side of each bowl.

NOTE

This recipe yields more chorizo purée than you need: toss what's left over with noodles, use it as a sauce for steak, chicken, or a hearty fish, or just dip bread in it! It will keep, covered in the fridge, for up to 2 days.

CELERY SALAD

3 celery stalks, peeled, cut lengthwise, and finely sliced on the bias

2 teaspoons sherry vinegar

1 teaspoon fresh lime juice

1 tablespoon finely sliced fresh chives

1 tablespoon olive oil

Kosher salt and freshly ground black pepper

GARNISH

25 celery heart leaves

SMOKED FISH SALAD

CRUDITÉS

SERVES 4 TO 6

CURING

SMOKING

Because bluefish is a fatty fish, I prefer eating it chilled, alongside something acidic and crunchy. This is slightly heartier than your basic summer salad but still light and refreshing.

BLUEFISH

3/4 cup kosher salt

Grated zest of 1 lemon

Grated zest of 1 orange

1 pound skin-on, boneless bluefish fillet

3/4 cup hickory-wood chips, soaked in cold water for 30 minutes and drained

Juice of 1 lemon

1 teaspoon finely chopped fresh flat-leaf parsley leaves

1 teaspoon finely sliced fresh chives

1 cup crème fraîche

3 tablespoons red wine vinegar

2 teaspoons whole-grain mustard

Fleur de sel

CRUDITÉS

5 baby orange carrots, 1/2 inch of the stem left on

5 red radishes, tops trimmed

4 baby fennel bulbs, trimmed and quartered lengthwise

8 to 12 caper berries

Combine the kosher salt, lemon zest, and orange zest in a bowl and mix well. Spread out one third of the salt mixture on a small sheet pan to create a bed of salt large enough to lay the fish on. Set the fish, skin-side down, on the salt. Lightly sprinkle the remaining salt mixture evenly over the flesh of the fish. Lay plastic wrap directly onto the fish and refrigerate for 6 to 7 hours.

When the fish has cured, rinse it well under cold running water and pat dry.

Set up your home smoking equipment and follow the method described on page 27 to smoke the fish. The smoking process will take 18 to 20 minutes, depending on the thickness of your fish: check it using an instant-read digital thermometer—you're looking for an internal temperature between 140°F and 155°F. Once smoked, remove the fish from the smoker and place in a covered container. Refrigerate for 40 minutes.

When the fish is completely chilled, peel the skin off and break the fish into large flakes into a bowl. Gently fold in the lemon juice, parsley, chives, crème fraîche, vinegar, mustard, and fleur de sel.

TO SERVE: Make 1 quenelle of the fish mixture per serving and place each on a small round plate. Arrange the vegetables to the side of the quenelle.

NOTE

The wood chips need to soak for at least 30 minutes ahead of smoking time, the fish needs to cure for 6 to 7 hours, and the smoking process will take up to 20 minutes. Plan accordingly.

SMOKED COD RILLETTES

CRÈME FRAÎCHE, DILL, ORANGE, CUCUMBER

SERVES 4 TO 6

One of my dad's favorite snacks is herring in cream—smoked herring brined in vinegar and tossed in a creamy white sauce. Like a lot of folks in the Great Lakes region, his ancestors were Eastern European, and every couple of weeks he would buy this delicacy by the half pint at D&W, a local grocery store in Kentwood, Michigan, where I grew up. I saw it every time I opened the refrigerator and thought it was just so gross. But it didn't stop me from sitting at the counter next to him as he enjoyed his herring with a stack of saltine crackers. I didn't get it, but there was still something intriguing about him loving it. Twenty years later . . . I get it!

SMOKE THE FISH: Using the smoking method outlined on page 27, smoke the cod for 20 minutes, or until fork-tender. Refrigerate until cold. Flake the fish in large pieces into a small bowl, then add the buttermilk, lemon zest, fried shallots, crème fraîche, chopped dill, and salt to taste. I like to keep the texture here slightly chunky, unlike traditional smooth rillettes. I don't whip it; instead I use a fork to mash and mix it together, a lot like how my mom makes tuna salad for sandwiches. Serve immediately or refrigerate until ready to use, preferably within 30 minutes of mixing; the fried shallots will soften the longer this sits.

PREP THE GARNISH: In a small saucepan over low heat, combine the crème fraîche with the heavy cream, season with salt, and cook until melted.

To dress the cucumber, I recommend combining the olive oil and red wine vinegar in a travel-size spray bottle and misting! This distributes the dressing nicely, while ensuring it doesn't weigh down the finely sliced cucumbers. I also avoid salting them to make sure they stay bright and crisp.

TO SERVE: Make quenelle of the smoked fish and set one off to the left side of each bowl. Pour 2 tablespoons of the warmed crème fraîche into the bottom of each bowl. Arrange 3 orange suprêmes in each bowl. Make a slit in each cucumber slice from the center out, and overlap the edges slightly to create a small cone shape. Scatter cucumber cones around the suprêmes. Garnish with dill fronds.

SMOKING

SMOKED COD RILLETTES

¾ cup applewood chips, soaked in cold water for 30 minutes and drained

8 ounces skin-on, boneless cod fillet

2 tablespoons buttermilk

Grated zest of 1 lemon

2 tablespoons fried shallots (see page 82), finely chopped

¼ cup crème fraîche

3 teaspoons finely chopped fresh dill

Kosher salt

GARNISH

½ cup crème fraîche

2 teaspoons heavy cream

Kosher salt

1 small Persian cucumber, unpeeled, finely sliced (⅛ inch thick) on a mandoline

1 teaspoon olive oil

1 teaspoon red wine vinegar

2 blood oranges, cut into suprêmes (see page 33)

8 to 12 fresh dill fronds

PASTA AND GRAINS

SWEET CORN CAPPELLACCI
CAMEMBERT, RADISH

TAGLIATELLE
CHAMPIGNON SAUCE

CREAMY BARLEY
BRAISED ONION, ONION SYRUP, PROSCIUTTO

RIGATONI
WALNUTS, BÉCHAMEL, SAGE, FRIED SHALLOT

CRAB FARAGLIONI
BROWN BUTTER, LEMON, CAPER

CAVATELLI
CORN, ROASTED TOMATO, THAI BASIL

RAVIOLI CON UOVO
DÉLICE DE BOURGOGNE, WHEAT BERRY, BRODO

ONION AND GRUYÈRE TORTELLONI
CHICKEN BRODO

PARISIAN GNOCCHI

SWEET CORN CAPPELLACCI

CAMEMBERT, RADISH

SERVES 6 TO 8

Having grown up in the Midwest, I have a deep reverence for Michigan corn—the unbeatable taste, yes, but also the nostalgia of jumping out of the car in the summertime, with the loose change my parents had given me, and buying corn from roadside farm stands. Usually it was an honor stand, where you just dropped coins into an old Maxwell House coffee can.

Once at home, I would sit outside with old brown paper grocery bags covering the back deck, shucking away. I remember loving and hating this process. The thought of eating the corn got me through the irritation of the corn silk itching my arms and blowing in the air. Being seven years old and destroying three or four ears of summer corn at the dinner table—pretty respectable.

Here I pair a sweet corn filling with al dente pasta (with a name that implies a hat, though I find they remind me of belly buttons), crunchy radishes, and a salty creamy cheese sauce (which is very similar in technique and flavor to the Époisses de Bourgogne in the rabbit recipe on page 205). It's a flavor that brings me back to Michigan, but in a more grown-up way.

MAKE THE CORN FILLING: Into a large sauté pan set over medium-low heat, pour in just enough olive oil to coat the bottom of the pan. Add the shallots and thyme and begin to sweat. Once the shallots are translucent, after about 5 minutes, add the corn kernels and salt and pepper to taste. Cook until just tender, 10 to 15 minutes. Discard the thyme. Transfer the corn mixture to a high-powered blender (a Vitamix is the best and worth the investment). Start blending and increase the speed as the corn begins to purée. You may need to add a bit of water to get things moving, but don't add too much as this will yield a purée too thin for stuffing the pasta. Taste for seasoning. Pass the purée through a fine-mesh sieve into a bowl. Press plastic wrap on top and refrigerate until chilled.

FORM THE CAPPELLACCI: On a floured surface, lay out a sheet of freshly rolled pasta (just thin enough to see your hand; on a KitchenAid attachment, I roll it to number 6). Cut out 2½-inch rounds, keeping them close together to use as much of the dough as possible. Put the corn filling in a piping bag fitted with a ½-inch tip,

recipe continues

EMULSIFYING

MAKING FRESH PASTA

SWEATING

NOTE

You will need a 2½-inch round cutter.

CORN FILLING

Olive oil

2 shallots, halved lengthwise and finely sliced

2 fresh thyme sprigs

6 fresh ears of corn, kernels sliced off the cob

Kosher salt and freshly ground black pepper

Basic Pasta Dough (page 158)

All-purpose flour, for the work surface and pans

or a zip-top plastic bag (cut off a corner to make a ½-inch opening). Pipe roughly ½ teaspoon of filling just off-center of each round of pasta toward the bottom. Dab the edge around the filling with water, which will act as the glue. Fold the top of the circle over onto the bottom, creating a half-moon shape. Holding the folded pasta in your hands with the rounded part facing upward, pull the two points under and press them together, using water, if needed, to stick them together. Put the pasta on a floured sheet pan. Repeat with the remaining dough and filling. You should have 35 to 40 cappellacci. Freeze the cappellacci on a parchment-lined and lightly floured sheet pan as you work through the batches. (Once frozen, transfer them to zip-top bags and freeze for up to 3 weeks if you make more than you need.)

CAMEMBERT SAUCE AND GARNISH

3 cups Roasted Chicken Stock (page 206) or store-bought low-sodium stock

5 radishes, some stem left on the radishes

Kosher salt and freshly ground black pepper

1 (8-ounce) wheel Camembert cheese, rind removed

1 lemon, halved

MAKE THE SAUCE: Pour the chicken stock into a medium saucepan. Bring to a simmer over medium-high heat. Add the radishes and simmer for 4 minutes. Using a slotted spoon, remove the radishes and set aside. Continue to simmer the stock for another 15 minutes or so, until the stock has reduced by a third, leaving you with 2 cups stock.

Meanwhile, bring a large pot of water to a boil to cook the pasta. Salt the water generously. Lower the heat so the water is at a rolling simmer. Add the cappellacci and cook until al dente, 3 to 4 minutes from frozen.

Whisk the cheese into the reduced stock until fully melted and incorporated. Season with salt and lemon juice to taste.

TO SERVE: Slice the radishes into eighths. Drain the pasta and toss immediately with the sauce and radishes. Garnish with freshly ground black pepper.

recipe continues

BASIC PASTA DOUGH

MAKES FOUR 24-INCH-LONG SHEETS OF DOUGH

In a humid kitchen in the summertime—if your AC isn't running or if you're cooking a lot—you will need a touch more flour, maybe an additional 2 tablespoons. Always start with the 2 cups and add more as necessary until the dough comes together.

2 cups all-purpose flour, plus more if needed

8 large egg yolks

2 large whole eggs

Semolina flour, for the pan

To begin, make a wide well with the flour on a clean surface. Add the egg yolks and egg to the center and, using a fork, begin to swirl the eggs, slowly incorporating the flour into the center of the well. When the flour is completely incorporated, knead it together to form a large ball. Knead until the dough has the consistency of Play-Doh, 3 to 5 minutes. Wrap the ball in plastic and refrigerate for at least 30 minutes and up to 1 hour.

Cut the dough into quarters. Roll out one piece at a time, keeping the rest covered with plastic wrap. Start on the widest setting of your pasta machine or attachment and dust with flour as needed to ensure the dough doesn't stick (but don't use too much, as you don't want the dough to become dry). Run the dough through the machine. Fold the sheet of dough in half onto itself, and roll it through this initial setting ten to fifteen times, folding it again after each pass! You will notice the dough go from a richer yellow color to a paler yellow, and the dough will also become tougher, which is what you want.

Once that initial stage is complete, change your setting to the next one up, and roll the sheet through once. You'll notice your sheet will become longer and longer as you work it through each successive setting. Keep rolling until you hit what on most pasta machines will be setting number 7: you want the sheet to be thin enough so you can just begin to see your hand through the sheet. Lay the pasta sheet out on a sheet pan heavily dusted with semolina flour (to keep the pasta from sticking). Repeat the rolling procedure with the remaining three quarters of dough. The dough can then be used to make cappellacci (page 155) or ravioli or cut into pappardelle or tagliatelle (see page 163) or other types of pasta.

TAGLIATELLE
CHAMPIGNON SAUCE

SERVES 8 TO 10

Back in 2012, when I was competing on *Top Chef*, I won my first elimination challenge a few episodes into the season, and it was the complete opposite of how I expected my big shining moment to go down. The task was to cook mushrooms along with french-fried onions. White. Button. Mushrooms.

As far as I knew, I cooked them just like anybody else would have. Except I didn't. I cooked the mushrooms twice: once to draw out moisture and once to caramelize and impart flavor. I won $10,000, and needless to say, my affinity for white mushrooms has doubled. I especially like them garnishing whole-wheat pasta, which has a nuttier flavor than regular pasta and makes a nice pairing with mushrooms.

MAKE THE TAGLIATELLE: Using the ingredients at right, follow the complete method outlined in the basic pasta dough recipe on page 158. Cut the sheets of pasta dough by hand into 8-inch sections, then cut ¼-inch-wide noodles by hand or with a pasta-cutting attachment fitted to your pasta maker. Toss the tagliatelle generously with semolina flour and set it aside on a sheet pan that is generously dusted with semolina flour.

MAKE THE SAUCE: Cut the mushrooms into sizable pieces—leave the smallest mushrooms whole, halve the medium-size ones, and quarter the largest ones. You want the pieces to be large enough to stand up to a rich sauce (keep in mind the mushroom pieces will shrink by a third or so during the cooking process).

In a large sauté pan, heat 2 tablespoons of the grapeseed oil until it begins to shimmer. Add a portion of the mushrooms, being careful not to overcrowd the pan, and a pinch of salt. Sweat the mushrooms over medium-high heat until the liquid begins to cook out; you will have to do this in three or four batches. For each batch, use 2 tablespoons of oil.

Let the mushrooms drain in the colander for 20 minutes.

BLANCHING

MAKING FRESH PASTA

SWEATING

WHOLE-WHEAT TAGLIATELLE

1 cup all-purpose flour

1 cup whole-wheat flour

7 large egg yolks

2 large eggs

Semolina flour, for dusting

CHAMPIGNON SAUCE

2 pounds white button mushrooms

8 tablespoons grapeseed or other neutral oil, plus more as needed

Kosher salt

recipe continues

6 ounces red pearl onions, blanched (see page 23), peeled, and halved from stem to root

2 tablespoons minced shallot

1 tablespoon minced garlic

1 teaspoon minced fresh thyme

¼ cup dry red wine

2 teaspoons dry vermouth

2 cups Roasted Chicken Stock (page 206) or store-bought low-sodium stock

2 teaspoons red wine vinegar

1 cup heavy cream

½ cup crème fraîche

2 tablespoons chopped fresh flat-leaf parsley leaves

Freshly ground black pepper

In a large, tall-sided sauté pan or Dutch oven, lightly coat the bottom of the pot with grapeseed oil. Heat over high heat until the oil is hot but not smoking. Add the mushrooms and cook until golden brown, 5 to 7 minutes. Add the pearl onions, season with salt, and cook until they are just browned on the edges and have become translucent, about 4 minutes.

Lower the heat to medium. Add the shallots and a splash more oil if necessary. Sweat the shallots until they are translucent and tender, about 4 minutes. Add the garlic and thyme, and sweat until the garlic is aromatic and no longer raw but not colored, 3 minutes. Deglaze the pan with the wine and vermouth, and simmer until the liquid has completely evaporated. Pour in the stock and vinegar. Simmer until the stock has reduced by one third. Add the heavy cream and continue to simmer until the sauce coats the back of a spoon, 10 to 15 minutes.

Meanwhile, bring a large pot of water to a boil for the pasta.

Reduce the heat under your sauce to low and add the crème fraîche to melt: do not let the sauce boil once you've added the crème fraîche or it will separate. Warm through gently instead, then turn off the heat and stir in the chopped parsley. Season with salt and pepper to taste. (FYI, you should have approximately 3 cups of sauce.)

When the pasta water begins to boil, salt it generously. Lower the heat so that the water is at a rolling simmer and add the pasta bit by bit. Cook until al dente, about 3 minutes. Remove the pasta using a slotted spoon or spider and transfer it directly into the sauté pan with the sauce, using splashes of pasta water to thin out the sauce if it has thickened too much.

GARNISH

Freshly grated Parmesan cheese

Freshly ground black pepper

TO SERVE: Portion the pasta into large shallow bowls and top with Parmesan and a couple of turns of freshly ground pepper to finish.

CREAMY BARLEY

BRAISED ONION, ONION SYRUP, PROSCIUTTO

SERVES 4 TO 6

This dish has a few involved steps, but making a large batch of onion stock ahead of time and freezing it in quart-size amounts will save you lots of time when, during a Boston winter—at least for me!—you're craving this. Here, barley is a vehicle for sweet onions, cooked a few different ways, alongside ham and cheese. The result is sweet, salty, and tangy, and the barley has such a great hearty-yet-delicate texture that it can carry the weight of richer ingredients while melting into them.

MAKE THE ONION SYRUP: The process of caramelizing onions properly takes time and some attention, but the end product is worth it! In a large sauté pan, heat the oil and butter over medium-high heat until foamy, then add the sliced onions, and cook them low and slow until dark amber in color, about 1½ hours. Be sure to keep an eye on your onions, stirring them often so they do not burn.

Once the onions have caramelized completely, drain off any excess fat, transfer them to a large saucepan, and pour in the onion stock. Bring to a boil, then decrease the heat to medium and reduce the cooking liquid to ½ cup, 30 to 35 minutes. Transfer the onions and reduced stock to a blender and purée until smooth; you're looking for the consistency of runny syrup. Adjust the consistency as needed, either by cooking it down further to thicken or by adding a splash of water to thin it. Season to taste with salt and pepper.

PREP THE GARNISH: Preheat the oven to 350°F.

Grease a small baking dish with the butter, then arrange the onion quarters in a single layer. Cover the onion quarters halfway with water. Drizzle the honey and sherry vinegar over the top, nestle the thyme sprigs in there, and season with salt and pepper. Cover with aluminum foil and bake until tender, about 40 minutes.

BRAISING
SWEATING

ONION SYRUP

Splash of grapeseed or other neutral oil

1 tablespoon unsalted butter

2 large white onions, finely sliced

2 quarts Onion Stock (page 168)

Kosher salt and freshly ground black pepper

NOTE

You will have extra onion syrup. You will thank me. Drizzle it over pasta tossed with Parmesan, or over meat or a cheese plate. It will keep, covered in the fridge, for up to a week.

GARNISH

1 tablespoon unsalted butter

1 large Vidalia onion, peeled, root intact, quartered lengthwise (pole to pole)

1 teaspoon honey

1 teaspoon sherry vinegar

2 fresh thyme sprigs

Kosher salt and freshly ground pepper

12 to 18 thin slices prosciutto

recipe continues

MEANWHILE, COOK THE BARLEY: Coat the bottom of a medium saucepan or deep-sided sauté pan (keep in mind, the barley will triple in volume as it cooks) with a splash of olive oil. Over medium heat, sweat the shallot, carrot, celery, and thyme, seasoning with salt and pepper to taste. Once the aromatics are becoming translucent, after 2 to 3 minutes, add the barley and stir, toasting it just slightly for 3 to 4 minutes. Deglaze with the sherry. Add the onion stock and simmer over medium heat, slightly covered (with a lid or some foil), until the barley is just tender, 35 to 45 minutes.

Once the barley is cooked, there should be roughly 1 cup of stock that hasn't cooked in; this is the point at which to add the cream. Uncover, stir, and cook further, until the cream and unabsorbed stock start to create a binding sauce, 10 to 15 minutes. Stir in the cheese and butter, and season to taste.

TO SERVE: Divide the barley evenly among bowls. Top each bowl with petals of the braised onion and 2 or 3 slices of prosciutto, and drizzle with the onion syrup to finish.

BARLEY

Olive oil

1 tablespoon minced shallot

1 tablespoon carrot, cut into brunoise (see page 32)

1 tablespoon celery, cut into brunoise (see page 32)

1 fresh thyme sprig, leaves only, chopped

Kosher salt and freshly ground black pepper

1¼ cups pearl barley

1 tablespoon sherry

1 quart Onion Stock (recipe follows)

½ cup heavy cream

¼ cup grated Gruyère cheese

1 tablespoon unsalted butter

ONION STOCK

MAKES 4 QUARTS

5 yellow onions, cut in half along the equator (see Note) and peeled

2 large leeks, pale green and white parts only, sliced and rinsed

8 shallots, finely sliced

Grapeseed or other neutral oil

4 quarts Roasted Chicken Stock (page 206) or store-bought low-sodium stock

NOTE

To cut an onion along its "equator," think of the onion as Earth, and the stem end as the North Pole, and the root end as the South Pole. This kind of cut is used mostly for onion rings and, like here, onion brûlée (see page 32), to enhance the flavor and color of your stock.

Use this stock as you would any flavorful cooking liquid, and especially to cook rice or grains.

Line a large sauté pan (you may need two pans to fit all 10 onion halves) with three layers of aluminum foil, place the onion halves, cut-side down, into the pan, and cook over high heat, simply letting the onions be. Once the onion faces start to blacken, after about 10 minutes, you can reduce the heat to medium-high and let them sit for 25 to 30 minutes. You want to burn those onion faces completely.

Meanwhile, in a stockpot, cook the leeks and shallots in a splash of oil over medium heat until the vegetables become soft and just begin to color, 3 to 4 minutes. Add the onion brûlée to the pot. Cover with the chicken stock. Bring to a boil, then reduce the heat and simmer, periodically skimming the surface of foam and any impurities, for 1½ hours. Strain and let cool. The stock can be covered and refrigerated for up to 2 days or frozen for up to a month.

RIGATONI

WALNUTS, BÉCHAMEL, SAGE, FRIED SHALLOT

SERVES 4 TO 6

I love the textures of the chewy pasta, lightly crisped sage, and crunchy shallots and walnuts. The béchamel marries all the various flavors of bitter and sweet together, making this a recipe I crave.

MAKE THE RIGATONI: In a large bowl, mix together the flour and water with your hands, or pulse them in a food processor until the mixture looks like slightly damp sand. You don't want this to be too wet or it will stick to the machine and clog it up. It should be drier than you might expect: when you squeeze a small amount in your fist, it should hold together, though it will feel and look far drier than a typical egg pasta dough. Bring the dough together into a ball and wrap in plastic. Let it rest at room temperature for 30 minutes.

In the meantime, fit your pasta extruder with the rigatoni plate, and attach it to your stand mixer. Sprinkle a heavy dusting of semolina onto a large sheet pan or two so you can arrange the rigatoni in a single layer. Extrude the pasta, cutting it every 2 inches. If you aren't using a stand mixer, follow the manufacturer's instructions for your particular pasta machine. Allow the pasta to sit out to dry for 3 to 4 hours. You can freeze it now, if you'd like, on the sheet pan; once firm, transfer to a zip-top bag and return to the freezer for up to a few weeks.

MAKE THE BÉCHAMEL: In a medium saucepan, melt the butter over medium heat, then add the flour and whisk together until incorporated. Cook for a minute until you have a blond roux. Steadily stream in the milk while whisking constantly. Increase the heat to medium-high and bring to a simmer. Cook, whisking, for 3 to 4 minutes, until the flour is cooked and you can no longer taste it. Reduce the heat to low and add the Fontina cheese. Whisk until the sauce is smooth. Season with salt to taste. Keep warm in a double boiler.

FRYING

RIGATONI

2 cups semolina flour, plus more for dusting

¼ cup water, or more as needed

Kosher salt

NOTE

The pasta recipe above is far easier to make than the more traditional Basic Pasta Dough (page 158), as it has only two ingredients. But it admittedly does require a machine that pumps out the shape for you. The pasta-extruder attachment on a stand mixer works well. Failing that, you can substitute 1 pound store-bought fresh rigatoni in place of the homemade.

BÉCHAMEL

2 tablespoons (¼ stick) unsalted butter

2 tablespoons all-purpose flour

1½ cups whole milk, at room temperature

4 ounces Fontina cheese, grated

Kosher salt

recipe continues

GARNISH

½ cup olive oil

15 large fresh sage leaves

½ cup walnuts, toasted, coarsely chopped

¾ cup freshly grated Pecorino cheese

3 large shallots, fried (see page 82)

Kosher salt and freshly ground black pepper

PREP THE GARNISH: In a small sauté pan, heat the olive oil over medium heat until it begins to shimmer. Add the sage leaves and fry until crisp, 1 to 2 minutes. Remove and drain the leaves on a paper towel. When the sage has cooled to room temperature, crumble it into a bowl and gently toss with the walnuts, Pecorino cheese, and fried shallots. Season with salt and pepper.

Meanwhile, bring a large pot of water to a boil to cook the pasta. Salt the water generously. Lower the heat so the water is at a rolling simmer. Add the pasta to the boiling water and cook until al dente, 3 to 4 minutes. Drain, reserving some of the cooking water.

TO SERVE: Mix the drained pasta with the béchamel. Use a ladle of pasta water to thin out the sauce, if necessary. You want to immerse the pasta in a generous amount of sauce, more than just a coating. Divide the pasta and sauce among bowls. Sprinkle equal amounts of the walnut garnish over each portion.

CRAB FARAGLIONI

BROWN BUTTER, LEMON, CAPER

SERVES 8 TO 10

This square-based pyramid shape is one of my favorite stuffed pastas to make: my inner perfectionist challenges me to get the dough pieces perfectly square so the corners will then match up just so. My guess is the chef who taught me to make these was probably inspired by crab Rangoon dumplings, as I'm pretty sure this shape doesn't exist in the classic Italian pasta repertoire—but these little pyramids do remind me of *faraglioni*, those rock formations off Capri and in the Adriatic. So I've decided to call them that. As for the stuffing: crab, cream, lemon, and capers—need I say more?

PREPARE THE FILLING: In a medium bowl, gently mix the crabmeat, crème fraîche, lemon zest, lemon juice, chives, capers, and salt to taste.

Trim the pasta sheets into 2-inch squares. I like to use a metal ruler, dusted in flour and laid directly on the sheet of pasta. I slide a small knife along the edge and then reposition the ruler to measure the next 2 inches.

Working in batches, line up a few squares (keeping the remaining squares covered with a towel). Scoop 1 teaspoon of filling in the center of each square of pasta dough. Once the filling is in place, lightly mist the surface of the squares with water from a spray bottle. Bring together the tips of two opposing corners of the square. Press the tips lightly together. Next bring the remaining two corners to the center, indenting the sides inward, and then delicately seal all the edges to create a square-based pyramid shape. Lay the faraglioni on a semolina flour–dusted sheet pan as you work. I recommend you freeze them until cooking time—this will help preserve the shape during cooking. Once firm, they can be transferred to a zip-top bag and returned to the freezer for up to 2 weeks.

Bring a large pot of water to a boil for the pasta.

EMULSIFYING

MAKING FRESH PASTA

NOTE

If you want to make this for 4 or so people, extra faraglioni freeze well.

CRAB FILLING

¾ pound crabmeat

¼ cup crème fraîche

Grated zest of 1 lemon

1 teaspoon fresh lemon juice

1 tablespoon finely sliced fresh chives

2 tablespoons brined capers, rinsed, drained, and minced

Kosher salt

Basic Pasta Dough (page 158)

Semolina flour, for dusting

Kosher salt

NOTE

You'll need a small spray bottle to mist your pasta dough with water before sealing the dough into shape.

recipe continues

BROWN BUTTER SAUCE

½ cup heavy cream

¾ cup Brown Butter (page 92), cold, cut into ½-inch cubes

1 teaspoon fresh lemon juice

Kosher salt

GARNISH

20 fresh celery leaves

MAKE THE SAUCE: In a medium saucepan set over medium heat, bring the cream to a boil. Reduce until the cream coats the back of a spoon. Reduce the heat to low and add the cubes of brown butter while whisking constantly: you're emulsifying the cold butter in the hot liquid to get a rich velvety sauce. Once the butter is incorporated, whisk in the lemon juice. Season with salt to taste. Keep warm.

When the pasta water begins to boil, salt it generously. Lower the heat to a rolling simmer and gently add the pasta, bit by bit. Cook until al dente, about 2 minutes if fresh and 3 to 4 minutes if frozen.

TO SERVE: Drizzle 2 tablespoons of the sauce into a large bowl. Remove the pasta using a slotted spoon or spider, and transfer it to the bowl. Gently toss the pasta in the bowl prior to serving. Arrange 5 or 6 faraglioni in each shallow medium bowl. Spoon some brown butter sauce into each bowl just until it starts to rise above the base of the pasta. Garnish with the celery leaves.

CAVATELLI

CORN, ROASTED TOMATO, THAI BASIL

SERVES 4 TO 6

When I worked at Stir, Barbara Lynch's cooking class and event space, we would offer a corn, tomato, and rosé menu every summer: five courses all paired with beautiful rosés (which I strongly urge you to drink with this dish). It was one of our most popular events—and one of the most fun for me; the flavors are intense, and I always have tons of ideas for these seasonal favorites. Here, corn and tomato are draped with an eggy pecorino sauce—not unlike a carbonara—and served over handmade cavatelli pasta.

MAKE THE CAVATELLI: In a large bowl, use your hands to combine the flour, ricotta, eggs, Parmesan, salt, and pepper, mixing until the ingredients come together and form a well-blended dough. Shape into a ball, wrap in plastic, and refrigerate for 30 minutes to 1 hour.

To form the cavatelli, cut the dough into quarters. Working with a quarter at a time and keeping the rest covered, shape the dough into a roll between your hands. Next, using the palms of your hands and your extended fingers, roll the dough back and forth on a lightly floured counter until you have a ½-inch-diameter rope. Next cut the rope into ¼-inch pieces using a knife or dough scraper. With your thumb, press and drag each nugget of dough on a generously flour-dusted gnocchi paddle, applying firm pressure to form an oblong shape. As you work, place the cavatelli on a parchment-lined and lightly floured sheet pan or tray that will fit in your freezer. Repeat with each piece of dough. Transfer the sheet pan to the freezer until you're ready to cook. Cavatelli can be made a week ahead of time, covered, and kept frozen until use.

Bring a large pot of water to a boil for the pasta.

MAKING FRESH PASTA

NOTE
You'll need a gnocchi paddle to shape the cavatelli, or you can substitute 1 pound store-bought fresh cavatelli, if you prefer.

CAVATELLI

2½ cups all-purpose flour, plus more for rolling

12 ounces fresh ricotta

2 large eggs

½ cup freshly grated Parmesan cheese

2 heaping teaspoons kosher salt, plus more for boiling the pasta

½ tablespoon freshly ground black pepper

recipe continues

START THE SAUCE: Into a large sauté pan, pour just enough olive oil to lightly coat the bottom of the pan. Over high heat, char the corn kernels, 2 to 3 minutes. Season with salt and pepper, remove from the heat, and keep warm.

Preheat the broiler.

Toss the tomatoes in the ½ cup olive oil, season with salt, and pour the tomatoes and oil onto a rimmed sheet pan. Set under the broiler until the skins just begin to burst, 1 to 2 minutes. Transfer the tomatoes to a small bowl, keep warm, and reserve the oil in a separate bowl.

In a large bowl, mix together the egg yolks, Pecorino cheese, 3 tablespoons of the reserved olive oil from the tomatoes, and salt and pepper to taste.

When the water has come to a boil, season it heavily with salt and drop the pasta into the water, stirring a few times to ensure the cavatelli aren't sticking to the bottom of the pot or to one another. Once they've floated to the top, give them 20 more seconds of cooking before you pull them out using a spider or a slotted spoon and transfer them directly into the bowl with the egg mixture, stirring constantly to make sure the egg yolks don't scramble. (I recommend enlisting a friend for this task, while you add the rest of the pasta.) Toss the corn in with the cavatelli, adding a few drops of the pasta water if the sauce seems too thick.

TO SERVE: Divide the pasta among bowls. Garnish each with 4 or 5 of the roasted tomatoes, 3 or 4 Thai basil leaves, and, to finish, some pecorino on top. Don't forget the rosé!

SAUCE

½ cup olive oil, plus more for sautéing the corn

3 fresh ears of corn, kernels cut off the cob

Kosher salt and freshly ground black pepper

20 to 30 cherry tomatoes

4 large egg yolks

1 cup freshly grated Pecorino cheese, plus more for serving

GARNISH

16 to 20 small Thai basil leaves

RAVIOLI CON UOVO

DÉLICE DE BOURGOGNE, WHEAT BERRY, BRODO

SERVES 8

EMULSIFYING

MAKING FRESH PASTA

NOTE
For this recipe you will need three round cutters: 1½ inches, 3¾ inches, and 4 inches.

¾ cup wheat berries

2 quarts plus 2 cups Roasted Chicken Stock (page 206) or store-bought low-sodium chicken stock (if you prefer, you can use 2 cups of water)

Kosher salt

1 pound Délice de Bourgogne cheese

1 tablespoon heavy cream, if needed

Semolina flour, for dusting

Basic Pasta Dough (page 158)

8 large egg yolks

1 (4 × 1-inch) Parmesan cheese rind

3 tablespoons cold unsalted butter, cut into pieces

1 teaspoon sherry vinegar

Freshly ground black pepper

½ cup freshly grated Parmesan

White truffles, if in season (obviously optional)

Is there anything sexier than cutting into a delicately chewy *raviolo* and releasing a golden runny yolk into your sauce? Maybe for you there is, but, for me, this is damn near perfection. Here is my take—unique because of the Délice de Bourgogne, the sultriest of the French triple cream cheeses—on a classically luxurious and decadent dish.

In a small saucepan, combine the wheat berries and 2 cups of stock with 1 tablespoon salt. Bring to a simmer over medium-high heat, cover, and reduce the heat to medium low. Simmer until the wheat berries are al dente, 40 to 45 minutes. The liquid should be perfectly absorbed by the end; drain if needed.

The Délice de Bourgogne is the moat that's going to hold your egg yolks in place. To begin, remove the rind, scraping all the cheese from the rind walls. Scoop the cheese into a bowl and, using a wooden spoon or a sturdy spatula, work the cheese into a smooth creamy mass—kind of like you're softening cream cheese. Depending on how fresh your cheese is and where you got it, it may be crumbly like a goat cheese. If that's the case, add the heavy cream to help the cheese along. Transfer the cheese to a piping bag fitted with a ¾-inch tip or to a zip-top bag (cut off a corner to make a ¾-inch opening).

Start assembling the ravioli. Dust your work surface with semolina flour. Lay half of the sheets of pasta down, keeping the remaining sheets covered with a damp towel so they don't dry out. Take the 4-inch round cutter and lightly score the pasta eight times at well-spaced intervals, leaving plenty of space around each one. This helps you map out where to place your 8 ravioli. Next, using the 1½-inch round cutter, very lightly score the center of each circle: this is where your egg yolk will sit.

Pipe a ring of cheese following the outside outline of each 1½-inch circle, making sure to leave 1 inch of space between the cheese ring and the outer ring. Next, use your fingers to delicately place an egg yolk right inside each of the cheese wells. If an egg yolk happens to burst, scoop it out and replace it with a new one. Once all

recipe continues

NOTE

Please, please do not freeze
this pasta. It will change the
texture drastically, and when
you are ready to cook the
ravioli, you won't get that sexy
burst of yolk . . . just a gross crust.

the yolks are in place, brush a bit of water around each cheese circle. This is the glue that will help seal the dough.

Lay the next sheet of pasta over the top, keeping in mind that the top sheet has to cover and also dip in between each ravioli. Use your fingers to press out any air as you go and nudge the yolk in place. Finally, using the 3¾-inch round cutter, fully cut through the pasta to make each ravioli. Transfer them to a semolina flour–dusted tray. Refrigerate until needed, up to 6 hours. Do not cover and do not freeze.

Bring a large pot of water to a boil.

In a large saucepan, simmer the remaining 2 quarts of chicken stock and Parmesan rind over medium heat until the stock has reduced from 8 to 6 cups, about 30 minutes. Discard the rind, then whisk the cold butter into the stock until it's emulsified. Add the cooked wheat berries to the stock. Season with the vinegar, salt, and pepper to taste, and keep warm.

Salt the water generously and gently lower the ravioli into the pot. Cook in heavily simmering water until the pasta is al dente but the yolk is still runny, about 3 minutes. How can you tell? By touching the outer edge of the pasta: it should feel like the floppy ear of a dog, and if you press lightly on the yolk it will feel like a soft-poached egg.

TO SERVE: While the pasta is cooking, ladle the stock and wheat berries into four shallow bowls. Scoop the ravioli out of the water and gently transfer 3 ravioli to each bowl. Sprinkle Parmesan over the top. To make this dish truly luxurious, let it rain white truffle shavings, if desired, over each bowl!

ONION AND GRUYÈRE TORTELLONI

CHICKEN BRODO

SERVES 6 TO 8

What's better than French onion soup on a cold winter's day? French onion soup stuffed inside tortelloni!

MAKE THE TORTELLONI: In a food processor, combine the onions and Gruyère, and process until you have a smooth purée.

Generously dust a small sheet pan with semolina flour to ensure a nonstick surface for your stuffed pasta.

Working with one sheet of pasta at a time on a lightly floured surface, and keeping the rest covered, trim the pasta into 3-inch squares. Use a metal ruler, dusted in flour, and lay it directly on the pasta, creating straight edges by sliding a small knife along the edge, and then repositioning the ruler to measure the next 3 inches. Scoop 1 teaspoon of the filling in the center of each square of pasta dough.

Next mist the surface of each square with water from a spray bottle. Bring together opposite corners of each square, creating a triangle. Press the edges lightly to seal, making sure to press out any air. Fold the top point of the triangle down over the plump stuffed part of the triangle. Holding the folded point down, wrap the two remaining points in the other direction, around your finger, to form a ring, pressing firmly to set the seal. You should now have something that looks like, well, tortelloni. If you don't get perfect shapes at first, don't despair—just practice. I can assure you they will still taste good. Transfer the assembled tortelloni to the semolina flour–dusted tray, keeping it in the freezer as you work to cut and fill the remaining pasta dough. Once the tortelloni are firm, you can transfer them to zip-top bags and freeze for 2 to 3 weeks.

EMULSIFYING

MAKING FRESH PASTA

TORTELLONI

1 cup caramelized onions (see page 165)

4 ounces Gruyère cheese, finely grated

Semolina flour, for dusting

Basic Pasta Dough (page 158)

All-purpose flour, for rolling

Kosher salt

1 tablespoon olive oil

NOTE

You'll need a small spray-bottle to mist your pasta dough with water before sealing the dough into shape.

recipe continues

PREP THE BRODO: Heat the chicken stock in a medium saucepan over medium to a simmer, and reduce by one third, until you have 1 quart stock. Skim off any impurities that come to the surface with a ladle.

Bring a large pot of water to a boil to cook the pasta.

Whisk the cold butter into the hot broth, switching to a hand blender to completely emulsify the butter and create a creamy rich broth. Add the sherry vinegar and season with salt to taste. Remove from the heat and cover to keep warm.

When the pasta water begins to boil, salt it generously and then lower the heat so the water is at a rolling simmer. Add the pasta gently in batches and cook until al dente, 2 to 3 minutes.

Using a slotted spoon or spider, transfer the pasta from the water directly to a bowl and toss with the 1 tablespoon olive oil.

TO SERVE: Portion 6 to 8 tortelloni into medium shallow bowls (high edges will keep the pasta hotter longer). Pour brodo into each bowl. Garnish with a heavy pinch of chives, a few turns of black pepper, and Gruyère shaved over the top using a vegetable peeler.

BRODO

1½ quarts Roasted Chicken Stock (page 206) or store-bought low-sodium stock

3 tablespoons cold unsalted butter, cut into pieces

1½ teaspoons sherry vinegar

Kosher salt

GARNISH

2 tablespoons finely sliced fresh chives

Freshly ground black pepper

1 (3-ounce) block Gruyère cheese

PARISIAN GNOCCHI

MAKES 40 TO 45 GNOCCHI

POACHING

SEARING

NOTE

Prior to sautéing, these gnocchi will keep, well oiled and covered with plastic wrap, for up to 2 days in the fridge.

½ cup water

3 tablespoons unsalted butter, plus more for sautéing the gnocchi

Kosher salt

½ cup all-purpose flour, plus more as needed

3 large eggs

Grated zest of 1 lemon

1 tablespoon whole-grain mustard

1 tablespoon finely chopped fines herbes (a mix of fresh parsley, chives, tarragon, chervil)

Olive oil, for the pan

Grapeseed or other neutral oil

This French variation on gnocchi is made exclusively with *pâte à choux* dough, which turns out fluffy and light dumplings and doesn't involve messing with hot potatoes and a ricer; the good news is they are very easy to make. In fact, I made these for the first time in culinary school, learning how to squeeze the dough into the water and cut off little gnocchi. Once you find that groove, the feeling is so satisfying. (Or maybe I'm just weird.) I like to serve these with Poulet (page 201), but these gnocchi are also great simply tossed in extra butter, garnished with some grated Parmesan cheese and a grind of pepper, and served as an entrée.

In a medium saucepan, combine the water, 3 tablespoons butter, and 2 teaspoons salt, and bring to a simmer over medium heat. Using a wooden spoon, add the flour, stirring vigorously until the mixture forms a dough. Then stir some more until the mixture dries slightly, 3 to 4 minutes; you'll notice a light skin forming on the bottom of the pan.

Transfer the dough to a stand mixer fitted with the paddle attachment. Mix on medium-high speed for 1 to 2 minutes to cool the dough slightly before you start adding the eggs.

Continue mixing, now adding 1 egg at a time. After each egg is incorporated, stop the mixer and scrape down the sides and bottom of the bowl with a spatula. Continue to mix the dough until it looks like a loose paste, 3 minutes or so, and the outside of the bowl feels cooler to the touch.

Reduce the speed to low and incorporate the lemon zest and mustard.

Stop the mixer, remove the bowl and, using a spatula, gently fold in the fines herbes. Season with salt. (I don't mind tasting raw dough for seasoning, but you can also lightly poach a small piece of dough if you don't feel comfortable eating raw eggs.)

Transfer the batter to a piping bag fitted with a ½-inch round tip or a zip-top bag (cut off a corner to make a ½-inch opening). Try to get any and all air bubbles out of the bag and dough. Twist the open end underneath and refrigerate for at least 20 minutes and up to 4 hours.

Set up a gnocchi cooking station: Bring a large pot of water to a boil. Prepare an ice bath. Coat a sheet pan with a good amount of olive oil to keep the gnocchi from sticking to it.

Season the boiling water lightly with salt. Adjust the heat so the water simmers. With a butter knife or the back of a paring knife in one hand and the piping bag in the other, pipe and slice ¾-inch pieces of dough directly into the hot water. You want to apply constant and even pressure to the piping bag while you run the knife down the piping tip and across to lob off the batter.

You should aim to get a batch of gnocchi into the water in 30 seconds. The faster you go, the easier it actually is. Once the gnocchi float to the top, give them another 30 seconds in the water and, using a slotted spoon or spider, transfer them to the ice bath. After 2 to 3 minutes, transfer them to the oiled tray. Repeat the poaching procedure until you have run out of batter. Transfer the cooked gnocchi to a sealed container and refrigerate until ready to use. They will keep for up to 2 days.

To sauté the gnocchi, pour ⅛ inch of grapeseed oil into a medium sauté pan set over medium-high heat. When the oil shimmers, add the first batch of gnocchi in a single layer, making sure not to overcrowd the pan. Brown the gnocchi on each side; this will happen fairly quickly, and you'll notice them puffing up also. Once you turn them all over, add 1 tablespoon of butter to the oil, and when it starts to foam, baste the gnocchi with a spoon. The whole browning process should take about 4 minutes per batch.

Using a slotted spoon, transfer the gnocchi to a paper towel–lined sheet pan set in a warm place. Dump out the cooking fat, wipe out the pan, and repeat the procedure with the remaining gnocchi. Serve hot.

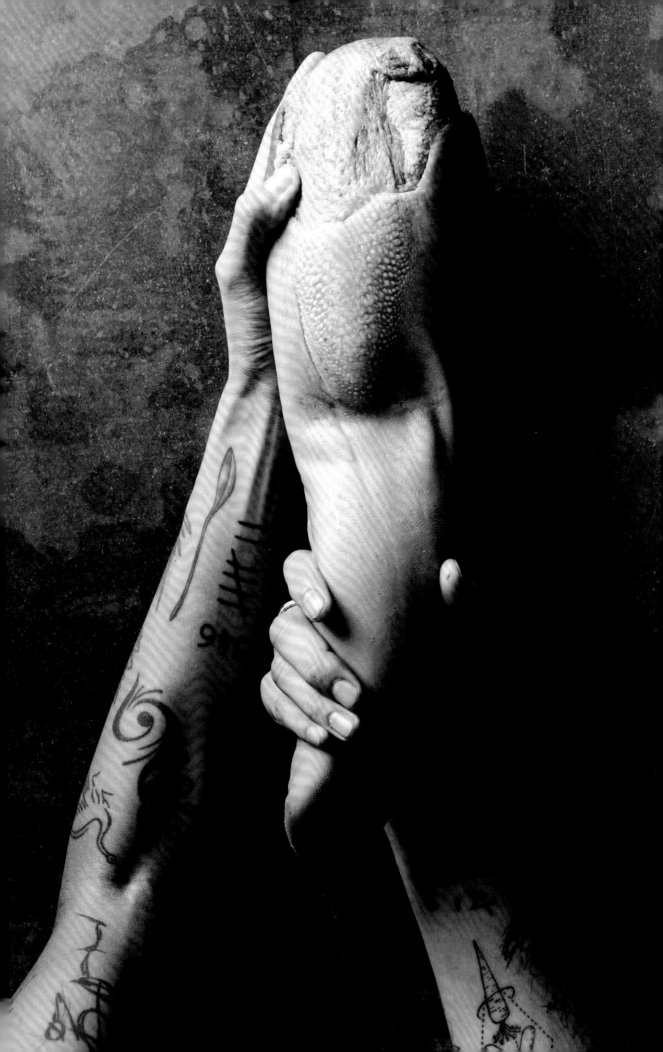

SEARED FOIE GRAS
HONEY TEA BROTH, HUSK CHERRY, BRIOCHE CRUMBLE

SEARED CHICKEN LIVERS
DRIED-FRUIT CREAM, BLACKBERRY, HERBS

GLAZED VEAL SWEETBREADS
RIESLING, WALNUTS, GREEN GRAPES

BEEF TONGUE
RED BEET PICKLES, HORSERADISH, MASCARPONE

POULET
GARLIC SAUCE, PARISIAN GNOCCHI, CHESTNUT

RABBIT LOIN
ÉPOISSES, MUSTARD, CARROT

CORNISH GAME HEN
PARMESAN SAUCE, CIPOLLINI ONION, CELERY

SQUAB

FRIED CHICKEN THIGH
CARAMELIZED HONEY, CALABRIAN CHILE, LABNEH

SEARED MUSCOVY DUCK BREAST
PLUM, PINK PEPPERCORN, HAZELNUT

SLOW-ROASTED PORK LOIN
KOREAN MELON, CHORIZO, ASIAN PEAR

VEAL
ESCARGOT RAGOÛT, WASABI, SWEETBREADS

BRAISED BEEF CHEEKS
FINES HERBES, WHITE MISO POTATO PURÉE

BERKSHIRE PORK LOIN
FAVA BEANS, GREEN GARLIC, BABY SPINACH

BEEF RIB EYE STEAK
LEEK FRITTER, MUSTARD SABAYON

STUFFED CABBAGE ROLLS

SEARED FOIE GRAS

HONEY TEA BROTH, HUSK CHERRY, BRIOCHE CRUMBLE

SERVES 4

I have cleaned more foie gras lobes than I can count. I've loved foie gras *hard*, and this is one of my favorite recipes for preparing it. It's fatty, sweet, and tart. When the foie has a good dark sear—which is how I like it—it is nutty, rich, decadent.

In a small saucepan, combine the tea leaves and Sauternes, and bring to a boil over medium-high heat. Stir in the honey, lemon zest, orange zest, lemon juice, and pink peppercorns. Pour in the water. Turn the heat up to high and boil for 2 minutes. Season with kosher salt to taste: you are looking for an even balance between sweet, salty, and tart. Strain. Reserve the liquid and keep warm.

Set a cast-iron or a heavy-bottomed sauté pan over high heat for a good 2 to 3 minutes.

Season the foie gras with kosher salt and pepper on both sides and put the foie in the pan. Warning: it will smoke a lot. Let a good 60 to 90 seconds elapse before you touch it to take a peek: you're looking for a dark crust. Using an offset spatula, gently turn the foie over and cook for an additional 30 seconds. If too much fat is melting into the pan, carefully drain it off (and save it, especially if you want to make the Almond Brown Butter Cake on page 278) and return the pan to the heat.

To determine if the foie is cooked enough, press the top and the sides: you want them to have some give but to feel a little firm in the center. This will continue to cook long after it's taken off the heat— you don't want to end up with a mushy puddle. From the side, the foie should resemble an ice-cream sandwich: a thin layer of dark crust on the top and bottom and flesh-colored creaminess in the center.

TO SERVE: Spoon 3 tablespoons of the honey-tea broth into each small bowl. Lay down 2 halves of the husk cherry to create a small pedestal for the foie to rest on in each bowl. Blot the bottom of the foie on paper towels to remove any excess fat (so it doesn't bleed into your sauce). Set the foie on the husk cherry halves, season with fleur de sel, then arrange 3 husk cherry halves on top of each. Sprinkle 1 tablespoon of the brioche crumble over each and garnish each with 2 or 3 sweet anise hyssop leaves, if using.

SEARING

1 tablespoon loose Earl Grey tea leaves

2 tablespoons Sauternes

¼ cup honey

2 strips lemon zest

1 strip orange zest

1 teaspoon fresh lemon juice

1 teaspoon pink peppercorns, crushed

1 cup water

Kosher salt and freshly ground black pepper

10 ounces grade A foie gras, cleaned (see Note) and cut into 2½-ounce portions

10 husk cherries or Cape gooseberries, husked and halved

Fleur de sel

¼ cup Brioche Crumble (recipe follows)

Anise hyssop leaves (optional)

NOTE

You can buy a whole lobe of foie gras and use leftovers and trimmings to make Almond Brown Butter Cake (page 278) or Seared Lobster (page 115). To prepare, separate the two lobes along their natural separation point. Carefully remove any of the excess yellow fat. Look for large veins running through the lobes and use a wooden skewer to push them out; discard. Using a knife, slice the lobes into portions, approximately 1 inch thick. Keep cold.

BRIOCHE CRUMBLE

MAKES 2 CUPS

I put this on almost anything, from roasted vegetables to ice cream, for a little crunch. It will keep in a sealed container for a week.

4 cups (1-inch-diced) torn stale brioche, homemade (page 45) or store-bought

1 cup all-purpose flour, plus more for rolling

6 tablespoons (¾ stick) cold unsalted butter, cut into ½-inch cubes

1 teaspoon kosher salt

1 large egg yolk

Preheat the oven to 350°F.

Combine the brioche, flour, butter, and salt in a food processor, and pulse until the butter resembles small peas. Add the egg yolk and pulse until the mixture comes together.

Turn out the mixture onto a floured surface and knead it until a dough ball forms. Flatten it into a disk, then wrap in plastic and refrigerate for at least 30 to 40 minutes, until the butter chills and sets, or up to 2 days.

Using your fingers, crumble the dough onto a sheet pan lined with parchment paper or a silicone baking mat. The pieces should be the size of large peas. Bake until lightly golden brown, 10 to 12 minutes. Remove from the oven and allow to cool completely.

Store the crumbs in an airtight container in a cool, dry place until ready to use, or for up to 3 days.

SEARED CHICKEN LIVERS

DRIED-FRUIT CREAM, BLACKBERRY, HERBS

SERVES 4 TO 6

SEARING

I have a deep love for chicken livers. In fact, during my time on *Top Chef*, I cooked chicken livers not once, not twice, but three times—and two of those landed me a win. I can go sweet or savory with liver. For this recipe, I give them a simple sear and serve them with a slightly jammy cream, tart blackberries, and a bright herb salad.

DRIED-FRUIT CREAM

5 pitted prunes, coarsely chopped

4 dried figs, coarsely chopped

2 dried apricots, coarsely chopped

1 tablespoon dried cherries

1 cup heavy cream

1 teaspoon grated orange zest

MAKE THE FRUIT CREAM: In a medium saucepan over medium heat, combine the dried fruit with the cream and orange zest. Cook at a low simmer until the fruit has rehydrated and is soft, 10 to 15 minutes.

Using a blender or an immersion blender, blend the fruit cream until smooth. Keep warm.

CHICKEN LIVERS

1½ pounds chicken livers, cleaned, rinsed, and patted dry

Kosher salt and freshly ground black pepper

½ cup all-purpose flour

Grapeseed or other neutral oil

4 fresh thyme sprigs

4 tablespoons (½ stick) cold unsalted butter

Maldon salt

COOK THE CHICKEN LIVERS: Season each liver with kosher salt and pepper. Dredge each one individually in the flour, shaking off any excess flour. Heat two cast-iron or heavy-bottomed sauté pans over high heat. I recommend two pans to ensure plenty of room between livers, so you can get a good sear on each, and the livers are then all ready at the same time as well. Pour in just enough grapeseed oil to coat the bottom of the pans. Just as the oil begins to let off wisps of smoke, add half the livers to each pan.

Sear the livers on the first side until they look golden and form a crust, 2 to 3 minutes. Turn over each liver, add 2 thyme sprigs to each pan, and cook for 1 additional minute.

Add 2 tablespoons of the butter to each pan. Allow it to foam, then, using a spoon, baste the livers four or five times. Remove the pans from the heat. I like to stop cooking the livers at medium-rare, as they will continue to cook to just under medium, which is ideal, while resting. Transfer the livers to a paper towel to drain and sprinkle with some Maldon salt as soon as they come off the heat.

PREP THE GARNISH: In a small bowl, toss together the blackberries, vinegar, and olive oil.

TO SERVE: In bowls, spoon 2 or 3 tablespoons of the fruit cream, then arrange 3 or 4 livers (depending on size) in the center of each bowl. Scatter blackberry halves over the livers and cream. Evenly distribute the herbs over the top.

GARNISH

12 to 18 blackberries, halved lengthwise

1 teaspoon red wine vinegar

2 teaspoons olive oil

12 to 18 fresh chervil leaves

3 sorrel leaves, torn into bite-size pieces

9 to 12 small tarragon leaves

8 to 10 watercress sprigs (optional)

GLAZED VEAL SWEETBREADS
RIESLING, WALNUTS, GREEN GRAPES

SERVES 4

Sweetbreads are like the silkiest and tastiest version of a chicken nugget. Yes, I realize it's the thymus gland of a calf, but you should not let that stop you from trying it. For this recipe, I channeled my love of fast-food chicken nuggets dipped in bright sweet-and-sour sauce and made something far better. If that doesn't sell you, take a look at the picture—pretty, no?

PORTION THE SWEETBREADS: Cut them into 1-ounce nuggets, approximately the size of 1-inch cubes.

MAKE THE GLAZE: In a small saucepan over medium-low heat, combine the sugar with a splash of water so the texture resembles that of wet sand. Cook the sugar until it turns to caramel and reaches a dark amber color, 12 to 15 minutes. Add the wine slowly and carefully, then increase the heat to medium-high and reduce the liquid by half, 6 to 7 minutes.

Next add the vinegar, and reduce by a third, or until it has the consistency of a loose syrup, another 4 to 5 minutes. Remove from the heat and swirl in the lemon juice and butter. You should have approximately ½ cup of glaze. Cover and keep warm.

SEAR THE SWEETBREADS: Season the sweetbreads with salt and pepper, then dust them lightly with flour. Heat a large sauté pan over medium-high heat and coat with grapeseed oil. When the oil is shimmering, sear the sweetbreads until golden brown on both sides, 3 to 4 minutes total. The sweetbreads should have a bit of give—not too squishy to the touch nor too firm. Toss the sweetbreads in a bowl with a few tablespoons of the glaze.

SEARING

NOTE

The sweetbreads need to be soaked in milk and refrigerated overnight. Plan accordingly.

SWEETBREADS

1 pound veal sweetbreads, soaked, poached, and peeled (see page 223)

Kosher salt and freshly ground black pepper

All-purpose flour, for dusting

Grapeseed or other neutral oil

GLAZE

3 tablespoons sugar

1 cup dry Riesling wine

¼ cup white wine vinegar

1 teaspoon fresh lemon juice

1 teaspoon cold unsalted butter

recipe continues

GARNISH

Maldon salt and freshly ground black pepper

¼ cup finely chopped toasted walnuts

20 large green grapes, sliced ¼ inch thick

20 small fresh flat-leaf parsley leaves

1 small skinny baguette or ficelle

4 tablespoons (½ stick) unsalted butter, preferably cultured, at room temperature

TO SERVE: Divide the sweetbreads among individual small plates, spooning a little more glaze over the sweetbreads. Season with Maldon salt and a couple turns of black pepper. Garnish with the walnuts, grape slices, and parsley leaves. Serve with a tear of ficelle, some butter, and Maldon salt. I like to butter a chunk of bread, pile on a piece of sweetbread, dunk it in the sauce, sprinkle a bit more salt on, and get after it.

BEEF TONGUE

RED BEET PICKLES, HORSERADISH, MASCARPONE

SERVES 10 TO 12

My inspiration here is a great deli sandwich—like the ones I ate in Montreal while working with Meredith, my coauthor. Maybe a terrine sandwich with sliced cornichon from Boucherie Lawrence. Or a Reuben from Lester's or Schwartz's, complete with pickled kraut.

In the deli of my mind, I serve tongue with pickled beets and a creamy horseradish. In reality, this is more of a deconstructed sandwich, but feel free to encase it in a Kaiser roll if that's what turns you on.

Also, try not to let tongue scare you; with a little time and effort, it turns silky and starts to taste a lot like braised short ribs. The flavor is intensely beefy.

BRINE THE TONGUE: Combine the water, apple cider vinegar, and ¼ cup salt in a large pot, bring to a boil, and simmer long enough to dissolve the salt, 3 minutes. Transfer to a container large enough to hold the tongue and let the brine cool completely. Submerge the tongue in the brine. Refrigerate for at least 8 to 10 hours, or overnight.

Remove the tongue and pat dry. Discard the brine.

Preheat the oven to 325°F.

In a Dutch oven large enough to fit the beef tongue, pour in just enough grapeseed oil to coat the bottom of the pot. Add the onion brûlée, carrot, and celery, and cook over medium-high heat until the vegetables begin to caramelize around the edges, 5 to 6 minutes.

Add the peppercorns, coriander seeds, and fennel seeds, and toast them lightly in the oil, 2 minutes. Then add the tomato paste, stirring for 3 to 4 minutes to cook out any metallic taste acquired in the can. Deglaze with the red wine and cook until the liquid has evaporated (au sec). Add the thyme, rosemary, and enough water to fill the pot halfway (the tongue should have enough liquid to swim in, but not too much); stir well. Season with salt to taste. Add the tongue to the pot and cover tightly with a lid or foil. Transfer to the middle rack of the oven and braise for 5 to 6 hours, until the tongue is completely tender.

BRAISING

BRINING

PICKLING

NOTE

The tongue should be brined for 8 to 10 hours before cooking begins. It's then braised in the oven for 5 to 6 hours. Plan accordingly.

TONGUE

3 quarts water

3 tablespoons apple cider vinegar

Kosher salt

1 small beef tongue (about 2 pounds)

Grapeseed or other neutral oil

1 large onion brûlée (see page 32)

1 large carrot, cut into large dice

2 celery stalks, cut into large dice

2 teaspoons black peppercorns

2 teaspoons coriander seeds

1 teaspoon fennel seeds

½ cup tomato paste

½ cup red wine

4 fresh thyme sprigs

1 fresh rosemary sprig

Sherry vinegar

recipe continues

BEETS

2 large red beets

1 teaspoon black peppercorns

1 teaspoon coriander seeds

4 fresh thyme sprigs

1½ cups white wine vinegar

2 teaspoons kosher salt

GARNISH

1 (8-ounce) container mascarpone cheese

2 teaspoons fresh lemon juice

2 tablespoons prepared horseradish

Kosher salt and freshly ground black pepper

20 fresh flat-leaf parsley leaves

1 ounce fresh horseradish, peeled, for grating

MEANWHILE, COOK THE BEETS: Combine the beets, peppercorns, coriander, and thyme in a medium saucepan. Add the vinegar and salt and top with enough water to rise about 1 inch over the beets. Bring to a boil, lower the heat to medium, and simmer the beets until just barely tender, roughly 35 to 40 minutes. Turn off the heat and allow the beets to cool completely in the liquid.

MAKE THE MASCARPONE GARNISH: Mix the cheese, lemon juice, and prepared horseradish until fully blended, then add salt and pepper to taste. Refrigerate until plating time.

PEEL THE COOLED BEETS: Using a mandoline, slice each one into paper-thin rounds.

Once the tongue is completely tender, remove it from the pot, and strain the braising liquid into a clean pot. Bring to a boil and then lower the heat to medium. Reduce the liquid, skimming it regularly to remove any impurities and fat, until it has the consistency of a loose syrup. It should take about 20 minutes and yield roughly 1 cup. Season with salt and sherry vinegar to taste. Keep warm.

While the liquid is reducing, peel off the outer membrane of the tongue. Next, using a sharp knife, slice it ⅛ inch thick across the grain (think French-dip-shaved-beef-sandwich thickness).

TO SERVE: Drop the beef tongue into the reduced braising liquid to warm through. The key is to allow the shaved tongue to soak and then hold onto that sauce as you put it on the plate. Mound the beef tongue slices in the center of individual round plates. Drizzle a small circle of braising syrup on and around the meat.

Drape 3 slices of beet over each portion of meat and garnish with parsley. Place a tablespoon-size quenelle of mascarpone off-center to the other side of the tongue. Using a Microplane zester, grate fresh horseradish over each plate.

POULET

GARLIC SAUCE, PARISIAN GNOCCHI, CHESTNUT

SERVES 4

A beautifully executed chicken dish is a mark of a great cook, second only to a classic green salad, as one of my former chefs used to say to me. It's true that the simplest items are often the easiest to screw up. People typically scoff at the thought of bland, boring chicken breast, but a skin-on chicken breast that's been cooked low and slow and well cared for is something to love. It can be silky and luscious and, when paired with the right sides, makes for a very rich and satisfying dish. This is where technique comes in; you don't have anything to hide behind. Time, instinct, proper seasoning, and knowing when to maneuver the pan on and off the heat lead to moist and tender flesh and a crispy paper-thin crust of skin.

RENDERING

SEARING

MAKE THE GARLIC SAUCE: Put the garlic cloves in a small saucepan and cover them with cold water. Bring to a boil over a medium-high heat. As soon as the water boils, strain the cloves, return them to the saucepan, and repeat this process five times. You are cooking out the pungency of the garlic, rendering it smooth in taste and soft in texture.

Drain the garlic and return it to the pan. Pour in the heavy cream and bring to a simmer over medium heat. Reduce the heat to low and simmer until the garlic is soft and the cream has thickened slightly, 5 to 6 minutes. If you find the cream has reduced too much, loosen it with a splash of water.

Transfer the garlic and cream to a high-speed blender and, starting on low speed, begin to blend. Add the tofu, gradually increasing the speed to high, and blend until completely smooth and slightly aerated. Season with salt to taste.

Return the sauce to a small clean saucepan, using a spatula to get it all out of the blender, and cover it with plastic wrap pressed against the surface to prevent a skin from forming. Leave it at room temperature if it's going to be used within the hour; otherwise, refrigerate and heat it back up when you are ready.

GARLIC SAUCE

10 large garlic cloves

½ cup heavy cream

4 ounces silken tofu

Kosher salt

recipe continues

CHICKEN BREAST

2 (6-ounce) boneless, skin-on chicken breast halves (preferably from a local farm)

Kosher salt and freshly ground black pepper

Grapeseed or other neutral oil

2 shallots, halved lengthwise

6 fresh thyme sprigs

6 tablespoons (¾ stick) unsalted butter

COOK THE CHICKEN BREASTS: Preheat the oven to 425°F.

Season the chicken breasts, sprinkling salt on both sides but pepper only on the skin side. (I think pepper on cooked white chicken flesh looks ugly.)

Coat the bottom of a large cast-iron or heavy-bottomed sauté pan with grapeseed oil and heat over medium heat.

Put the chicken breasts in the pan, skin-side down. They will sizzle just slightly—you don't want the pan to be too hot. To avoid a dry chicken breast, the key is low and slow, so no high-heat searing, please. Resist the temptation to move the chicken around or touch it: let the skin render for 8 to 10 minutes. Around the 4- to 5-minute mark, you may lift up the edge of each breast to make sure the oil is reaching all of the skin and to check its color. When the skin looks lightly golden, you can start shifting the breasts around and moving the pan to make sure the heat is in fact reaching all parts of the skin. You don't want pockets of white on golden brown skin: you want the browning to be perfect!

Once the chicken skin is a perfectly toasted-hazelnut color, use a spoon to start basting the chicken flesh with the hot oil and rendered fat. You'll want to do this forty or so times to each breast (patience!) to help the flesh cook, focusing especially on the thicker parts. Turn the chicken breasts over and transfer the pans to the oven. Cook until the internal temperature of the chicken registers 140°F on an instant-read digital thermometer, 5 to 8 minutes more.

Remove the pans from the oven and return to the stove over medium heat. Immediately add 2 shallot halves, 3 thyme sprigs, and 3 tablespoons of butter to each pan. When the butter starts to foam, baste the skin sides fifteen to twenty times each, or until the internal temperature of the breasts rises to 145°F.

Transfer the breasts to a cutting board and let rest in a warm place for 10 minutes. The internal temperature should reach 150°F to 155°F—anything above that and the chicken will taste like sawdust. Slice each breast lengthwise in half. Reheat the sauce and gnocchi as needed.

TO SERVE: On a large round plate, arrange a chicken breast portion vertically just to the left of center. Spoon a few tablespoons of garlic sauce onto the center of each plate, right next to the chicken. Arrange the gnocchi around the right side, following the contour of the sauce, roughly 8 to 10 pieces per plate. Using a mandoline, shave the chestnuts very thinly directly over the plate. Finish with a sprinkling of the fresh herbs.

GARNISH

Parisian Gnocchi, (page 184), sautéed

2 large chestnuts, roasted and peeled

12 small fresh flat-leaf parsley leaves

12 fresh chervil leaves

12 small fresh tarragon leaves

RABBIT LOIN

ÉPOISSES, MUSTARD, CARROT

SERVES 4 TO 6

I created a version of this dish when I was at Menton. I just love this combination of Époisses cheese and rabbit. You'd think a stinky French cheese would overpower the delicate rabbit meat, but I find that the funk of the cheese actually underscores some of the meat's flavors. Also, sometimes I love emulsifying cheese into a sauce in place of butter—they both round out a sauce and make it richer, but cheese adds dimensions and layers of flavor that butter can't always provide.

MAKE THE SAUCE: In a small saucepan, combine the chicken stock and mustard, and bring to a boil over high heat. Decrease the heat to medium and reduce to ½ cup.

Reduce the heat to medium-low, and whisk in the cheese until it becomes completely emulsified. Whisk in the parsley, lemon zest, sherry, and salt to taste. Keep warm in a double boiler.

COOK THE RABBIT: Over medium-high heat, pour in enough grape-seed oil to lightly coat the bottom of a large sauté pan. Season the rabbit loins with salt. Brown lightly on all sides, about 2 minutes per side. Add the thyme, shallot, and butter to the pan, and baste the loins for 2 to 3 minutes, or until the internal temperature registers 145°F to 147°F.

Remove from the heat (you can discard the thyme and shallot) and let the rabbit rest for 5 to 6 minutes; the final internal temperature should be 150°F.

WHILE THE RABBIT IS RESTING, GLAZE THE CARROTS: Lightly coat the bottom of a medium sauté pan with grapeseed oil and sear the carrots over medium-high heat, seasoning with salt to taste, 4 to 5 minutes. The carrots should be just browned. Add the vermouth and butter, and roll the carrots in the pan to glaze them. Cook until almost tender, 5 to 6 minutes.

EMULSIFYING

SEARING

CHEESE-MUSTARD SAUCE

2 cups Roasted Chicken Stock (recipe follows) or store-bought low-sodium stock

2 tablespoons whole-grain mustard

4 ounces Époisses de Bourgogne cheese, rind removed, large diced

1 tablespoon finely chopped fresh flat-leaf parsley leaves

½ teaspoon grated lemon zest

¼ teaspoon fino sherry

Kosher salt

RACK OF RABBIT

Grapeseed or other neutral oil

4 to 6 rabbit loins

Kosher salt

2 fresh thyme sprigs

1 shallot, quartered lengthwise

2 tablespoons unsalted butter

GLACÉ CARROTS

Grapeseed or other neutral oil

8 to 12 baby orange carrots, trimmed, keeping 1 inch of stem (optional)

Kosher salt

1 tablespoon dry vermouth

2 tablespoons unsalted butter

recipe continues

GARNISH

15 to 18 carrot leaf tops

TO SERVE: Ladle a couple tablespoons of sauce onto each plate. Slice the rabbit into thick medallions and place them on top of the sauce. Stack 2 or 3 carrots to the right of the rabbit. Garnish each with a few leaves of the carrot tops.

ROASTED CHICKEN STOCK

MAKES 6 QUARTS

This freezes well. Make a big batch so you can have homemade chicken stock on hand whenever you need it. Count on 6 to 8 hours of simmering time, followed by an overnight rest in the refrigerator.

5 pounds raw chicken bones (wings, rib cage, necks, feet, etc.)

2 carrots, cut into a large dice

1 onion, cut into a large dice

3 celery stalks, cut into a large dice

5 fresh thyme sprigs

5 fresh flat-leaf parsley sprigs

3 garlic cloves, smashed

1 tablespoon black peppercorns

Preheat the oven to 425°F.

On a rimmed sheet pan or in a roasting pan, spread out the chicken bones in a single layer. Use a second sheet pan as needed; if the bones are too close together, they will end up steaming instead of roasting—and you don't want that to happen.

Roast the bones in the oven until they take on a deep golden color, 45 minutes to 1 hour.

Remove the sheet pan from the oven carefully: there'll be hot fat on it! Transfer the roasted bones to a stockpot and add the carrots, onion, celery, thyme, parsley, garlic, and peppercorns.

Next drain off the fat from the pan, and scrape off the *fond* on the bottom: that's all the crusty, tastiest bits of concentrated chicken flavor. Add a splash of water to loosen things up, then pour the water and fond into the stockpot.

Cover the contents of the pot with cold water. Over medium-low heat, bring to a simmer (not a boil). Reduce the heat to low, cover, and simmer gently for 4 hours, periodically skimming the surface of foam and any impurities.

Strain the stock through a fine-mesh sieve into a container that will fit in your fridge; discard the solids. Let cool completely. Transfer to the refrigerator overnight. Any remaining fat will rise to the top and congeal. The next day, spoon off the fat cap and return the stock to the fridge for up to 2 days or freeze for up to a month.

CORNISH GAME HEN

PARMESAN SAUCE, CIPOLLINI ONION, CELERY

SERVES 4

A game hen is the perfect size for two (and so two game hens for four) and takes so much less time in the oven than a whole chicken. This is a go-to holiday recipe for a small gathering, when a whole turkey, for example, would just be too much. And it does not come easier than this Parmesan sauce—which is how I satisfy my craving for pairing chicken and cheese these days, a love forged at a young age by dipping chicken fingers in cheese soup.

PREPARE THE GAME HENS: Preheat the oven to 400°F.

Pat the game hens dry. Season the inside of each cavity liberally with salt and pepper and add half the head of garlic, 2 lemon wedges, 3 thyme sprigs, and 1 rosemary sprig. Rub 1 tablespoon of butter per bird in between the breast meat and skin. Using your hands, rub 1 tablespoon of olive oil on the outside of each bird. Season the outsides with salt and pepper. On a sheet pan positioned horizontally, line the celery stalks vertically ½ inch apart. Place the cipollini onions in between the celery. Drizzle the grapeseed oil and balsamic vinegar over the top of the vegetables. Season with salt and pepper. Set the hens on top of the vegetables. Roast until the juices run clear when the thighs are pierced and the outside is a dark brown, 40 to 45 minutes. Remove from the oven and let rest for 15 minutes.

MEANWHILE, MAKE THE SAUCE: In a small saucepan over medium heat, melt the butter. Add the flour and whisk while it slowly bubbles for 2 minutes to make a blond roux. At a steady pace, stream in the milk while continuously whisking to avoid lumps. Once the milk has been added, continue to whisk so it doesn't scald on the bottom and slowly simmer it over medium-low heat until the raw flour taste has been cooked out, 5 to 7 minutes.

Begin to whisk in the cheeses, a little at a time, until it has all been added. Continue to cook until everything comes together, 3 to 4 minutes more. Add the lemon zest, a few grates of nutmeg, some salt, and a couple dashes of sherry.

ROASTING

CORNISH HEN

2 (2-pound) Cornish game hens

Kosher salt and freshly ground black pepper

1 head of garlic, split in half crosswise

1 lemon, quartered

6 fresh thyme sprigs

2 fresh rosemary sprigs

2 tablespoons unsalted butter, at room temperature

2 tablespoons olive oil

6 celery stalks, leaves reserved for garnish

12 to 16 cipollini onions

4 tablespoons grapeseed or other neutral oil

2 tablespoons white balsamic vinegar

PARMESAN SAUCE

2 tablespoons unsalted butter

1½ tablespoons all-purpose flour

1½ cups whole milk, at room temperature

½ cup freshly grated Parmesan cheese

¼ cup finely grated Comté cheese

½ teaspoon grated lemon zest

Freshly grated nutmeg

Kosher salt

Sherry wine

recipe continues

TO SERVE: Carve the breast halves off the rib cage. Carve off the legs, separating the thighs and drumsticks. French the leg and remove the thigh bones (see Note, page 211), if you'd like. Spoon 3 tablespoons of the sauce into the center of each plate. Arrange the thigh and drumstick on top. Trim the celery so each piece is 5 inches long. Set next to the chicken. Quarter the cipollini onions and pull apart the "petals" from each quarter. Garnish the celery with the onion petals and reserved celery leaves.

SQUAB

CONFIT LEG, ONION MARMALADE, PICKLED CHERRY

SERVES 4 TO 8

I love every part of this bird: the head, liver, breast, heart. The meat is so beautifully silky and delicate, yet also subtly rich and gamey. The legs benefit from being made into confit before being crisped in a hot pan, while the breasts are made for searing and then roasting them until medium-rare. If you're not pro-squab, the onion marmalade and the pickled cherry are perfect for a cheese board.

CONFIT THE SQUAB: Cut the legs off of the squabs. Cover and return the rest of the squab to the refrigerator. Toss the squab legs with 1 tablespoon kosher salt. Lay them flat on a small sheet pan or plate, cover with plastic wrap, and refrigerate for 8 hours.

The next day, preheat the oven to 220°F.

Remove the legs from the salt, rinse, and pat dry. Arrange them in a small ovenproof dish, one that can hold 8 small squab legs in a single layer. In a small saucepan over medium-low heat, gently melt the duck fat. Pour it over the squab, making sure they are completely submerged. Nestle the thyme and bay leaves into the fat. Cover with a lid or foil and cook in the oven for 4 hours, or until the meat is tender. Remove the dish from the oven and allow the legs to cool in the fat. Refrigerate for at least 6 hours and up to 4 days.

CURING
EMULSIFYING
MAKING CONFIT
PICKLING
ROASTING
SEARING

SQUAB

4 whole squabs, each roughly 1 pound

Kosher salt

3 cups rendered duck fat

3 fresh thyme sprigs

1 bay leaf

Grapeseed or other neutral oil

NOTE
You must confit the legs 2 days prior to serving. Plan accordingly.

NOTE
Frenching the bones is optional. (Nope, not kissing. Rather, cleaning meat from the bone, in this case squab legs, but this technique is also used with rack of rabbit or lamb.) I do this purely for aesthetics. At home, it's a slight hassle, but when you come to my restaurant, we'll take this extra step for you. It's in the details. Using a sharp knife, starting where the bulk of the leg meat begins (roughly ¼ to ½ inch), score the excess fat and skin around the bone. Scrape upward toward the top of the leg bone, removing the excess flesh and exposing the bones. Lightly scrape until the bone is completely bare. Carefully cut off the very tip of the leg bones, making a clean cut. Your knife must be sharp; otherwise the bone will split and no longer look as clean, and it can also create some sharp bone points. I also remove the thighbone but keep the leg bone in. To do this, gently arrange the leg with the meat-side facing up. I use my fingers and gently push a little of the meat aside that is surrounding the bone. With a few twists of the fingers and some delicate maneuvering, the bone will pop right out.

recipe continues

ONION MARMALADE

3 tablespoons olive oil

2 tablespoons unsalted butter

2 red onions, halved and finely sliced

2 fresh thyme sprigs

1 tablespoon sugar

Kosher salt

1 cup port

¼ cup red wine vinegar

MAKE THE MARMALADE: Warm the oil and butter in a sauté pan over medium-high heat. Add the onions, thyme, sugar, and a pinch of salt. Once the onions start to wilt, turn the heat down to medium-low and cook, stirring regularly, until they are completely caramelized, 45 minutes to 1 hour. This process takes time and patience! The onions will shrink in size drastically. Once caramelized, deglaze with the port and reduce until the liquid evaporates completely. Add the vinegar, and let all the liquid reduce until the onion mixture is dry. Season with salt to taste. Discard the thyme. The marmalade should be served warm, but it can be prepared ahead of time, cooled, covered, and refrigerated for up to 3 days. Reheat as needed.

COOK THE BREASTS: Preheat the oven to 425°F.

Season the breasts (still attached to the rest of the body) with salt and pepper on both sides. Over high heat, warm enough grapeseed oil in a small skillet to coat. Add the squab, breast-side down. Since it won't rest on both breasts simultaneously, hold up one breast with tongs and sear the other breast until golden brown, 3 to 4 minutes. Then repeat with the other breast. Transfer to a parchment-lined sheet pan, breast-side up, and continue searing the remaining squabs. Transfer the sheet pan to the oven and roast the squabs until medium-rare, 8 to 10 minutes. Let the squabs rest for 10 minutes.

BROWN BUTTER–LIVER SAUCE

½ cup Brown Butter (page 92)

4 squab livers

1 teaspoon finely diced shallot

1 tablespoon port

¼ cup Roasted Chicken Stock (page 206) or store-bought low-sodium stock

Kosher salt

Fresh lemon juice

WHILE THE SQUABS ARE RESTING, MAKE THE SAUCE: In a food processor, blend the brown butter with the squab livers until smooth.

In a small saucepan over medium heat, combine the shallot and port. Simmer to allow the alcohol to cook off a bit, about 30 seconds, and then add the stock. Bring to a simmer. Whisk in the brown butter mixture gradually, over a light simmer, to create an emulsified butter sauce. Simmer gently until the sauce coats the back of a spoon. Remove from the heat, cover, and keep warm. Season with salt and a small squeeze of lemon juice.

To finish the legs, remove them from the duck fat. French the legs (see Note, page 211), if desired. Heat a sauté pan over medium-high heat with enough grapeseed oil to liberally coat the bottom. Add the squab legs, skin-side down, and shallow-fry, turning once, until the skin is crispy, about 2 minutes. Transfer to paper towels to absorb the fat and season immediately with a touch of salt, but not too much; remember that the curing also added salt.

TO SERVE: Carve the breast halves off the rib cages. Spoon the brown butter sauce onto the base of each plate, then top with 2 squab breasts, arranging 2 pickled cherries (stem-side up) alongside. Add a quenelle of onion marmalade to each plate. Prop one leg up against an onion quenelle and the other against one of the breasts.

GARNISH

8 Pickled Cherries (recipe follows), warmed

PICKLED CHERRIES

MAKES 3 CUPS

To prepare the cherries for pickling, slice off the very bottom of the cherry (the end opposite the stem) so that it stands up straight. Using a tiny Parisian scoop (melon baller) or a pair of tweezers, coax out the pit from the bottom of each cherry—this maintains the original shape of the cherry. Transfer the cherries to a container. In a small saucepan, bring the water, vinegar, sugar, and spices to a boil. Remove from the heat and pour over the cherries. Let cool, then cover and refrigerate for at least 2 hours and up to 2 days.

3 cups bing cherries

3 cups water

1½ cups red wine vinegar

1 cup sugar

2 tablespoons juniper berries

6 cloves

2 star anise

FRIED CHICKEN THIGH

CARAMELIZED HONEY, CALABRIAN CHILE, LABNEH

SERVES 4

ROASTING

This frying-without-frying dish came about by mistake. I was roasting chicken thighs at home for my dinner and then . . . I forgot all about them! I left them in too long, but to my surprise, instead of being overcooked and dry, they were still so crispy and juicy that they almost reminded me of Korean fried chicken. I guess those little thighs are pretty damn resilient. The lemon juice here works so well with the honey. If you can't find Calabrian chiles in a jar, you can substitute pepperoncini.

CHICKEN

8 skin-on, bone-in chicken thighs

Grated zest of 1 lemon

2 tablespoons fresh lemon juice

2 tablespoons grapeseed or other neutral oil

3 garlic cloves, smashed

3 fresh thyme sprigs

Kosher salt and freshly ground black pepper

COOK THE CHICKEN: Preheat the oven to 420°F.

In a bowl, toss together the chicken thighs, lemon zest, lemon juice, grapeseed oil, garlic, and thyme. Season with salt and pepper. Massage the chicken with your hands for a couple of minutes. Set aside for 15 minutes at room temperature.

Arrange the thighs on a sheet pan, leaving ample space in between them. Transfer to the hot oven and forget about them as I did—just kidding! Bake until the meat is cooked through, the chicken fat has rendered, and the skin is crisp, 30 to 35 minutes. Let the chicken rest for 10 minutes.

GLAZE

¼ cup honey

1 jarred Calabrian chile in oil, drained and finely chopped

½ tablespoon fresh lemon juice

1 tablespoon cold unsalted butter

Kosher salt

MAKE THE GLAZE: In the meantime, in a small saucepan over medium heat, bring the honey to a simmer and then allow the honey to lightly bubble for 2 minutes. Remove from the heat and stir in the chopped chile, lemon juice, and butter. Season with salt. Using a pastry brush, brush the rested thighs thoroughly with this glaze.

GARNISH

1 cup labneh

1 tablespoon oil from jar of Calabrian chiles or olive oil

TO SERVE: I prefer to serve this family-style. Spread the labneh on a platter and drizzle the chile oil over it. Then simply pile the thighs on top and serve with leftover honey glaze on the side for those who want more sweetness and heat.

SEARED MUSCOVY DUCK BREAST

PLUM, PINK PEPPERCORN, HAZELNUT

SERVES 4

One of the best duck dishes I've ever had was at Eleven Madison Park in New York. I went there with Barbara Lynch while we were in town for a cooking event. It was my first time at this incredible restaurant, and I remember being in awe of everything, from the crisp white linens to the unparalleled service, which was calm yet very attentive. What also stuck with me was their technique of crusting duck skin in an array of flavors. Here, honey provides the sweetness that I think complements duck so well, while also helping floral pink peppercorns and rich hazelnuts (fat on fat—more is more) adhere to the duck. The plum syrup is a final sweet-tart note wrangling everything together.

Cooking a duck breast properly is one of those things that takes practice—it requires attention and a little bit of babysitting. The good news is it can be cooked to medium-rare entirely on the stovetop.

MAKE THE PLUM SYRUP: In a small saucepan, combine the plums, prunes, sugar, and water. Bring to a boil over medium-low heat, then reduce the heat and simmer until the fruit breaks down completely, 15 to 20 minutes.

Transfer the mixture to a blender and purée until smooth. Clean your small saucepan, then pass the purée through a fine-mesh sieve into the saucepan. Simmer over low heat until the sauce has the consistency of a thin maple syrup, 6 to 8 minutes. Remove from the heat and stir in the vinegar. Season with kosher salt to taste. This syrup will thicken as it cools but loosens again when reheated.

RENDERING
SEARING

PLUM SYRUP

2 plums, pitted and coarsely chopped

3 pitted prunes

2 teaspoons sugar

3 tablespoons water

1 tablespoon ume plum vinegar or red wine vinegar

Kosher salt

NOTE
Air-drying your duck breasts a few days ahead of time is key here. To do so, refrigerate the duck breasts, fat-side up and uncovered, on a rack over a small sheet pan or plate for 3 to 4 days. This intensifies the flavor of the meat (like aging beef) and dries out the fat cap, which will make for excellent rendering and crisping of the skin. This technique works great with other meats and birds such as squab and chicken.

recipe continues

SPICE-CRUSTED DUCK

1 tablespoon pink peppercorns, crushed

3 tablespoons hazelnuts, toasted and finely ground

½ teaspoon ground coriander

2 teaspoons fleur de sel

2 boneless Muscovy duck breast halves, air-dried (see Note, page 217)

Kosher salt and freshly ground black pepper

3 tablespoons honey

GARNISH

1 pluot, halved and pitted

12 to 16 fresh anise hyssop leaves (optional)

NOTE

You will have extra plum syrup. Drizzle it over a cheese board or ice cream, or swap it for the cranberry jam in the Almond Brown Butter Cake recipe (page 278).

COOK THE DUCK: In a small bowl, combine the pink peppercorns, hazelnuts, coriander, and fleur de sel. Spread the spice mixture out on a plate.

Season both sides of the breasts with kosher salt and black pepper. Put the breasts, fat-side down, in a cast-iron skillet over medium heat. As the pan heats up, the fat will start to render slowly. As the fat starts to accumulate, drain it out of the pan every 5 minutes or so. You are looking for the duck fat to render out almost completely. This entire process will take 20 to 25 minutes, depending on how thick the fat cap and breast is. Lower and raise the heat as you see fit and as the duck needs.

Check the duck with an instant-read digital thermometer: I like my duck medium-rare, so I take it out at 125°F; the temperature will rise another 4 to 5 degrees as the meat rests. Just before the duck reaches the desired doneness, use the last round of fat in the pan to baste the flesh side of the duck. Flip the breast over, and baste the skin side. Remove the duck from the pan and rest, fat-side up, in a warm place for 6 to 7 minutes.

In a large sauté pan set over medium heat, warm the honey until it loosens up. Arrange the duck breasts, skin-side down, and make sure the skin is completely coated in honey—10 seconds tops. Using a spoon or tongs if you prefer, remove the duck breasts from the pan and press them, skin-side down, in the spice mixture to coat.

Transfer the duck breasts to a cutting board. Cut horizontally into ½-inch slices.

TO SERVE: Shave each pluot half into ⅛-inch-thick slices using a mandoline. On four large round plates, spoon a tablespoon of plum syrup onto each plate. Shingle 4 to 6 slices of the pluot into the center of the plate and then shingle one fourth of the duck in a straight line overlapping the pluots. Garnish with 3 anise hyssop leaves, if using.

SLOW-ROASTED PORK LOIN

KOREAN MELON, CHORIZO, ASIAN PEAR

SERVES 4 TO 6

Asian pears aren't too sweet and have floral notes and a texture that can stand up to meat. Korean melons are a beautiful pale yellow and have white stripes running down the side, like a fruit version of a delicata squash, and they also hold a floral note that some describe as a cross between a cucumber and a honeydew melon. Look for these in Asian markets.

    I like to slow-roast the pork before searing it because you can begin to render the fat out as well as avoid the gray ring that high-heat searing can create. Low and slow ensures an even roast.

ROAST THE PORK: Preheat the oven to 275°F.

    Rub the pork loin all over with grapeseed oil and season generously with salt and pepper. Make a bed of rosemary on a sheet pan and set the pork on top, fat cap up. Roast until the meat reaches an internal temperature of 125°F, 35 to 45 minutes.

WHILE THE PORK IS COOKING, START THE SAUCE: Combine the chorizo and the vegetable stock in a medium saucepan and bring to a boil. Reduce the heat and simmer until tender, 20 to 25 minutes.

RENDERING
ROASTING
SEARING

PORK

2 pounds pork loin, fat cap left on (Berkshire pork has a great fat cap!)

Grapeseed or other neutral oil

Kosher salt and freshly ground black pepper

8 fresh rosemary sprigs

2 shallots, halved lengthwise

8 fresh thyme sprigs

2 tablespoons unsalted butter

SAUCE

6 ounces Spanish (cured) chorizo, small diced

2 cups vegetable stock, homemade (page 89) or store-bought

½ cup heavy cream

Kosher salt and freshly ground black pepper

recipe continues

1 small Asian pear

3 teaspoons fresh lemon juice

3 teaspoons olive oil

½ small Korean melon, cut in half and seeded

16 leaves of purple mustard greens or any peppery greens, like arugula or mizuna

Kosher salt and freshly ground black pepper

NOTE

If you don't have a vacuum sealer to compress the Asian pear, you can simply marinate the pear wedges in the lemon juice and olive oil.

PREP THE GARNISH: Halve the Asian pear (stem to root) and use a melon baller or measuring spoon to remove the core. Cut each half into 6 wedges. Place in a vacuum sealer with 2 teaspoons of the lemon juice and 2 teaspoons of the olive oil. Seal the bag airtight and let it sit at room temperature for about 30 minutes.

Cut each melon half lengthwise into 8 wedges, then cut each wedge in half. Using a paring knife, remove and discard the rind.

Add the cream to the chorizo mixture and simmer for 15 minutes longer. Transfer to a blender and blend until smooth. Strain through a fine-mesh sieve into a clean saucepan and season with salt and pepper to taste. Set aside and keep warm.

Remove the pork from the oven. Discard the rosemary. Heat a heavy-bottomed skillet (I prefer cast iron) over high heat and coat the bottom with grapeseed oil. Once very hot, put the pork in the pan, fat cap down, reduce the heat to medium, and add the shallots and thyme, and slowly render out the fat, occasionally stirring the shallots and thyme, until the fat cap begins to crisp, 10 to 15 minutes.

To finish, add the butter and, using a spoon, baste the meat twenty or so times. Check the internal temperature again: it should be at 135°F. Remove from the heat, tent with foil, and allow to rest 15 minutes.

Unseal the Asian pears, drain, and pat dry. In a small bowl, toss the mustard greens with the remaining 1 teaspoon olive oil and 1 teaspoon lemon juice; season with salt and pepper to taste.

TO SERVE: Spoon a few tablespoons of chorizo sauce onto the center of each plate. Slice the meat into 6 to 8 pieces, depending on the number of guests, and place a piece over half the sauce, just off to the left. Alternate the melon and the Asian pear wedges around the other half of the sauce. Lay a few leaves of greens around the pork and fruit.

VEAL

ESCARGOT RAGOÛT, WASABI, SWEETBREADS

SERVES 4 TO 6

This dish is inspired by the first time I tried snails. When I was working as a line cook at Sensing, the chef de cuisine, Gerard Barbin, created a dish of poached veal, seared escargots, mashed potato, and phyllo dough—I hadn't had anything like it before! As I was very green to the finer-dining side of food, snails weren't part of my repertoire, but I instantly loved their bouncy texture and subtle folds that pick up whatever sauce you choose to toss them in. The thought of combining veal with snails seemed jarring initially, but the finished dish was so simple and beautifully executed that the pairing has stuck with me ever since. This ragoût can also simply be enjoyed with a crusty piece of bread.

PREP THE SWEETBREADS: Soak the sweetbreads in the milk and refrigerate, covered, for at least 8 hours or overnight.

Drain the sweetbreads and rinse off the milk. In a medium stockpot, combine the shallots, carrot, celery, thyme, parsley, lemon zest, salt, peppercorns, and water. Bring to a light simmer, then add the sweetbreads. Poach the sweetbreads for 6 minutes. Meanwhile, prepare an ice bath. Drain and shock the sweetbreads in the ice bath. Once cool enough to handle, peel and discard any outer membranes, cleaning the sweetbreads completely. Portion into 2-ounce servings, each roughly the size of a semideflated ping-pong ball.

COOK THE VEAL: Preheat the oven to 350°F.

Season the veal generously with salt and pepper. Heat an ovenproof sauté pan over high heat with enough grapeseed oil to coat the bottom. Sear the veal loin on all sides until a rich golden brown, 3 to 4 minutes. Add the thyme and shallots to the pan, then add the butter. When the butter has foamed, baste the meat a handful of times, then transfer the pan to the oven until the internal temperature of the meat reaches roughly 120°F, 2 to 4 minutes (this will vary depending on your oven, pan, and thickness of the cut of veal). Transfer to a cutting board to rest for 5 to 8 minutes before carving portions.

POACHING
SEARING
SWEATING

SWEETBREADS

10 to 12 ounces veal sweetbreads

2 cups whole milk

2 shallots, quartered lengthwise

½ carrot, large diced

1 stalk celery, large diced

3 fresh thyme sprigs

2 fresh flat-leaf parsley sprigs

Zest of 1 lemon, removed with a vegetable peeler

Kosher salt and freshly ground black pepper

1 tablespoon black peppercorns

3 quarts water

All-purpose flour, for dusting

Grapeseed or other neutral oil

3 tablespoons unsalted butter

VEAL

1½ pounds trimmed veal loin

Kosher salt and freshly ground black pepper

Grapeseed or other neutral oil

4 fresh thyme sprigs

2 shallots, halved lengthwise, keeping the root intact

3 tablespoons unsalted butter

recipe continues

ESCARGOT RAGOÛT

Grapeseed or other neutral oil

2 tablespoons onion cut into brunoise (see page 32)

1 tablespoon celery cut into brunoise

1 tablespoon carrot cut into brunoise

1 garlic clove, minced

1 (7½-ounce) can large or extra-large snails, drained

1 teaspoon chopped fresh thyme

2 teaspoon grated fresh wasabi, or ½ tablespoon wasabi powder

2 teaspoons dry vermouth

¼ cup Roasted Chicken Stock (page 206) or store-bought low-sodium stock

½ cup heavy cream

1 teaspoon apple cider vinegar

1 tablespoon chopped fresh flat-leaf parsley leaves

Kosher salt and freshly ground black pepper

GARNISH

16 fresh chervil leaves

8 fresh tarragon leaves

8 fresh flat-leaf parsley leaves

6 fresh chives, cut into ½-inch bâtons

NOTES

The sweetbreads require at least 8 hours of soaking. Plan accordingly.

My go-to snail source is Doug the Snailman, a lovable importer who brings in snails from Burgundy: www.potironne.com.

WHILE THE VEAL IS IN THE OVEN, COOK THE ESCARGOTS: Coat the bottom of a medium saucepan with grapeseed oil and heat over medium heat. Once the oil begins to shimmer, add the onion, celery, carrot, and garlic, and sweat the vegetables. Once they start to become translucent, 2 to 3 minutes, add the escargots, thyme, and wasabi. Cook until the ingredients begin to perfume, a minute or so. Deglaze with the vermouth and cook until the liquid has evaporated (au sec), then add the chicken stock and heavy cream and reduce slightly until the sauce coats the back of a spoon, 5 to 7 minutes. Finish with the vinegar, parsley, and salt and pepper to taste.

Season the sweetbreads with salt and pepper, then dust them lightly with flour. Heat a sauté pan over medium-high heat and coat with grapeseed oil. When the oil is shimmering, sear the sweetbreads until golden brown on both sides, 3 to 4 minutes. Add the butter and, when it starts to foam, baste the sweetbreads a handful of times before removing from the heat. The sweetbreads should have a bit of give—neither too squishy to the touch nor too firm.

TO SERVE: Cut the veal into medallions. Place a slice of veal on one side of each plate and a sweetbread on the other. In the middle, spoon the escargot ragoût. Garnish with the chervil, tarragon, parsley, and chives.

BRAISED BEEF CHEEKS

FINES HERBES, WHITE MISO POTATO PURÉE

SERVES 4 TO 8

This is the ultimate stay-at-home-in-your-sweats, snowy winter evening comfort food. Invite friends and family over early, while it's still braising in the oven, so you can all bask in its aroma. To seal the deal: potato purée and fines herbes—the classic French blend of fresh parsley, chives, tarragon, and chervil. It's a combo I love so much that I had it tattooed on my forearm!

Miso to me is a nonfatty version of salted butter. It's salty and rich, acts as a thickener, and has a sweet undertone and a huge umami factor. Why not use it like you would salt and butter?

BRAISE THE BEEF CHEEKS: Preheat the oven to 325°F.

Season the beef cheeks on both sides with salt and pepper.

In a large Dutch oven, heat enough grapeseed oil to coat the bottom of the pot in a thin layer over high heat. When the oil is almost smoking hot, sear the beef cheeks on both sides until nicely browned, 6 to 8 minutes. Transfer the beef cheeks to a plate. Add the onion, celery, carrots, and garlic to the pot. Caramelize the vegetables and cook until they have slightly softened, 5 to 6 minutes. Stir in the tomato paste and cook until it takes on a slightly darker color, about 4 minutes.

Next add the thyme, rosemary, parsley, and bay leaves. Pour in the wine to deglaze the pot: using a spatula, scrape any brown bits off the bottom of the pot and stir in with the vegetables, then return the beef cheeks to the pot. Add the stock, making sure that the meat is covered by the liquid—add water as needed. Bring to a heavy simmer. Put the lid on the Dutch oven and transfer to the oven. Let the beef cheeks braise for 4 to 6 hours, or until very tender.

BRAISING

EMULSIFYING

NOTE

The beef cheeks require 4 to 6 hours of braising time, and you also need time to reduce the braising liquid to a sauce. Plan accordingly.

BEEF CHEEKS

8 beef cheeks (about 3 pounds), cleaned of any sinew

Kosher salt and freshly ground black pepper

Grapeseed or other neutral oil

1 large yellow onion, cut into a medium dice

2 stalks celery, cut into a large dice

2 carrots, large diced

4 garlic cloves, smashed

4 ounces tomato paste

6 fresh thyme sprigs

3 fresh rosemary sprigs

6 fresh flat-leaf parsley sprigs

3 bay leaves

2 cups dry red wine

2 quarts Roasted Chicken Stock (page 206), store-bought low-sodium stock, or water

3 tablespoons unsalted butter

Sherry vinegar

1 teaspoon honey

recipe continues

POTATO PURÉE

3 large Yukon Gold potatoes

1 tablespoon kosher salt

1 teaspoon black peppercorns

1 bay leaf

2 thyme sprigs

1 cup heavy cream

¼ cup white miso

4 tablespoons (½ stick) cold unsalted butter, cubed

Kosher salt and freshly ground white pepper

NOTE

You'll need a potato ricer for the potato purée.

FINES HERBES

25 small fresh flat-leaf parsley leaves

5 fresh chives, cut on the bias into ½-inch bâtons

20 fresh chervil leaves

10 fresh tarragon leaves

AN HOUR BEFORE SERVING, COOK THE POTATOES: In a large pot of water, combine the potatoes, salt, peppercorns, bay leaf, and thyme, bring to a boil, and then simmer over medium heat. Cook the potatoes until tender when pierced with a fork, 20 to 25 minutes. Remove from the heat and drain. Discard the bay leaf and thyme.

In a small saucepan, combine the cream and miso and bring to a simmer over medium heat, whisking to blend.

Peel the potatoes while still hot and put them through a ricer and then through a tamis or fine-mesh sieve, using a spatula, into a medium bowl. Add the hot cream mixture gradually, in small batches, stirring with a wooden spoon until you have stiff peaks. Working quickly, while the potato purée is still hot, add the butter, a few cubes at a time and, using a spoon, stir to emulsify. Season with salt and white pepper to taste. Keep warm in a double boiler.

Remove the meat from the pot and transfer to a bowl. Strain the braising liquid through a fine-mesh sieve into a large clean saucepan. Over high heat, bring to a light simmer, turn the heat to low, and gently reduce this liquid, skimming any impurities off the top as it simmers, until it becomes a glaze, 20 to 25 minutes.

Whisk in the butter, a splash of sherry vinegar, and the honey. Add the beef cheeks and cover completely with the sauce.

TO SERVE: In a small bowl, toss the fines herbes together. I trim the cheeks to make straight edges for presentation, but this is optional. In a wide shallow bowl, spoon ¼ cup of the potato purée in the center. Place 1 or 2 glazed beef cheeks on top (if you are serving 2 per person, stack them on top of each other). Sprinkle a generous amount of fines herbes over the beef, along with 3 tablespoons of the beef sauce.

BERKSHIRE PORK LOIN

FAVA BEANS, GREEN GARLIC, BABY SPINACH

SERVES 4 TO 6

This dish is a technique bonanza; it completely encompasses the basics of cooking. In that way, it is very simple. But when executed properly, the results are revelatory, making the ultimate spring dinner. The fava beans, green garlic, and spinach create a rich but bright purée to accompany a fatty yet delicate slow-roasted piece of rosy pork. Add a crisp glass of Grüner Veltliner, and you've got perfection.

BRINE THE PORK: In a large saucepan, combine 1 quart of the water, the salt, and the thyme, and bring to a simmer over medium-high heat. Simmer until the salt is completely dissolved, 6 to 8 minutes. Transfer the brine to a large stainless steel bowl and add the remaining 2 quarts cold water to it.

Put the pork in a container large enough to hold it and the brine, and pour the brine over it, making sure it's completely submerged. Refrigerate and brine for 8 to 12 hours.

Remove the pork loin from the brine and pat dry.

Preheat the oven to 300°F.

Transfer the pork to a rack set on a sheet pan and into the oven. Slow-roast the meat until the internal temperature reaches 130°F, 30 to 35 minutes. Remove from the oven and let it sit out until you're ready to sear.

START THE CHICKEN SAUCE: In a small saucepan, bring the chicken stock to a boil, and simmer hard to reduce the stock to ¾ cup, 15 to 20 minutes.

BLANCHING
BRINING
EMULSIFYING
RENDERING
ROASTING
SEARING
SWEATING

PORK

3 quarts water

1 cup kosher salt

6 fresh thyme sprigs

1½ pounds Berkshire pork loin, fat cap left on

Grapeseed or other neutral oil

NOTE
Prior to cooking, the pork should be brined for 8 to 12 hours. Plan accordingly.

CHICKEN SAUCE

2 cups Roasted Chicken Stock (page 206) or store-bought low-sodium stock

3 tablespoons cold unsalted butter, cubed

1 teaspoon apple cider vinegar

1 teaspoon coarsely ground black pepper

Kosher salt

recipe continues

GREENS PURÉE

Kosher salt

2 pounds fresh fava beans in their pods

2 tablespoons olive oil

4 ounces green garlic, trimmed, coarsely chopped, rinsed, and patted dry

1 teaspoon fresh lemon juice

½ pound baby spinach

2 tablespoons cold unsalted butter, cubed

MAKE THE GREENS PURÉE: Bring a large pot of generously salted water to a boil. While the water is heating, set up an ice bath and shuck the fava beans.

Blanch the fava beans in the boiling salted water until the outer skin just softens, 30 to 35 seconds. Using a slotted spoon or spider, transfer the fava beans to the ice bath. Reserve 1 cup of the blanching water. Once cold, peel the skin off the beans and discard the skins.

In a large sauté pan, heat the olive oil over medium heat. Add the green garlic and sweat until tender, 6 to 8 minutes. Add the fava beans, and continue to sweat until just tender, 3 to 4 minutes. Remove from the heat and add the lemon juice.

Transfer the beans and green garlic to a blender, starting to purée on low speed and gradually increasing the speed to medium-high. You may need to add a splash or two of the reserved blanching water to get the blending going. Add the spinach and continue to blend. Next add the cold butter and blend on high until the purée is very smooth. Season with salt to taste. Keep warm.

Using a hand blender, emulsify the 3 tablespoons butter into the reduced chicken stock. Blend in the vinegar and pepper. Season with salt to taste. Keep warm.

To finish the pork loin, heat a cast-iron skillet or a heavy-bottomed sauté pan over medium-high heat. Lightly coat the bottom of the pan with grapeseed oil. If the fat cap is quite thick, you may need to score it slightly with a knife to help the fat render. Put the pork loin, fat-side down, in the pan and sear, adjusting the heat as required until it turns a light golden brown, 12 to 15 minutes. You don't want to render the fat out completely. Transfer to a cutting board.

TO SERVE: Slice the pork loin into 4 to 6 portions. Put the pork pieces to the left of center in dinner bowls. Spoon a quenelle of greens purée off-center to the right. Carefully spoon 2 or 3 tablespoons of the sauce over the meat, allowing it to pool slightly in the bottom of the bowl.

BEEF RIB EYE STEAK

LEEK FRITTER, MUSTARD SABAYON

SERVES 4 TO 6

When I don't know what to make for dinner, I make a recipe like this: a roasted or seared meat, a simple sauce, and a side. It's my go-to combo when I want something quick and I don't have much time—like if I offer to cook for friends last minute.

The leek fritters are inspired by Yotam Ottolenghi's recipe. The first time I made them, I kept thinking that such large chunks of leeks wouldn't stay in the batter or cook evenly. I should have known better than to doubt Yotam. This is how we learn and stay inspired—from other cooks and chefs.

TEMPER THE MEAT: Take the meat out of the refrigerator 1½ hours ahead of time.

AFTER 1 HOUR, GET STARTED ON THE LEEK FRITTERS: Soak the leek disks in water for 20 minutes, lightly swishing them in the water with your hands. Drain the water and repeat once more. Drain and lay the leek disks on a kitchen towel or paper towels to dry.

In a large bowl, whisk together the flour, baking powder, cumin, coriander, and caraway. Whisk in the milk and add soda water as needed: the consistency should be smooth and like that of thick pancake batter. Stir in the leeks. Refrigerate for 20 minutes.

Put a medium saucepan filled with a few inches of water on to boil over medium heat—you'll need this when you make the mustard sabayon after the steak is cooked.

COOK THE MEAT: Place a large cast-iron or heavy-bottomed pan over high heat, pouring in a thin layer of grapeseed oil. Season the rib eye generously with salt and pepper. When the pan is very hot and the oil is shimmering, sear the steak until a golden-brown crust has formed, 3 to 4 minutes. Reduce the heat to medium-high and turn over the steak. Arrange the shallots, garlic (cut-sides down), thyme, and sage around the steak. Continue to cook for 3 to 4 minutes. I like my meat medium-rare. Using a digital meat thermometer, when the internal temperature of the steak hits 118°F, add the butter, allowing it to foam, then baste the steak fifteen to twenty times. Transfer the

EMULSIFYING

FRYING

SEARING

NOTE

The meat will need to be brought to room temperature before you cook it. Plan accordingly.

MEAT

1 (2-pound) beef rib eye steak

Grapeseed or other neutral oil

Kosher salt and freshly ground black pepper

2 shallots, quartered lengthwise

1 head of garlic, halved crosswise

8 fresh thyme sprigs

3 fresh sage sprigs

3 tablespoons unsalted butter

LEEK FRITTERS

2 leeks, white and light green parts only, sliced ¾ inch thick

1 cup all-purpose flour

1 teaspoon baking powder

½ teaspoon ground cumin

¼ teaspoon ground coriander

¼ teaspoon ground caraway

¾ cup whole milk

Soda water

1 cup grapeseed or other neutral oil, plus more as needed

Kosher salt

recipe continues

meat to a cutting board and allow it to rest for 10 to 15 minutes. The final internal temperature will climb to 123°F to 126°F.

MUSTARD SABAYON

4 large egg yolks

¼ cup whole-grain mustard

¼ cup dry vermouth

1 tablespoon honey

Kosher salt

NOTE

The fritters are also great as a snack with the saffron aioli (see page 41).

WHILE THE MEAT IS RESTING, MAKE THE SABAYON: In a stainless steel or heat-resistant bowl, whisk together the egg yolks, mustard, vermouth, honey, and a pinch of salt. Set it over the pan of hot water over medium-low heat. Make sure the bottom of your bowl does not come into contact with the simmering water to ensure the egg mixture doesn't curdle. Whisk constantly until the sabayon nearly triples in volume and turns a pale yellow, about 10 minutes. The sauce will become thick enough to hold a ribbon: when you raise your whisk and let the sabayon pour off the end of the whisk back into the bowl, that ribbon of sauce should sit on the surface of the sabayon for a couple of seconds before melting back into the mixture. Turn the heat off but keep the bowl sitting on top of the saucepan to keep warm. Press a piece of plastic wrap against the sabayon to prevent a skin from forming.

Using a new pan or cleaning out the pan you used to cook the steak, bring the 1 cup of grapeseed oil up to 350°F over medium-high heat. Drop 2-tablespoon dollops of leek batter into the hot oil and shallow-fry, flipping the fritters over if they're not completely submerged in the oil, until golden brown, 3 to 4 minutes. Transfer to paper towels to drain and season with salt immediately.

TO SERVE: Serve family-style: slice the rib eye on the cutting board, stack a pile of the leek fritters next to the meat, and add a bowl of the mustard sabayon and a spoon.

STUFFED CABBAGE ROLLS

SERVES 6 TO 8

My grandmother taught me how to make this before I was ten years old, and it's been my favorite ever since. We would eat this at nearly every Christmas gathering. Her house was so warm and inviting—perfumed with sauerkraut! When I was really small, she'd have me stand on a step stool (which doubled as my chair at large family dinners, since I was the youngest and smallest) to watch her cook this, meticulously peeling the cabbage leaves so they wouldn't tear. The rolls would then simmer away for hours, and waiting for them to be ready was almost unbearable: I would sit in my grandmother's light blue chair, eating candy, while she sat next to me crocheting a blanket. She used Jimmy Dean pork sausage, so I make this dish a little differently—adding my own spices to the meat with some additional flavors to balance. Of course, you can just buy your favorite sausage. I like to serve this with creamy pickled cucumbers: my grandmother wouldn't have one without the other, so neither do I.

START THE CABBAGE ROLLS: You'll need 12 to 15 nice large leaves to make these rolls. Gently peel off the outer leaves of the cabbage, then steam these over a pot of boiling water until pliable, roughly 15 minutes. Lay them out on a kitchen towel to cool and dry. Chop up the remaining cabbage (up to ½ head) into medium chunks.

MAKE THE STUFFING: In a large bowl, mix together with your hands the pork, beef, paprika, fennel seeds, red pepper flakes, coriander, black pepper, garlic, onion, and rice, adding a generous sprinkling of salt. Shape a very small patty of the mixture and, in a hot small frying pan lightly coated with oil, cook it for 2 minutes on each side. Taste for salt and adjust your overall mixture accordingly.

Preheat the oven to 350°F.

Roll up ¼ cup of the stuffing into each steamed cabbage leaf, like you would roll a burrito, and tuck each roll into a deep baking dish, seam-side down. Pour a light layer of the sauerkraut juice and all of the tomato juice over the rolls. Insert small pieces of the cabbage heart(s) in between each roll, then top with the sauerkraut and more

BRAISING

STEAMING

NOTES

If you don't love sauerkraut, no worries: a beautiful rich tomato sauce is a great alternative.

Also, I encourage you to serve the cabbage rolls directly from your baking vessel. So if you're aesthetically inclined, choose your wares accordingly!

CABBAGE ROLLS

1 or 2 large green cabbages, enough for 12 to 15 large leaves

4 cups of your favorite sauerkraut

2 cups tomato juice

5 smoked bacon slices (optional)

STUFFING

1 pound ground pork shoulder (Boston butt)

1 pound ground beef

1 tablespoon sweet, smoked, or hot paprika (I like a mix)

2 teaspoons ground fennel seeds

½ teaspoon crushed red pepper flakes

½ teaspoon ground coriander

1 teaspoon freshly ground black pepper

2 garlic cloves, finely grated

recipe continues

¼ cup grated white onion

1¼ cups uncooked white rice

Kosher salt

Grapeseed or other neutral oil

of its juices: the overall amount of liquid should come three fourths of the way up the cabbage rolls. I like to add some slices of smoked bacon over the top to add flavor while the dish cooks, but it's your choice. Cover tightly with a lid or buttered foil, and bake for 2½ to 3 hours, until tender.

CREAMY CUCUMBERS

1 English cucumber

¼ cup red wine vinegar

2 tablespoons sugar

3 teaspoons kosher salt

1 (8-ounce) container sour cream

2 tablespoons finely chopped fresh dill

Freshly ground black pepper

IN THE MEANTIME, MAKE THE CREAMY CUCUMBERS: Slice the cucumber into rounds about the thickness of a nickel. Combine in a nonreactive bowl with the vinegar, sugar, and 1 teaspoon of the salt. Allow to sit for 20 to 30 minutes at room temperature.

Drain off the cucumber liquid. Mix the cucumbers with the sour cream, dill, remaining 2 teaspoons salt, and the pepper. Cover and refrigerate for 1 hour.

TO SERVE: Serve family-style right from your cooking vessel, with the creamy cucumbers on the side.

WHIPPED MASCARPONE
FIG, ROSE WATER, PISTACHIO

PINK PEPPERCORN ICE CREAM
COCOA NIB, HAZELNUT, TAHINI

SPONGE CAKE
STRAWBERRY ICE CREAM, MERINGUE,
CRÈME ANGLAISE

JASMINE TEA ICE CREAM
TOASTED RICE PUDDING,
SEVILLE ORANGE

HAZELNUT CAKE
BANANA ICE CREAM, WHIPPED
CHOCOLATE GANACHE, RAS EL HANOUT

MATCHA CUSTARD
BERRIES, SABLÉ, OLIVE OIL

PEACH PÂTE DE FRUIT
ROSEMARY SUGAR

POACHED CHERRIES
MERINGUE, LAVENDER, LEMON THYME

SOUR CREAM CAKE
PECAN, MALTED MILK CRÈME FRAÎCHE

SPROUTED GRAIN CAKE
CHOCOLATE PEANUT CARAMEL MOUSSE,
SALTED VANILLA CUSTARD ICE CREAM

ORANGE SHERBET
GOAT MILK SODA, FENNEL

POACHED PEAR
CORNMEAL AND ALMOND CAKE,
FROMAGE BLANC

ROASTED QUINCE
BUCKWHEAT HONEY, FARRO PUDDING

ALMOND BROWN BUTTER CAKE
FOIE GRAS, CRANBERRY, ORANGE

FRIED BUNS

WHIPPED MASCARPONE

FIG, ROSE WATER, PISTACHIO

SERVES 4 TO 6

There is a cardinal rule with rose water: less is *far* more. Used correctly, it adds just what you need in floral accents. Because it's such a powerful scent, mixing it into a light, fluffy mascarpone will soften it a bit. Ripe, juicy figs and crunchy salty-sweet pistachios both add dimension and textures. This is one of my simplest desserts.

1 (8-ounce) container mascarpone cheese

¾ cup heavy cream

⅓ cup confectioners' sugar

1½ teaspoons rose water

½ cup plus 3 tablespoons shelled pistachios, toasted

Kosher salt

¼ cup dark honey

8 to 12 whole fresh figs, each cut into 4 slices

In a stand mixer fitted with the paddle attachment, beat the mascarpone until it loosens up and becomes smooth. Transfer to a medium bowl. Combine the heavy cream, confectioners' sugar, and rose water in the mixer bowl. Switch to the whisk attachment and whip the cream to medium-stiff peaks. Fold the whipped cream mixture into the mascarpone until the texture becomes mousse-like. Transfer to a covered container and chill for at least 2 hours or up to 2 days.

Using a high-speed blender, blend ½ cup of the pistachios with just enough water to help things along—anywhere from 2 teaspoons to 1 tablespoon. Season the pistachio butter with a pinch of salt.

Coarsely chop the remaining 3 tablespoons pistachios.

TO SERVE: Using medium white flat plates, scoop 3 quenelles of whipped mascarpone onto each plate, just slightly left of center. Spoon 1½ tablespoons pistachio butter in the center of each plate. Lightly drizzle 2 teaspoons honey over the quenelles. Then sprinkle 1 to 2 teaspoons chopped pistachios over the mascarpone and pistachio butter. Finish by stacking fig slices over the pistachio butter.

PINK PEPPERCORN ICE CREAM

COCOA NIB, HAZELNUT, TAHINI

SERVES 6 TO 8

The first time I made a version of this dessert was on *Top Chef Duels* in 2014. For those who haven't seen it, the premise of this show is to take former *Top Chef* contestants and pit them against each other in series of scenarios. I was competing against the wildly talented, badass Chicago chef Stephanie Izard in a Garden of Eden theme. As far as I can remember, our food had to include "masculine" and "feminine" elements. My interpretation of the challenge? For the starter, I poached swordfish (a penis!) and served it with caviar (eggs!), lemon, and *bavarois* (Bavarian cream). (I may have actually said these things on national television.) For the main: seared fluke with a miso potato purée, asparagus, and fried oysters—a sort of sensual aphrodisiac. And for dessert, this here ice cream: pink peppercorns mixed with nuts, chocolate, and tahini. (Nuts and berries . . . get it?) By the way, I lost. By one vote—but this dessert is still a winner!

MAKE THE ICE CREAM: In a medium saucepan, bring the half-and-half, milk, sugar, and pink peppercorns to a simmer over medium heat and cook for 2 to 3 minutes. Turn off the heat, cover, and allow the peppercorns to steep for 15 minutes.

While the peppercorns are steeping, whisk the egg yolks in a medium heatproof bowl.

Return the milk mixture to a simmer over medium heat, then slowly pour it over the yolks while whisking constantly. Stir in the salt.

Return the custard to the saucepan. Clean the egg bowl and set it aside. Prepare an ice bath.

Over medium-low heat, stir the custard constantly with a spatula until it coats the back of a spoon. Do not boil. Strain through a fine-mesh sieve into the clean reserved bowl, set it in the ice bath, and stir a few times to help the custard cool.

Once cool, refrigerate the custard until cold, then pour it into an ice cream maker. Follow the manufacturer's instructions to churn ice cream. Transfer it to a lidded container and freeze for a minimum of 6 hours and up to 5 days.

MAKING CUSTARD

NOTES

You will need an ice cream maker. The ice cream should be made and chilled a minimum of 6 hours ahead of serving. Plan accordingly.

The xanthan gum is optional. It creates that artificial Cool Whip texture, which I just love. Look for Bob's Red Mill brand at your local supermarket.

PINK PEPPERCORN ICE CREAM

2 cups half-and-half

2 cups whole milk

¾ cup granulated sugar

3 tablespoons pink peppercorns, crushed, plus more for garnish

5 large egg yolks

¼ teaspoon kosher salt

recipe continues

HAZELNUT COOKIE

½ cup all-purpose flour

¼ cup raw hazelnuts

3 tablespoons granulated sugar

2 tablespoons cocoa nibs

½ teaspoon baking powder

¼ teaspoon baking soda

½ teaspoon kosher salt

4 tablespoons (½ stick) cold unsalted butter, cubed

1 large egg yolk

TAHINI CREAM

1 cup heavy cream

3 tablespoons confectioners' sugar

½ teaspoon xanthan gum (optional)

1 tablespoon tahini

Pinch of kosher salt

MAKE THE COOKIE: Preheat the oven to 350°F.

In a food processor, combine the flour, hazelnuts, sugar, cocoa nibs, baking powder, baking soda, and salt. Process for 10 seconds, and then pulse until the mixture looks like fine sand.

Next add the butter and pulse until the butter is the size of small peas. Add the egg yolk and pulse until the dough just starts to come together. If it still looks too dry, add a teaspoon of water and pulse some more. Repeat as required. Use your hands to shape into a ball, cover with plastic wrap, and refrigerate for 20 minutes.

Crumble the dough onto a parchment-lined sheet pan. Bake until golden brown, 10 to 12 minutes. Set aside to cool. The cookie crumbs will keep in an airtight container for about a week.

WHIP THE TAHINI CREAM: Using a stand mixer, a hand mixer, or a whisk (my personal favorite), whip the heavy cream until it begins to thicken but hasn't yet formed peaks. Add the confectioners' sugar, xanthan gum (if using), tahini, and salt. Continue whipping until the mixture reaches medium to stiff peaks. Refrigerate until ready to serve, or for up to 2 days.

TO SERVE: Into each deep, narrow bowl, sprinkle 3 tablespoons of the hazelnut cookie crumbs. Scoop a quenelle of ice cream on top of the crumbs and, next to it, lay a quenelle of the tahini cream. Garnish with a light sprinkle of pink peppercorns.

A NOTE ABOUT ICE CREAM

Please note: I have no standard base ice cream recipe in this book.

You may be thinking, *Hey, Kristen! Why no standard ice cream base through-out the book? Why half-and-half in some but whole cream in others? Why fewer or more eggs or egg yolks? Why no streamlined recipe we can reference to make any number of tasty chilled delights in splendid variation?*

Fair enough. But let me answer your questions with another question: have you ever had a gelato . . . and then an ice cream from the local stand down the street . . . then homemade ice cream in a restaurant . . . or a Mickey Mouse ice-cream pop from Disney world? My guess is that you have had many different ice creams and have loved or hated them for so many different reasons: how velvety each one was, how the fat dissolved on your tongue, if there were little crystals in it. Was it clean and refreshing or was it rich and overly satisfying? Well, in order to make all these different variations of the sweet eaten around the world, you have to play with the types of sugars, amounts of eggs to egg yolks, cream to milk. It's the sum of all of your ingredients that affects the outcome.

SPONGE CAKE

STRAWBERRY ICE CREAM, MERINGUE, CRÈME ANGLAISE

SERVES 8

MAKING CUSTARD

MAKING MERINGUE

NOTES

You will need an ice cream maker for this recipe. The ice cream should be made and chilled a minimum of 6 hours ahead of serving. Plan accordingly.

You also will need one 8-inch round cake pan.

MERINGUE

1¼ cups granulated sugar

2 tablespoons water

3 large egg whites

Pinch of cream of tartar

Pinch of kosher salt

Sponge cake, a cousin to angel food cake, for me is the white bread of desserts. Many of us can cast our minds back fondly to the classic Cool-Whip-plus-store-bought-angel-food-cake-plus-strawberry combination. This is my tricked-out version of that little slice of nostalgia.

A word on the meringue technique: There are many styles of meringues. Here we make a hot simple syrup from the sugar to incorporate with the whites. It lends a shinier, smoother, slightly more stable meringue than straight sugar grains hitting your egg whites. With the latter, the sugar will eventually begin to dissolve, and excess liquid could come into play in your meringue; I'd rather control the amount of liquid at the beginning. When incorporating meringue or transferring it into piping bags, handle with care: you don't want to knock out the air.

MAKE THE MERINGUE: Preheat the oven to 250°F.

In a small saucepan, combine the granulated sugar and water. Bring to a boil over medium-high heat and cook until the mixture reaches 235°F on a candy thermometer.

Meanwhile, in a stand mixer fitted with the whisk attachment, whip the egg whites on medium speed until frothy. Add the cream of tartar and salt. With the mixer still going, add the hot syrup in a slow and steady stream, aiming for the inside of the bowl (as opposed to the whisk or whites themselves). Increase the speed to high and beat until stiff, glossy peaks form and the bowl is cool to the touch, 6 to 8 minutes.

On a 12 × 17-inch sheet pan lined with a silicone baking mat (or parchment paper sprayed with nonstick cooking spray), spread the meringue in a thin layer, about ¼ inch thick. Bake for 3 to 4 hours, or until dry. Keep in mind the meringue will crisp up more as it cools. Once cool, wrap the sheet pan well with plastic wrap and store in a cool, dry place.

recipe continues

SPONGE CAKE

Unsalted butter, for the pan

⅓ cup granulated sugar, plus more for the pan

5 large egg whites

1½ tablespoons confectioners' sugar

¼ teaspoon cream of tartar

Pinch of kosher salt

½ teaspoon lemon extract (vanilla works great, too)

½ cup plus 1 tablespoon all-purpose flour

CRÈME ANGLAISE

4 large egg yolks

¼ cup granulated sugar

½ cup whole milk

½ cup half-and-half

½ vanilla bean, split lengthwise, seeds scraped

GARNISH

Strawberry Ice Cream (recipe follows)

1 fresh tarragon sprig, leaves only

1 pint small strawberries, stemmed

BAKE THE SPONGE CAKE: Preheat the oven to 350°F. Butter an 8-inch round cake pan and sprinkle with granulated sugar. Tap out any excess.

In a stand mixer fitted with the whisk attachment, beat the egg whites on medium speed until frothy. In a small bowl, mix together the granulated and confectioners' sugars. As the mixer is running, slowly add the sugars to the whites, and then add the cream of tartar and salt. Increase the speed to high and beat the egg whites until stiff peaks form, 4 to 6 minutes. Whip in the lemon extract.

Remove the bowl from the mixer. In two additions, sprinkle the flour over the beaten whites, folding gently with a stiff spatula to incorporate. Make sure there's no remaining flour visible. Spread the batter into the prepared cake pan, smoothing the top. Bake until the cake is pale gold and firm but springy to the touch, 15 to 18 minutes. A cake tester inserted into the cake should come out clean. Cool the cake in the pan on a wire rack.

MAKE THE CRÈME ANGLAISE: Whisk the yolks and granulated sugar in a medium bowl until very pale in color and thick, 4 to 5 minutes. Set up an ice bath.

In a medium saucepan, combine the milk and half-and-half. Add both the vanilla seeds and the bean to the pan, set it over medium-high heat, and bring to a simmer. Quickly remove the pan from the heat.

Slowly pour the milk mixture into the yolk mixture while whisking constantly. Return the custard to the saucepan and cook over medium-low heat, stirring constantly with a wooden spoon or spatula until the custard coats the back of a spoon. Pour the crème anglaise through a fine-mesh sieve into a bowl set over the ice bath and stir for 5 to 6 minutes to cool. When the custard has cooled, press a sheet of plastic wrap directly on its surface to prevent a skin from forming, and refrigerate until cold, at least 2 hours or overnight.

TO SERVE: Unmold the sponge cake and cut it into 1-inch cubes. Break the meringue into shards. Spoon ¼ cup crème anglaise into each bowl, topping it with pieces of cake, meringue shards, and a scoop of ice cream. Finish each with a tarragon leaf and 4 or 5 strawberries.

STRAWBERRY ICE CREAM

MAKES 1 QUART

Combine the strawberries, 1 tablespoon granulated sugar, and the water in a high-speed blender and blend at high speed for 2 to 3 minutes. Strain the purée through a fine-mesh sieve into a medium bowl; discard the solids.

In a saucepan, combine the milk, heavy cream, and remaining ¾ cup granulated sugar. Over medium heat, bring the mixture to a light simmer, whisking just until the sugar has dissolved. Set up an ice bath.

In a medium bowl, whisk the eggs, ¾ cup of the strawberry purée, the lemon zest, and a tiny pinch of salt. Temper the milk mixture into the eggs, whisking constantly. Return the custard to the saucepan and cook over medium-low heat, stirring constantly with a spatula, until the custard coats the back of a spoon. Do not boil. Strain through a fine-mesh sieve into a clean bowl set over the ice bath and stir a few times to help the custard cool.

Once cool, refrigerate until cold, then pour the mixture into an ice cream maker. Follow the manufacturer's instructions to churn ice cream. Transfer it to a lidded container and freeze for a minimum of 6 hours and up to 5 days.

¾ pound ripe strawberries, stemmed and halved, or defrosted frozen berries

¾ cup plus 1 tablespoon granulated sugar

2 tablespoons water

2 cups whole milk

1½ cups heavy cream

4 large eggs

Grated zest of 1 lemon

Pinch of kosher salt

JASMINE TEA ICE CREAM

TOASTED RICE PUDDING, SEVILLE ORANGE

SERVES 6 TO 8

Typically when I plan private dinners, I rarely repeat recipes I've cooked before. I'm always confident that any idea I have can be executed and never nervous to try new things on new diners. That's what I love and thrive on.

Normally, in a professional kitchen, I use a Pacojet to make ice cream in no time at all. It's an industrial (and incredibly expensive) machine that takes a frozen-solid ice cream base and whips it into smooth ice cream in seconds. There's no way I would buy one for home (nor do I expect you to). For a particular dinner in Boston's South End, we couldn't get our hands on a Pacojet, so my sous chef Robeisy brought her home kitchen ice cream maker, which I thought would be fun to try for a change! But hours later, the custard was still soup. So, a dessert that was meant to be ice cream became a tea-infused crème anglaise instead. And it was still delicious! The moral of the story: You can enjoy these flavors and textures whether or not you own an ice cream maker. And never be afraid to try something new!

MAKE THE ICE CREAM: In a medium saucepan, bring the milk, cream, sugar, tea leaves, and corn syrup to a heavy simmer over medium-high heat. Turn off the heat and allow the tea to steep for 15 minutes, so that some of the astringency of the tea is drawn out; this will balance out the inherent sweetness of the ice cream.

While the tea is steeping, whisk the eggs and egg yolks in a bowl. When 15 minutes have elapsed, strain the tea leaves from the milk mixture. Return the milk mixture to the saucepan and simmer for 20 seconds, then slowly pour the milk mixture into the eggs while whisking constantly.

Clean your saucepan, and return the custard to the saucepan. Next clean out your egg bowl and set it aside. Prepare an ice bath.

Over medium-low heat, stir the custard constantly with a spatula until the custard coats the back of a spoon. Do not boil. Strain it through a fine-mesh sieve into the reserved clean bowl, set it over the ice bath, and stir a few times to help the custard cool.

MAKING CUSTARD

NOTES
You'll need an ice cream maker if proceeding with the ice cream. The ice cream should be made and chilled a minimum of 6 hours ahead of serving. Plan accordingly.

If you cannot find Seville oranges, substitute navels.

ICE CREAM

2 cups whole milk

2 cups heavy cream

½ cup sugar

2 tablespoons loose jasmine tea leaves

2 tablespoons light corn syrup

3 large eggs

2 large egg yolks

recipe continues

Once cool, refrigerate until cold, then pour it into an ice cream maker. Follow the manufacturer's instructions to churn ice cream. Transfer it to a lidded container and freeze for a minimum of 6 hours and up to 5 days.

RICE PUDDING

¾ cup short-grain rice

2¼ cups water

1½ cups whole milk

½ cup heavy cream

¼ cup sugar

½ vanilla bean, split lengthwise, seeds scraped

Grated zest of 1 Seville orange

3 tablespoons Seville orange juice

1 tablespoon unsalted butter

1 egg yolk

Kosher salt

MAKE THE RICE PUDDING: In a large sauté pan over medium heat, dry-toast the rice until it's golden brown and has a nutty fragrance, 15 to 20 minutes. (You could do this on a sheet pan in the oven, but I like being able to move the rice around in a pan regularly rather than having to open and close the oven several times.) Allow the rice to cool.

Put the toasted rice into a medium saucepan and combine with the water. Cook over medium-low heat, stirring occasionally, until the rice is tender and the water has been fully absorbed, about 20 minutes.

Next add the milk, cream, sugar, vanilla bean and seeds, orange zest, and orange juice. Simmer until the mixture begins to thicken, 15 to 20 minutes.

Remove from the heat and finish the pudding by stirring in the butter, egg yolk, and salt to taste. I like to serve the rice pudding warm for a temperature contrast with the ice cream, but enjoy it hot or chilled.

GARNISH

2 Seville oranges, cut into suprêmes (see page 33)

Rice Crackers (page 63; optional, but great for textural contrast)

Handful of tiny fresh mint leaves

TO SERVE: Discard the vanilla bean pod. Spoon ½ cup of rice pudding into each deep, narrow bowl. Place a quenelle of ice cream right in the middle of the rice pudding. Lay a few orange suprêmes around the ice cream. Garnish with rice cracker shards, if using, and 4 or 5 tiny mint leaves.

HAZELNUT CAKE

BANANA ICE CREAM, WHIPPED CHOCOLATE GANACHE, RAS EL HANOUT

SERVES 8 TO 12

This dessert comes straight from my love for Nutella and bananas. Adding ras el hanout to any recipe featuring nuts is a winner every time. This North African spice blend warms a dish up and creates interesting notes. *Ras el hanout* translates to "head of the shop"—that is, the best that the spice store has to offer—and the blend tends to be a mix of dozens of different spices that vary from region to region. I first used ras el hanout in a peanut butter dish at Sensing, and I've been obsessed with it ever since.

BAKE THE CAKE: Preheat the oven to 350°F and prepare a 9 × 13-inch cake pan with a little cooking spray, placing a rectangle of parchment to fit the bottom, and then spraying it again.

Using a whisk, combine the all-purpose flour, hazelnut flour, baking powder, baking soda, and salt in a large bowl.

In a separate medium bowl or in a stand mixer, whisk together the eggs and sugar until the mixture is pale yellow in color, has thickened, and you've reached the ribbon stage: when lifting the whisk up, the batter will drip off and form a slow-dissolving ribbon on the surface of the batter.

Whisk the milk, buttermilk, and olive oil into the egg batter. Using a spatula, fold a third of the flour mixture into the batter, and repeat with the remaining two thirds.

Pour the batter into the prepared cake pan and bake until a cake tester inserted in the center comes out clean, 30 to 35 minutes. Let cool in the pan on a wire rack.

WHILE THE CAKE IS COOKING, START THE GANACHE: Put the chocolate in a small mixing bowl.

Combine the heavy cream, ras el hanout, and salt in a small saucepan, and bring to a heavy simmer over medium-high heat. As soon as the cream mixture is simmering, pour it over the chocolate, making sure the chocolate is completely submerged. Allow to sit for 3 to 5 minutes.

Using a rubber spatula, stir gently to blend the cream and melted chocolate until smooth. Refrigerate the ganache until it sets, 1 to 2 hours.

MAKING CUSTARD

NOTES

You'll need an ice cream maker. The ice cream should be made and chilled a minimum of 6 hours ahead of serving. Plan accordingly.

You'll also need a 9 × 13-inch cake pan.

HAZELNUT CAKE

Nonstick cooking spray

1¼ cups all-purpose flour

¾ cup hazelnut flour, plus more for garnish

1½ teaspoons baking powder

1 teaspoon baking soda

1 teaspoon kosher salt

4 large eggs

1¼ cups sugar

1 cup whole milk

½ cup buttermilk

½ cup olive oil

CHOCOLATE GANACHE

8 ounces bittersweet (I like to use 70%) cacao chocolate, broken into small chunks

1 cup heavy cream

1 teaspoon ras el hanout

½ teaspoon kosher salt

Banana Ice Cream (recipe follows)

recipe continues

Transfer the ganache to a stand mixer fitted with the whisk attachment. Whisk on high until the ganache begins to look like chocolate mousse and has lightened in color and doubled in volume, 2 to 4 minutes. Keep for up to an hour at room temperature until ready to use or in the fridge for up to 8 hours. If the ganache is chilled, it will set up and no longer be light and mousse-like. You can certainly enjoy this chilled but it will be firmer in texture.

To serve use a bowl with a small lip to prevent melting ice cream from running all over. Portion and plate your cake slices (or rounds—whatever shape you desire!). This is a casual dessert: make quenelles from the ganache and ice cream and serve them alongside the cake. Sprinkle with a pinch of hazelnut flour.

BANANA ICE CREAM

MAKES 1 QUART

1 cup mashed ripe bananas (from 2 medium bananas)

2 tablespoons cornstarch

1 vanilla bean, split lengthwise, seeds scraped

2 cups heavy cream

½ cup whole milk

¾ cup sugar

5 large egg yolks

2 large eggs

1 teaspoon fleur de sel

Combine the bananas, cornstarch, and vanilla bean seeds in a food processor, and process until smooth.

In a saucepan, combine the heavy cream, milk, and sugar. Over medium heat, bring the mixture to a light simmer, whisking just until the sugar has dissolved. Set up an ice bath.

In a medium bowl, whisk the egg yolks, eggs, and fleur de sel. Temper the milk mixture into the eggs, whisking constantly. Return the custard to the saucepan and cook over medium-low heat, stirring constantly with a spatula until the custard coats the back of a spoon. Do not boil. Stir in the banana purée. Strain through a fine-mesh sieve into a bowl set over the ice bath and stir a few times to help the custard cool.

Once cool, refrigerate until cold, then pour into an ice cream maker. Follow the manufacturer's instructions to churn ice cream. Transfer it to a lidded container and freeze for a minimum of 6 hours and up to 5 days.

MATCHA CUSTARD

BERRIES, SABLÉ, OLIVE OIL

SERVES 4 TO 6

The first time I made this was for a *Top Chef* challenge to create a dish showcasing a tayberry—the love child of a blackberry and raspberry. The only information we had was that the event would be outside—on a farm—and we would be serving a couple hundred people. And so this is how my brain mapped it out in seconds: I thought *farm,* then I pictured a goat. Okay … goat milk. The tayberry is sweet and tangy, and I wanted something bitter that would pair well with a creamy element: matcha. And because I'm not a super-sweet dessert person, the spice and savory notes of extra-virgin olive oil came to mind. Add a little texture with a crumble—something more sophisticated than oats, like a sablé mixture—and there you have it: the dish that won me the challenge.

MAKE THE CUSTARD: Bring the cream and the goat milk to a simmer in a small saucepan. Whisk together the egg yolks, matcha, granulated sugar, and cornstarch in a medium bowl. Temper the milk mixture over the yolks, whisking constantly.

Return the mixture to the saucepan and stir over low heat until the custard coats the back of a spoon, 3 to 4 minutes. Do not boil.

Remove from the heat and stir in the drained gelatin until it is fully melted and well combined.

Prepare an ice bath.

Strain the custard through a fine-mesh sieve into a bowl set over the ice bath. Stir until cool to the touch, then transfer the mix to quart containers and refrigerate. Chill, covered, in the refrigerator until fully set, at least 4 hours or overnight.

BERRIES: Close to serving time, combine the blackberries and raspberries with the confectioners' sugar and olive oil in a bowl and macerate for 30 minutes, or until the confectioners' sugar has completely dissolved.

MAKING CUSTARD

CUSTARD

1 cup heavy cream

1½ cups goat milk

4 large egg yolks

3 tablespoons matcha powder

¼ cup granulated sugar

1 tablespoon cornstarch

4 gelatin sheets, bloomed (see page 31), or 1 teaspoon powdered gelatin, bloomed according to the instructions on packet

BERRIES

1 pint fresh blackberries, sliced in half horizontally if large

1 pint fresh raspberries

3 tablespoons confectioners' sugar

¼ cup as-fancy-as-you-can-get extra-virgin olive oil

recipe continues

½ to ¾ cup Sablé Crumbs
(recipe follows)

15 small fresh micro shiso leaves
(available at Asian grocers) or
small fresh mint or basil leaves

TO SERVE: Spoon out a large scoop of custard into each shallow bowl. Spoon the berries and olive oil mixture around the custard. Crumble the sablé over top. Garnish with the shiso.

SABLÉ CRUMBS

MAKES 2 CUPS

½ cup potato flour

½ cup all-purpose flour, plus more for dusting

3 tablespoons granulated sugar

½ teaspoon baking powder

Pinch of kosher salt

3 tablespoons cold unsalted butter, diced

1 large egg yolk

1 tablespoon extra-virgin olive oil

Preheat the oven to 350°F.

Mix together the potato flour, all-purpose flour, sugar, baking powder, and salt. Using your hands or a stand mixer fitted with the paddle attachment, incorporate the butter until it is the size of small peas. Add the egg yolk and olive oil and mix together just until a dough begins to form.

Crumble the dough in an even layer onto a parchment-lined sheet pan. Bake until golden brown, 9 to 12 minutes. Remove from the oven and cool completely. The sablé crumbs will keep in an airtight container for about a week.

PEACH PÂTE DE FRUIT

ROSEMARY SUGAR

MAKES ABOUT FIFTY 1-INCH JELLIES

I first learned how to make these classic fruit jellies while working at Sensing with chef de cuisine Gérard Barbin. We used them as *mignardises* to serve guests at the end of the meal, alongside coffee and liqueurs. We kept creating new flavors—tart cherry, passion fruit, black pepper, lime, raspberry—and would change our offering once or twice a week. Here is the base recipe; you can substitute any other fruit purée of your liking and have fun with the sugar coating. These make an impressive addition to any meal or a great food gift.

MAKE THE ROSEMARY SUGAR: Put the sugar in a bowl. Use the back of a chef's knife to lightly bruise the rosemary sprigs to release some of their essential oils. Toss the sprigs in the sugar, cover, and set aside for 24 hours at room temperature.

MAKE THE PÂTE DE FRUIT: Prepare an 8-inch square cake pan by lightly spraying it with cooking spray. Combine the plain sugar in a bowl and stir in the pectin; this prevents the pectin from clumping.

In a large saucepan, bring 3 quarts water to a boil. Set up an ice bath. Drop the peaches into the boiling water. After 20 seconds, remove them from the water, plunge them into the ice bath to cool, then peel and pit the peaches. Cut the peaches into manageable chunks. Transfer them to a blender or a food processor and purée until smooth. Pass through a fine-mesh sieve into a bowl.

In a large saucepan over medium heat, combine 2¼ cups of the peach purée with the sugar/pectin mix. (You will have leftover purée; transfer it to a lidded container and refrigerate to use later in cocktails or to spoon over ice cream.) Cook the purée, whisking regularly, until the sugar had dissolved, about 10 minutes. Secure your candy thermometer to the edge of the saucepan (you can use an instant-read digital thermometer instead to check the temperature at regular intervals). Add the butter. As the mixture begins to bubble, reduce the heat to low. Whisk constantly, ensuring that, as the mixture cooks, it doesn't burn. Cook until the mixture reaches a temperature of approximately 220°F. Remove from the heat and stir in the lemon juice.

BLANCHING

ROSEMARY SUGAR

2 cups granulated sugar

2 fresh rosemary sprigs

PÂTE DE FRUIT

Nonstick cooking spray

2 cups granulated sugar

1 tablespoon powdered apple pectin

1 pound ripe peaches (about 4)

1 tablespoon unsalted butter

2 teaspoons fresh lemon juice

NOTES

The rosemary needs a minimum of 24 hours to infuse the sugar coating. Plan accordingly.

You'll need a candy thermometer for this recipe.

recipe continues

Carefully pour the hot jelly into the prepared cake pan. Be extra careful: this mixture is fucking hot! Don't even think about trying to taste it at this stage—trust me. Let the pan sit out at room temperature until the mixture has cooled somewhat, about 2 hours. Cover the container. You don't want the jelly to touch plastic wrap. The pâte de fruit will set overnight as it cools.

TO SERVE: Turn out the pâte de fruit onto a cutting board. Cut into desired shapes; my personal preference is 1-inch squares. Lightly spray your knife with cooking spray every two or three cuts. Also, when you notice the jelly sticking to your knife, take 30 seconds and wash it. The cleaner your knife is, the cleaner the cuts will be. The jellies will keep for up to a week in an airtight container at room temperature. Before serving, toss each jelly into the rosemary-perfumed sugar, coating completely.

POACHED CHERRIES

MERINGUE, LAVENDER, LEMON THYME

SERVES 4 TO 6

This recipe should be made in cherry season only. You're just letting the ingredients speak for themselves in this simple recipe that complements juicy cherries with a fluffy, light-as-air, soft meringue.

Slice off the very bottom of each cherry (the end opposite to where the stem attaches), so that it stands up straight. Using a tiny Parisian scoop, melon baller, or a measuring spoon, coax out the pit from the bottom of each cherry—this maintains the original shape of the cherry. Put the cherries in a heatproof bowl or a rimmed vessel.

In a large saucepan, combine the water, wine, lemon juice, 1½ cups of the sugar, the lavender, and vanilla bean and seeds. Bring to a boil, then reduce the heat, and simmer until the sugar has fully dissolved, 6 to 8 minutes.

Pour this hot poaching liquid directly over the cherries, and press a sheet of plastic wrap directly on top of the cherries to keep them submerged. Allow to cool at room temperature for 30 minutes, then transfer to the refrigerator and chill for 30 minutes or overnight, depending on how cold you like your finished dessert.

Fill a medium saucepan with water and bring to a boil, then reduce the heat to very low so the water simmers gently. Whisk together the egg whites and remaining 1 cup sugar using the mixing bowl from your stand mixer, holding it over the pot of simmering water. The bowl can be resting on the saucepan but shouldn't touch the water. Whisk over the heat until the sugar has dissolved, 10 to 12 minutes. Add the cream of tartar and transfer the bowl to a stand mixer fitted with the whisk attachment. Begin mixing on medium speed and gradually increase the speed to high. Whisk the mixture until it reaches stiff peaks, 6 to 8 minutes.

TO SERVE: Arrange 9 cherries in a circle at the bottom of each deep, narrow bowl. Spoon 3 or 4 tablespoons of the poaching liquid over the cherries. Next dollop ¼ cup meringue over the top and, using the back of a damp spoon, create large peaks and waves in the meringue. Zest some lemon directly over the top of the meringue. Carefully arrange 6 to 8 lemon thyme leaves over the meringue. This dessert can be served warm or at room temperature.

MAKING MERINGUE

POACHING

1 pound sweet cherries

1½ quarts water

2 cups dry red wine

2 tablespoons fresh lemon juice

2½ cups sugar

2 teaspoons lavender

1 vanilla bean, split lengthwise, seeds scraped

3 large egg whites

¼ teaspoon cream of tartar

Grated zest of 1 lemon

2 fresh lemon thyme sprigs, leaves only

SOUR CREAM CAKE

PECAN, MALTED MILK CRÈME FRAÎCHE

SERVES 8 TO 10

I love Pecan Sandies. But because I love cake even more than cookies, I wanted to take that great sweet-salty pecan flavor and turn it into a pound cake—specifically one that rivals Entenmann's coffee cake and is as perfect for breakfast as it is for dessert. Voilà!

CAKE

16 tablespoons (2 sticks) unsalted butter, at room temperature, plus more for the pan

2 cups all-purpose flour, plus more for the pan

2 teaspoons baking powder

½ teaspoon baking soda

1 cup granulated sugar

2 large eggs

1 cup sour cream

1 teaspoon vanilla extract

½ cup whole milk

1 cup pecans, coarsely chopped

½ cup packed dark brown sugar

1 teaspoon kosher salt

BAKE THE CAKE: Preheat the oven to 350°F. Butter and flour an 8-inch round cake pan.

In a medium bowl, whisk together the flour, baking powder, and baking soda. In a stand mixer fitted with the paddle attachment, beat the butter and granulated sugar on medium-high until pale yellow in color and slightly fluffy, 4 to 5 minutes, stopping the machine once or twice to scrape down the sides and bottom to make sure the sugar and butter are evenly mixed.

With the machine running on medium speed, add the eggs, one at a time, and continue mixing until each egg is fully incorporated. Next add the sour cream and vanilla and mix, again stopping the machine to scrape down the sides once or twice, until incorporated.

Switching to the lowest speed, add one third of the flour mixture. When it begins to incorporate, and with the machine running, add half of the milk and mix lightly. Add another third of the flour mixture, followed by the remaining milk. Then add the final third of the flour mixture and mix until the batter just begins to come together.

Stop the stand mixer and, using a spatula, fold the batter until all the ingredients are fully incorporated, being sure not to overmix it. Spread the batter evenly into the prepared cake pan.

In a small bowl, toss together the pecans, brown sugar, and salt. Sprinkle evenly over the batter, using your hand to press the nuts into the cake just so they begin to adhere and sink in slightly.

Bake until a cake tester inserted in the center comes out clean, 35 to 45 minutes. Cool in the pan on a wire rack.

MEANWHILE, PREP THE GARNISH: By hand, or using a stand mixer with a whisk attachment, whip the crème fraîche, confectioners' sugar, and malted milk powder until medium-stiff peaks form. Keep chilled until ready to serve.

TO SERVE: Cut the cake into desired portions. Scoop a large quenelle of the whipped crème fraîche alongside each serving.

GARNISH

2 cups crème fraîche

¼ cup confectioners' sugar

2 tablespoons malted milk powder

SPROUTED GRAIN CAKE
CHOCOLATE PEANUT CARAMEL MOUSSE, SALTED VANILLA CUSTARD ICE CREAM

SERVES 12

This dessert is inspired by a classic breakfast my mom would make: whole-wheat toast with peanut butter, warm maple syrup, and a tall glass of milk. I'd sit on a wooden stool at the kitchen counter, feet dangling. I remember it being a little cold; the house hadn't quite warmed up to the bustle of the day. I crave the simplicity of that breakfast and those peaceful quiet mornings.

BAKE THE CAKE: Preheat the oven to 350°F. Butter a 13 × 18-inch rimmed sheet pan lined with parchment paper. Butter the parchment paper well.

In a medium bowl, whisk together the flour, baking powder, baking soda, and salt. In a stand mixer fitted with the paddle attachment, beat the butter, honey, and sugar on medium speed until incorporated, about 3 minutes. Next, with the mixer still running, add the eggs and the yolks, one at a time. Stop the mixer and scrape down the sides of the bowl with a spatula. Add the vanilla.

With the mixer now running on slower speed, incorporate a third of the dry mixture into the bowl. Add the buttermilk. When that has been mixed in, add the remainder of the dry mixture. Remove from the stand mixer and give the batter a couple of stirs with a spatula. Pour the mixture into the prepared sheet pan and spread it evenly using the back of a spoon or the spatula. Bake until a cake tester inserted into the center comes out clean, 8 to 10 minutes. Allow the cake to cool in the pan on a wire rack for 30 minutes.

Run a sharp knife along the edges of the cake to separate it from the pan. Then lay a fresh sheet piece of parchment paper on top of the cake. Put a large cutting board over the sheet tray and quickly flip the cake over: the bottom of the cake is now the top. Remove the top sheet of parchment paper. Using a 3½-inch ring cutter, cut out 12 disks. Now, using a 1½-inch mold, cut out the middle of each disk, saving these donut holes.

CAKE

8 tablespoons (1 stick) unsalted butter, at room temperature, plus more for the pan

2 cups sprouted grain flour

1 teaspoon baking powder

1 teaspoon baking soda

½ teaspoon kosher salt

⅓ cup dark honey

⅓ cup sugar

2 large eggs

2 large egg yolks

½ teaspoon vanilla extract

1 cup buttermilk

NOTES

Sprouted grain flour has an extra-wheaty flavor. If you cannot find it, you can substitute whole-wheat flour.

You'll need an ice cream maker. The ice cream should be made and chilled a minimum of 6 hours ahead of serving. Plan accordingly.

If you want to plate the dish as shown in the photo, you will need a 3½-inch ring mold and a 1½-inch ring mold.

recipe continues

CHOCOLATE PEANUT CARAMEL MOUSSE

8 ounces bittersweet (I like to use 70%) chocolate, coarsely chopped

¾ cup sugar

¼ cup water

1 teaspoon fresh lemon juice

1½ cups heavy cream

1 tablespoon unsalted butter

¼ cup smooth peanut butter

Fleur de sel

NOTE

If you're paying me to cook for you, I'm going to make the peanut butter from scratch. But I'm not going to force you to make your own peanut butter for a few tablespoons. You can substitute store-bought (I'm a Jif Smooth girl).

GARNISH

Salted Vanilla Custard Ice Cream (recipe follows)

¼ cup roasted unsalted peanuts

2 tablespoons sesame seeds

Maldon salt to taste

MAKE THE MOUSSE: Put the chocolate in a medium heatproof bowl.

In a small saucepan, combine the sugar, water, and lemon juice. Over medium heat, cook until the mixture is a dark amber color, approximately 10 minutes. If you notice any sugar on the sides of the pot, brush it down with a pastry brush dipped in water. Watch the pan carefully, because if the caramel goes from deep amber to burning, you need to start over.

Remove from the heat and carefully add ½ cup of the heavy cream, whisking slowly so the sugar does not seize or boil over (though if it does seize, it will remelt). Add the butter and the peanut butter. Whisk until both butters begin to melt. Pour this mix over the chocolate. Add a pinch of fleur de sel and, using a wooden spoon, mix until smooth. Let the mixture cool at room temperature for about 20 minutes.

In the meantime, whip the remaining 1 cup heavy cream until stiff peaks form. Fold the cream into the peanut butter mixture. Refrigerate for a minimum of 20 minutes and up to 24 hours; if you chill it overnight, make sure to pull it out 30 minutes before serving to allow it to soften a bit.

TO SERVE: Set a donut hole just off-center of each plate. Either scoop or make a quenelle of the ice cream and place it atop the donut hole. Put the cake in the middle of the plate. Transfer the mousse to a piping bag fitted with a 1-inch tip or to a zip-top bag (cut off a corner to make a 1-inch opening) and pipe the mousse around the edge, so that the cake looks like a wreath; alternatively you can spoon dollops of the mousse in place. Using a Microplane zester, make it rain peanut dust. Sprinkle with some sesame seeds and Maldon salt.

SALTED VANILLA CUSTARD ICE CREAM

MAKES 1 QUART

In a saucepan, combine the milk, heavy cream, and sugar. Over medium heat, bring the mixture to a light simmer, whisking just until the sugar has dissolved.

In a medium bowl, whisk together the yolks, eggs, and cornstarch. Temper the cream mixture into the eggs. Return the custard to the saucepan and cook over medium-low heat, mixing constantly with a spatula until the custard coats the back of a spoon.

Prepare an ice bath. Strain the custard through a fine-mesh sieve into a bowl set over the ice bath. Add the vanilla seeds and fleur de sel, and stir a few times to help the custard cool.

When the custard has cooled, refrigerate until cold, then pour into an ice cream maker. Follow the manufacturer's instructions to churn into ice cream. Transfer the ice cream to a lidded container and freeze for a minimum of 6 hours and up to 5 days. Plan accordingly.

2 cups whole milk

2 cups heavy cream

¾ cup sugar

5 large egg yolks

2 large eggs

2 tablespoons cornstarch

1 vanilla bean, split lengthwise, seeds scraped

1 teaspoon fleur de sel

ORANGE SHERBET

GOAT MILK SODA, FENNEL

SERVES 4 TO 6

When I was growing up, my family would go to A&W for root beer floats, and that's where my love of a good ice cream float started. Once I had come to terms with the genius concept of ice cream combined with a fizzy drink, I couldn't stop; vanilla ice cream and just about anything was fair game: grape soda, cola, fruit punch, and—the most important—orange soda. This recipe is my updated version of an old friend. For novelty purposes, I like to serve this in a collins glass complete with a striped straw or in a sundae bowl.

BLANCHING

NOTES
You'll need an ice cream maker for this recipe. You'll also need a whipped cream dispenser (such as an iSi canister) or soda syphon.

ORANGE SHERBET

1½ cups fresh orange juice

¾ cup granulated sugar

¼ cup plus 2 tablespoons honey

Pinch of kosher salt

2 tablespoons grated orange zest

½ tablespoon fresh lemon juice

1 cup whole milk

1 cup heavy cream

MAKE THE SHERBET: Whisk together the orange juice, granulated sugar, honey, salt, orange zest, and lemon juice until the sugar begins to dissolve, 3 to 5 minutes. Whisk in the milk and heavy cream until well incorporated. Transfer to an ice cream maker and freeze following the manufacturer's directions. Transfer the sherbet to a lidded container and store in the freezer for at least 8 hours and up to 5 days. Plan accordingly.

CANDIED FENNEL

1 cup water

1½ cups granulated sugar

1 strip of lemon zest

2 fennel stalks, cut into ¼-inch coins, fronds reserved for garnish

CANDY THE FENNEL: Bring a small saucepan of water to a boil.

In a separate small saucepan, bring the 1 cup water and ½ cup of the granulated sugar to a boil. Add the lemon zest.

When the plain water has come to a boil, blanch the fennel coins for 30 seconds. Drain and transfer them to the lemon simple syrup, reducing the heat to medium-low. Simmer until tender, 5 to 8 minutes. Drain the fennel and set it on a paper towel to soak up any excess liquid. Transfer to a bowl and toss with the remaining ½ cup granulated sugar. Using a fork or an offset spatula, transfer the fennel coins from the sugar to a sheet pan lined with parchment.

recipe continues

GOAT MILK SODA

3 cups goat milk

¼ cup water

¼ cup granulated sugar

¼ teaspoon vanilla extract

1 teaspoon fresh lemon juice

WHIPPED CREAM

1½ cups heavy cream

¼ cup confectioners' sugar

½ vanilla bean, split lengthwise, seeds scraped

MAKE THE GOAT MILK SODA: Combine the goat milk, water, granulated sugar, and vanilla into a medium saucepan. Gently warm over medium heat, whisking gently until the sugar has dissolved, 6 to 8 minutes. Prepare an ice bath. Strain the milk through a fine-mesh sieve into a bowl. Stir in the lemon juice. Set the bowl into the ice bath. When the mixture is cool, transfer it to a whipped cream dispenser and follow the manufacturer's directions. Charge five times with a soda cartridge and keep chilled until ready to serve.

WHIP THE CREAM: By hand or using a stand mixer, whip the cream, confectioners' sugar, and vanilla bean seeds until the mixture holds medium peaks.

TO SERVE: Scoop the sherbet into your preferred serving vessels. Carefully dispense the goat milk soda around each scoop of sherbet. The texture is going to be that of a milky soda. Garnish with generous dollop of whipped cream, the candied fennel, and a fennel frond.

POACHED PEAR

CORNMEAL AND ALMOND CAKE, FROMAGE BLANC

SERVES 10

This dessert was inspired by my love for the classic French tart filling: frangipane, a delicious mixture of butter, sugar, eggs, and almond paste. I discovered it during pastry class in culinary school; we made a frangipane tart topped with pears poached in red wine and I pretty much devoured the entire thing. Why make it boozy? Think about those terrible fruit cups with the syrup, sitting in that sugary solution and soaking in that "flavor"; why not plunge that shit in champagne and allow some real flavor to soak in? The fromage blanc is rich and can stand up to the hearty pears and cake but also helps cut through the dessert, adding a subtle savory note.

POACH THE PEARS: In a large, tall saucepan, combine the pears, water, wine, granulated sugar, lemon juice, orange zest, vanilla bean seeds, and salt. Bring to a boil and then reduce the heat to low. Cover the pears with a cartouche (a round piece of parchment paper to cover the surface of the simmering liquid) and simmer until the pears are tender when pierced with a knife, 45 minutes to 1 hour.

MEANWHILE, MAKE THE CAKE: Preheat the oven to 350°F. Prepare an 8-inch round cake pan: Butter the bottom and sides of the pan, then fit a round of parchment on the bottom and butter that. Lightly dust with flour, tapping out any excess.

In a medium bowl, whisk together the flour, cornmeal, baking powder, baking soda, and salt.

In a stand mixer fitted with the paddle attachment, beat the almond paste to soften and smooth it, stopping the machine occasionally and scraping down the sides often with a spatula. This may take a little bit of time, depending on how thick the almond paste is. Add the granulated sugar and continue to mix until the paste is smooth.

With the machine running on medium speed, add one egg at a time, stopping the mixer and scraping down the edges after each one. Once the eggs are incorporated, increase the speed to medium-high and beat until the consistency is thoroughly blended, 3 to 4 minutes.

POACHING

PEARS

10 Seckel or other small pears, peeled and cored from the bottom

2 quarts water

1 cup dry white wine

1½ cups granulated sugar

2 tablespoons fresh lemon juice

2 strips orange zest, removed with a vegetable peeler

1 vanilla bean, split lengthwise, seeds scraped

Pinch of kosher salt

1 (750 ml) bottle dry sparkling wine or champagne

CAKE

Unsalted butter, for the pan

1½ cups all-purpose flour, plus more for the pan

½ cup fine cornmeal

1 teaspoon baking powder

½ teaspoon baking soda

½ teaspoon kosher salt

6 ounces almond paste

¼ cup granulated sugar

4 large eggs

1 cup whole milk

recipe continues

Next reduce the speed to low and add the milk little by little. Then slowly add the flour mixture. You don't want to overmix the batter, so add half the flour mixture with the machine still running. Then stop the mixer, add the remainder of the flour mixture, and use a spatula to gently fold it in by hand.

Transfer the batter to the prepared cake pan and bake until a cake tester inserted in the center comes out clean and the top is golden brown, 30 to 35 minutes. Let cool in the pan on a wire rack.

Transfer the pears from the poaching liquid to a bowl filled with the sparkling wine, making sure they are completely submerged. Let sit at room temperature for 2 hours.

In the meantime, vigorously simmer the poaching liquid to reduce it by two thirds, yielding ½ cup of syrup. Let cool.

MAKE THE GARNISH: Whisk together the fromage blanc with the confectioners' sugar. Refrigerate until ready to use.

TO SERVE: Take the pears out of the sparkling wine and pat them dry (save the sparkling wine for cooking at a future date in lieu of white wine, or for drinking). Reheat the syrup. Cut the cake into 10 triangular slices. Place each slice of cake into a shallow, wide bowl and stand a pear upright to one side, just opposite the cake. Spoon the warm syrup over both the pear and the cake. Scoop a nice quenelle of fromage blanc on top of each slice. Dust confectioners' sugar atop the cake and serve.

GARNISH

8 ounces fromage blanc (you can substitute Greek yogurt)

3 tablespoons confectioners' sugar, plus more for dusting

ROASTED QUINCE

BUCKWHEAT HONEY, FARRO PUDDING

SERVES 4

ROASTING

I'm not the kind of person who wakes up and eats a typical breakfast, especially a sweet one. However, come nighttime, I start to crave sweets ferociously, desperate for a dessert nightcap. My sweet tooth tends to rear its head too late, long after the breakfast joints have stopped serving (this is perhaps how my addiction to gas-station gummy candy started). That's when I make this recipe; a cross between breakfast and dessert: think sweet oats with melted butter, fruit, and granola. If you can't find buckwheat honey—which is bold, earthy, a little funky, and gorgeously sweet—you can substitute a subtler honey or molasses in a pinch.

ROASTED QUINCE

2 quince, peeled, halved, and cored

3 tablespoons granulated sugar

Grated zest of 2 lemons

2 tablespoons fresh lemon juice

2 tablespoons cold unsalted butter, small diced

ROAST THE QUINCE: Preheat the oven to 400°F.

On a small sheet pan, arrange the quince halves cut-side up and sprinkle with the granulated sugar, lemon zest, and lemon juice. Dot the butter over the top. Roast until the quinces are just tender but still keep their shape, 40 to 45 minutes.

FARRO PUDDING

¾ cup farro

3 cups water

1 vanilla bean, split lengthwise, seeds scraped

1 cup canned coconut milk

2 cups heavy cream

¼ cup lightly packed brown sugar

¼ cup buckwheat honey

¼ cup golden raisins

1 large egg yolk

MEANWHILE, COOK THE FARRO: In a saucepan, combine the farro and 3 cups water. Bring to a boil, then reduce the heat to medium-low and simmer until al dente, 30 minutes. Drain off any excess water.

In a medium saucepan, combine the cooked farro, vanilla bean seeds, coconut milk, heavy cream, brown sugar, and buckwheat honey. Cook over medium-low heat, stirring occasionally, until the mixture thickens, about 20 minutes.

Meanwhile, soak the raisins in warm water to cover until plump and softened, 10 minutes. Drain well and chop finely.

Remove the farro from heat and stir in the raisins and egg yolk.

GARNISH

3 tablespoons clarified butter, melted

¼ cup shredded unsweetened coconut, toasted

Maldon salt

TO SERVE: Cut each quince half in half lengthwise and put them off to the left in individual medium bowls. Spoon ½ cup of the farro pudding on the other side of each quince quarter. Drizzle 2 teaspoons clarified butter on top and sprinkle each with 1 tablespoon shredded coconut and a little Maldon salt.

ALMOND BROWN BUTTER CAKE

FOIE GRAS, CRANBERRY, ORANGE

SERVES 8 TO 10

I love the flavor of brown butter and the texture of almond flour. This cake is elegant but, still has some weight. The cakes are crisped on the outside because of the high fat content yet very moist in the center. I like to enhance the batter by adding foie gras. It brings a savory note to this sweet and decadent little cake. I like serving the cakes with homemade jam, Pickled Cherries (page 213), and/or a simple cheese and charcuterie board.

BROWN BUTTER CAKES

1 cup plus 2 tablespoons almond flour

1 cup minus 1 tablespoon packed dark brown sugar

1 cup plus 2 tablespoons all-purpose flour

¼ cup rendered foie gras fat (see Note)

¼ cup Brown Butter (page 92), melted

6 large egg whites

1 teaspoon kosher salt

Nonstick cooking spray

MAKE THE CAKE BATTER: In a stand mixer fitted with the paddle attachment, combine the almond flour, brown sugar, and all-purpose flour, and mix on low until combined. In a small bowl, whisk together the foie gras fat, brown butter, egg whites, and salt. With the mixer running on medium speed, add this to the dry ingredients and mix until a smooth batter forms—you'll have to stop the machine to scrape down the sides once or twice.

Transfer the batter to a piping bag fitted with a ¼-inch-round tip or to a zip-top plastic bag (cut off a corner to make a ¼-inch opening) and refrigerate for at least 2 hours or up to a day ahead of time. The batter will solidify slightly, making it easier to pipe into the molds without running all over the place.

CRANBERRY JAM

8 ounces fresh or frozen cranberries

¾ cup granulated sugar

Grated zest of 2 oranges

2 teaspoons fresh lemon juice

MAKE THE JAM: In a medium nonreactive saucepan, combine the cranberries, sugar, and orange zest. Cook this mixture over medium-high heat until it registers 220°F on a candy thermometer, 15 to 18 minutes. Stir in the lemon juice. Let the jam cool completely, then transfer to a jar, and refrigerate for up to a week.

When you're ready to bake the cakes, preheat the oven to 400°F.

Spray mini bread loaf pans or muffin tins (or financier pans) with cooking spray. Pipe the batter into the molds, filling each mold three fourths of the way. You should have 8 to 10 loaves (more if you use a mini muffin tin). Bake until a cake tester inserted in the center comes out clean and the cakes feel springy, 10 to 12 minutes.

TO SERVE: Warm the jam slightly and transfer it to a small plate. Slice the warm cakes and serve next to the jam or line a larger ramekin with a cloth napkin and arrange the warm slices inside and serve alongside a smaller ramekin of jam with a small spoon for serving.

NOTES

Bakers love any excuse to get a custom mold, and I strongly suggest you buy financier molds for this recipe: 2 × 4-inch shallow rectangles, each holding about 3 ounces. One should not fuck with French baking classics.

I render foie gras by putting it in a plastic zip-top bag, sealing it, placing it in a bowl, and running hot tap water over it for 5 to 6 minutes, or until it has melted. Strain out any solids from the fat.

FRIED BUNS

MAKES 15 TO 20 BUNS; SERVES 5 TO 6

This might be my favorite recipe in the book. It's my take on the buns you'll find in most traditional restaurants in Singapore, where they are served as a sort of spice mellower and a vehicle for the sauce in a chile crab with tomato sauce. But my version is for dessert buns. These beauties have the prettiest golden color, and when you break one open, steam billows out of the white interior. I'm marrying these buns with my other Singaporean obsession: *kaya* toast—aka toast, cold butter, and kaya, a coconut curd made from sugar, coconut milk, and eggs. I fell in love at first bite.

In a medium bowl, combine the water, yeast, granulated sugar, and honey. Let the yeast bloom until it starts to foam, about 10 minutes.

Stir in the coconut oil and flour with a spoon, eventually using your hands to turn the mixture into dough. Transfer to a very lightly floured work surface and knead the dough until it becomes smooth. Put in a lightly oiled bowl, cover with a clean dish towel, and set in a warm place until the dough doubles in volume, 25 to 30 minutes.

Turn the dough out on a lightly floured surface. Pinch off 1- to 2-ounce pieces—I like these buns to be bite-size. Roll each one into a tight ball: move your hand in a circular motion over the top of the bun on the counter. Transfer the balls to a lightly oiled sheet pan, placing them on their flat bottom sides and leaving plenty of space between each one, and cover with a lightly buttered piece of plastic wrap. Allow to rise in a warm place until doubled in size again, another 15 to 20 minutes.

In the meantime, heat the 3 cups of canola oil in a heavy-bottomed saucepan that can be used as a fryer. When the temperature registers 350°F on a deep-frying thermometer, reduce the heat to medium-low to maintain the temperature until you are ready to fry.

Working in batches, fry the buns, flipping them over to evenly color all sides, until dark golden brown, about 4 minutes. Using a spider or slotted spoon, transfer them to paper towels to drain.

TO SERVE: Allow 3 buns per person (though I once ate 6 of these in one sitting!). I like to put these on a simple bread plate, dust them with confectioners' sugar, a dollop of the kaya jam.

FRYING

NOTE
If you can't find *kaya,* you can substitute dulce de leche mixed with a couple of drops of coconut extract or some toasted coconut.

½ cup plus 1 tablespoon warm water

1 teaspoon active dry yeast

2 teaspoons granulated sugar

1 teaspoon honey

1 teaspoon coconut oil, warmed

2 cups all-purpose flour, plus more for kneading and rolling

3 cups canola oil, for frying, plus more for the bowl and pan

½ cup confectioners' sugar

¼ cup kaya jam (available in Asian supermarkets or online)

ACKNOWLEDGMENTS

Where do I begin? I owe an immense amount of gratitude to those who have worked on this book, all of whom came with more experience than I had in the cookbook process, all wonderfully skilled individuals who brought their expertise and eye for the smallest of details.

To Meredith, my cowriter: I remember our first conversation, the getting-to-know-you phase. You so quickly tapped into me, asking all the right questions and putting the answers down on paper to help me to tell my story. We have been in this for the long haul, meeting in Boston, New York City, and Montreal, clacking away at the computer keyboard. You captured my voice: stark, foul-mouthed, and to the point. To go from never having met me, to helping me tell my story in such a way that is so authentic, is no easy feat. You had so much patience and your kind yet strict approach kept me on track and focused. My cowriter and now my great friend.

To Kristin, my photographer: We worked together once before many, many years ago. Your work and friendship has stuck in my head and there was no one else who I would have rather worked with on my first cookbook. You and Joe make such a talented team that I feel honored to have been able to work with you. To Michelle, food stylist extraordinaire: Your attention to the smallest of movements in the styling is admirable, one that I wish I possessed. I am in awe of your eye for beauty and your understanding of the camera. You certainly made my job in the shooting of this book easier and allowed me to focus on just cooking. To Rebecca, the prop stylist: You nailed every prop and every vessel, giving the food and the camera something to marvel in. The choices of textures, colors, and shapes flow cohesively in a way that captures the light and certainly makes my food look more beautiful than I could have imagined.

To Robeisy: We have had so many adventures, cooking in so many places together, and now we get to add a cookbook to our résumé. You are an immensely talented cook and a great friend to me, one who challenges my decisions and helps me in finding the perfect balance of flavors and techniques. To the Smith family: Thank you for allowing us to use your home in Michigan. I could not have had a better setting to showcase the people I love.

To Rica, Marysarah, the entire team at Clarkson Potter (including Amy, Kim, Natasha, Erica, Carly, Raquel, Doris, and Aaron), Kim, Tory, and Jenna: All of you come with so many years of experience and I can't thank you enough for this opportunity to create something so special to me. I needed all of you in order for this book to be held by many. From the first moment of the idea of a book, to filling in all the gaps, to all of the conversations, to finding the right team, to the execution of art, to the inspiring challenges ensuring the words and feel of this book are just right, and to now, a book I am so very proud of.

To all of my restaurant friends who helped me order the copious amounts of food for shooting all of these dishes. To all of those who have influenced me and helped me grow into the chef I am. My food is a reflection of all of my experiences, cooking history, and the people with whom I have crossed paths. I learn and am inspired by you. To all the ones I love who offered support during this two-and-a-half-year process: Your words of encouragement and your opinions have impacted the final product greatly. You all have made my idea of a book far greater, better than what I could have done alone.

Thank you from the most honest part of my heart.

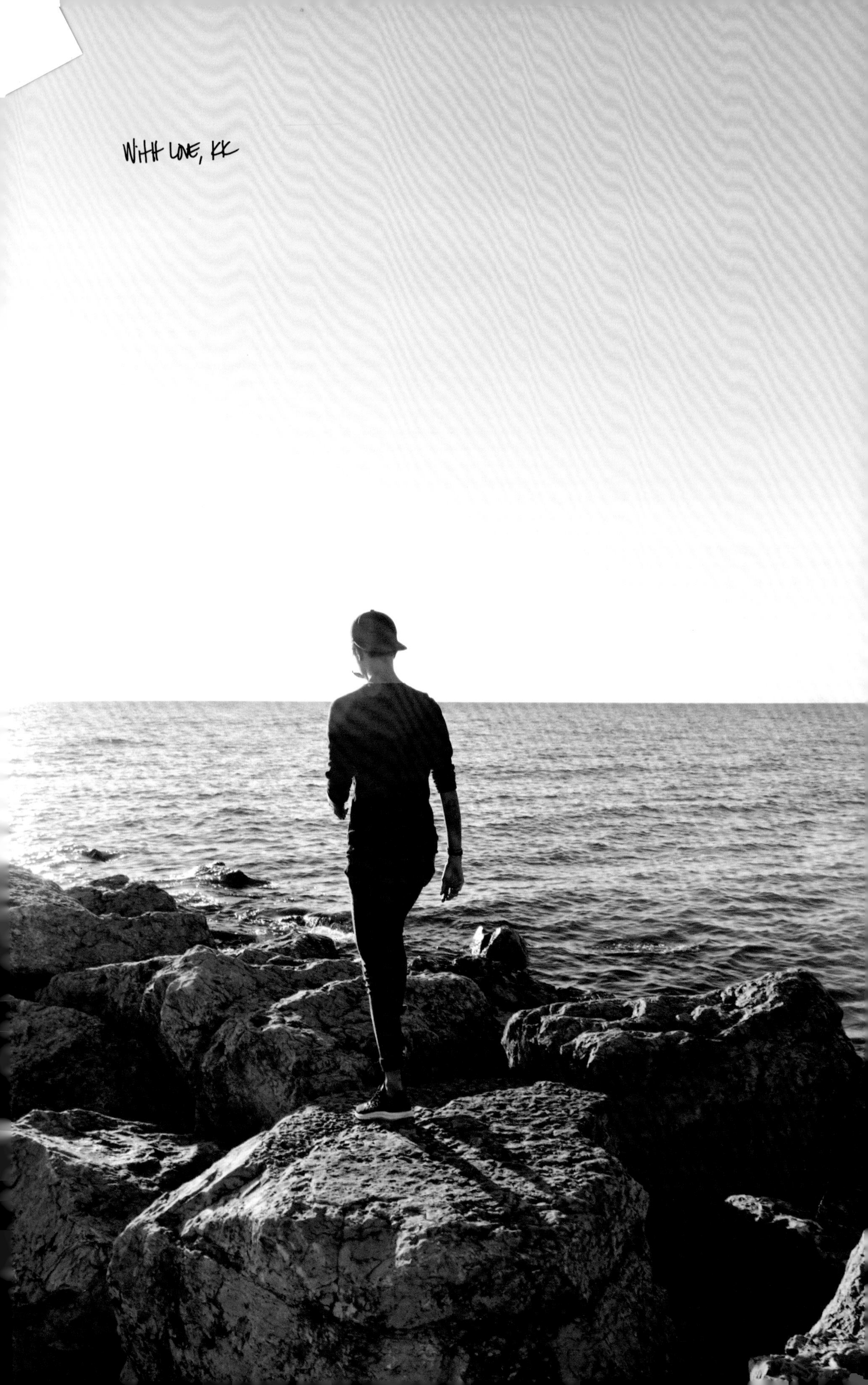
WITH LOVE, KK